# The Best
# 125
# Meatless
# Mediterranean
# Dishes

# Other Books by the Authors

*The Best 125 Meatless Pasta Dishes*
*The Best 125 Meatless Main Dishes*
*The Best 125 Fish and Seafood Dishes*
*The Best 125 Vegetable Dishes*
*The Best 125 Meatless Mexican Dishes*
*The Best 125 Meatless Italian Dishes*
*The Vegan Gourmet*
*A Cozy Book of Herbal Teas*
  (by Mindy Toomay)
*A Cozy Book of Coffees and Cocoas*
  (by Susann Geiskopf-Hadler)

## How to Order:

Single copies may be ordered from Prima Publishing, P.O. Box 1260, Rocklin, CA 95677; telephone (916) 632-4400. Quantity discounts are also available. On your letterhead, include information concerning the intended use of the books and the number of books you wish to purchase.

# The Best 125 Meatless Mediterranean Dishes

**Susann Geiskopf-Hadler**
**Mindy Toomay**

**Prima Publishing**

PRIMA PUBLISHING and its colophon are trademarks of Prima Communications, Inc.

**Library of Congress Cataloging-in-Publication Data**

Geiskopf-Hadler, Susann
    The best 125 meatless Mediterranean dishes / by Susann
Geiskopf-Hadler & Mindy Toomay.
        p.   cm. — (The best 125 dishes series)
    Includes index.
    ISBN 1-55958-637-0
    1. Vegetarian cookery.   2. Cookery, Mediterranean.
I. Toomay, Mindy.   II. Title.   III. Series.
TX837.G3797   1996
641.5'636—dc20                                              96-17710
                                                                  CIP


96 98 99 HH 10 9 8 7 6 5 4 3 2 1
Printed in the United States of America

All products mentioned in this book are trademarks of their respective companies.

Nutritional values have been rounded to the nearest whole number. Actual figures may vary slightly depending on the brands of food that are used.

*We dedicate this book to*
*Mediterranean cooks and explorers of ancient times*
*who disseminated recipes, plants,*
*and precious spices throughout the region;*
*and to today's creative cooks,*
*explorers in their own right,*
*who combine innovation with tradition*
*in countless delicious ways.*

# Contents

## Salads and Cold Vegetables  81

## Soups and Stews  116

## Pasta and Couscous    154

## Entrées from the Oven    182

## Hot Vegetable Dishes 227

## Grain and Bean Dishes 261

# Almost Instant Recipes

The following list is a guide to the recipes in this book that require 30 minutes or less to prepare, from start to finish. This earns them our Almost Instant designation, which appears under the titles on the recipe pages. Pizzas are included on this list because one can find good quality prepared pizza crust or frozen bread dough for pizzas at the supermarket.

In addition, this book includes many other quick-to-prepare recipes not labeled Almost Instant because they require some time for baking or marinating. These are great do-ahead recipes.

# Vegan Recipes

The vegan diet excludes meat, dairy products, eggs, and honey. We provide the following listing of vegan recipes as a convenience for those who have embraced this approach to healthful eating.

# Introduction

The Mediterranean Sea has played an important role in culinary history since ancient times. For centuries, explorers and traders roamed her waters, carrying foods and recipes from one port to the next. Aromatic spices such as cumin, coriander, and caraway; flavorful herbs such as rosemary, oregano, and thyme; vegetables of all kinds; rice and legumes; onions and garlic; lemons and oranges. Many crops that thrive in the sun have prospered near the Mediterranean Sea and have been enjoyed for ages by all her peoples.

These shared ingredients create much common ground among the cuisines of the region, though each of the Mediterranean countries—among them Spain, Italy, Greece, Turkey, Lebanon, Israel, Egypt, and Morocco—interprets the traditional foods in unique ways.

Today, nutrition researchers recognize "the Mediterranean diet" as one of the world's healthiest. Its commonsense rules are a joy to follow: eat fresh fruits and vegetables in season, consume plenty of whole grains and legumes, minimize meat and dairy products, and use olive oil as the primary fat. Our recipes are based on these practical guidelines, delivering the utmost in nutrition as well as flavor.

One chapter is devoted to the savory "small bites" served throughout the Mediterranean region. Such classics as Spiced Yogurt Cheese with Pita Crisps and Black Olive Tapenade provide inspiration for a memorable appetizer course or casual buffet meal. A tempting selection of soups and stews, salads, pasta and grain dishes, stuffed vegetables, casseroles, pizzas, and savory pastries complete the collection. Many are Almost Instant recipes, requiring 30 minutes or less to prepare.

We invite you to enter a world of flavor, where your senses and your imagination will soar beyond mere tradition. Take a journey with us through the riches of meatless Mediterranean cooking.

# Stocking the Pantry

Colorful outdoor food markets provide inspiration for cooks throughout the Mediterranean basin, from southern Europe to the Near East to North Africa. Seasonal fruits and vegetables, dried legumes and grains, fresh herbs, olives, and local field mushrooms are offered in abundant and beautiful displays.

Since parts of the United States have a Mediterranean-like climate, many of the classic ingredients of Mediterranean cooking are readily available here. We frequent the farmers' markets in our communities and grow seasonal vegetables and herbs in backyard gardens so that we may use the finest quality fresh ingredients in our daily cooking.

In addition to seasonal produce, our recipes are based on the pantry staples described below.

# Beans

Dried beans are wonderfully nutritious, delicious, and economical and have an important place in all the cuisines of the Mediterranean. The most popular varieties include garbanzo beans (also known as chickpeas), cannellini beans, and various kinds of lentils. Dried fava beans are a common ingredient, particularly in Egypt and the eastern Mediterranean countries. Dried lima beans are another common legume of the region.

Garbanzo beans, brown lentils, and limas are readily available in American supermarkets; cannellinis, dried favas, and the more exotic lentils may take some looking in specialty food stores. They are worth seeking out, however.

We also keep canned beans in our pantries for occasions when we don't have time for the rather lengthy soaking and cooking process required for dried beans. Select low-sodium or no-salt-added brands, and rinse canned beans before using them to remove any undesirable additives that may affect the flavor. Canned beans can be mushy, so they work best in soups or stews, where a firm texture is less crucial than it would be in a salad, for instance.

Cooking instructions for dried beans are provided on page 29.

# Dairy Products

Much of the Mediterranean region is rocky and steep and is not conducive to the raising of dairy cattle, so cow's milk products are not used extensively in these areas. Goat and sheep herds are a common sight, however, and the milk from these animals is consumed, primarily as cheese or yogurt. In the more northerly climes, cows are raised, and prized cheeses are produced from their milk.

**Feta cheese**   Feta is the cheese synonymous with Greek cuisine. It is made from sheep's milk and has a salty, piquant flavor and crumbly texture. There are Greek and French imported varieties, and domestic brands are also available.

**Goat cheese**   Chèvre is the French term for goat cheese. The semisoft, mild variety is called for in several of our recipes. Soft chèvre is now produced by goat farmers in America and various domestic and imported brands are readily available in supermarkets and specialty cheese shops.

**Gorgonzola cheese**   This blue-veined cow's milk cheese traditionally made in the Lombardy region of Italy is creamy, pungent, and aromatic. Imported gorgonzola is widely available, or another blue cheese can be substituted in our recipes, such as the fine Maytag variety now produced domestically.

**Parmesan cheese**   The very best and only true Parmesan is Parmigiano-Reggiano. It is made from skimmed cow's milk by specially trained artisans exclusively in the Emilia-Romagna region, where the city of Parma is located. Precise, centuries-old techniques are followed to produce this highly prized nutty, tangy, slightly salty cheese. Its texture is rather dry and its color is straw yellow. It combines deliciously with many regional foods and is the premier grating cheese of Italy. Buy it in small wedges, preferably cut directly from a large wheel, and grate it as needed. Fresh pregrated Parmesan is sold at well-stocked delicatessens, sometimes blended with Romano cheese, and it should be used within a few days of purchase for optimum flavor.

**Ricotta cheese**   Ricotta cheese is soft, unsalted, and somewhat grainy in texture. It is made from the whey of cow's milk and is highly perishable, so it is seldom imported from Italy. The American-made version is different from that available in Italy, but it is perfectly acceptable. Whole-milk and part-skim varieties are produced. Our recipes call for part-skim ricotta, which we find to be perfectly rich-tasting and delicious.

**Yogurt** Yogurt, a cultured milk product, has long been a staple food of the eastern Mediterranean. It has a creamy texture and tangy, pleasant taste that lends a cooling note to strongly seasoned foods. Because yogurt is cultured, it is more easily digested than milk. Our recipes call for plain nonfat yogurt. To maximize the nutritional benefits of yogurt, seek out a brand that specifies active or living cultures on the package label.

## Garlic and Onions

Garlic is a beloved ingredient in Mediterranean cooking. Its pungent punch defines many classic dishes of the region. Fresh garlic is sold in bulbs, which should be firm when you squeeze them. Garlic is past its prime when it dries and shrivels in the paper skin or when it begins to show green sprouts at the top. Store garlic bulbs in a dry, airy spot.

Onions, too, play an important role in Mediterranean cuisines. They are used in raw form where a crisp and tangy accent is desired; however, most often they are sautéed in olive oil or butter, which brings out their natural sugars and mellows their flavor. White, red, and yellow globe onions all have distinct flavors and textures. Select firm onions with no signs of sprouting. Store them in a cool, dry place.

Shallots have a more delicate flavor than globe onions and are more perishable. Purchase them in small quantities and store them in the refrigerator.

## Grains

Dried grains, staples for centuries in the Mediterranean region, keep very well when properly stored. All of the following grains are available at natural food stores, well-stocked supermarkets, and ethnic markets.

**Bulgur wheat**   Bulgur is produced from whole wheat kernels that are steam-cooked, then dried and cracked. Because of the initial steaming process, bulgur requires less cooking time than cracked or whole wheat. Bulgur is a common ingredient in the cooking of the eastern Mediterranean.

**Polenta**   Polenta is ground dried corn, known as cornmeal to most Americans. It has been a staple in Italy for hundreds of years, where it is boiled in water or broth until the grains swell and soften. Sweet or savory seasonings are then added to transform this humble cooked cereal into something quite delicious. Polenta may be made from either fine or coarse cornmeal, or you can simply buy a product labeled "polenta." Meal ground from either yellow or white corn is acceptable for polenta, though the yellow variety is much preferred in Italy.

**Rice**   Rice is enjoyed throughout the Mediterranean. Italy is world-famous for the classic creamy rice preparation called risotto. The variety most commonly used for risotto and for classic Spanish paella is a starchy, oval-shaped rice called arborio. In dishes where a creamy texture is not desired, such as the pilafs of the eastern Mediterranean, long-grain white rice is typically used. Do not substitute "instant" or "converted" rice, as their texture and flavor are inferior.

Brown rice is an excellent choice in dishes where a chewy, substantial texture is desired. It is only minimally processed and delivers good quantities of dietary fiber, vitamins, and minerals. Long-grain brown rice is a suitable substitute for the white variety in pilaf or steamed rice recipes, if you prefer it. Simply increase the cooking time from twenty minutes to forty-five minutes. The amount of liquid needed for cooking the rice will remain the same.

# Mushrooms

The white button mushrooms most common in American supermarkets are mild in flavor and are quite delicious in most recipes. In recent years new cultivation techniques have made fresh "field" mushrooms, with their distinctive earthy flavors, available to many American markets. Some of our recipes call for the big, meaty portobello mushrooms.

The porcini mushroom is a highly prized field variety frequently used, both fresh and dried, in Italian cuisine. Dried porcini are readily available and will keep indefinitely. They are reconstituted in hot water before using. The soaking liquid is extremely rich in flavor and is strained and used in recipes—never discarded.

# Nuts and Seeds

Nuts and seeds are common ingredients in the Mediterranean, used extensively in desserts and occasionally in savory dishes.

**Almonds and walnuts** We keep these common nuts on hand for a variety of uses. Shelled nuts should be stored in the refrigerator or freezer to prevent rancidity, or nuts may be shelled as needed.

**Pine nuts** Pine nuts are seeds harvested from the cones of the stone pine, common to the Mediterranean regions of Italy. These small, oval nuts have a creamy color and texture and a unique rich flavor. They are often toasted to intensify the taste. They, too, are best stored in the refrigerator or freezer.

**Sesame seeds** Sesame seeds are an ancient food and are important to the cuisines of Turkey and the Middle East, as well as Asia. Tahini, ground from either raw or toasted sesame seeds, has the texture of a nut butter and adds a wonderful rich note to some classic sauces and dips of the region. Whole sesame seeds and tahini are highly perishable and are best stored in the refrigerator.

## Olive Oil and Olives

Olive trees are a major feature of the Mediterranean landscape, and their fruits are used extensively.

**Olive oil** By far the most universal ingredient in Mediterranean cuisine, olive oil appears regularly in this book. Extra virgin olive oil comes from the first pressing of the best-quality unripe olives. It delivers a powerful olive color, aroma, and flavor that is delicious in salads and in other raw preparations. The olive oil termed "virgin" is from slightly riper olives and has a higher level of acidity. It is suitable for many cooked uses, such as sautéing. "Pure" olive oil is derived from the second or third pressing of the olives. Where the robust quality of extra virgin olive oil is essential in our recipes, we have so specified. Elsewhere, we simply call for olive oil, and any grade is suitable for these uses. The taste of olive oil can vary greatly from brand to brand. Sample several small bottles before deciding which you prefer.

**Olives** Green olives are unripe fruit while black olives have been left on the tree to ripen. Olives, whether green or black, must be cured—in salt, oil, or brine—to mellow their bitterness. Smooth-skinned, purplish-black calamata olives, dry oil-cured black olives, tiny piquant niçoise olives, and green varieties like the flavorful French *picholines* are used in the recipes in this book. Look for these distinctive olives at specialty food stores or delicatessens. The black olives canned in water common to

American supermarkets are not acceptable substitutes for the varieties called for in our recipes.

## Pasta and Couscous

Wheat is a centuries-old Mediterranean staple, primarily used in breads, pasta, and couscous.

**Pasta**　Dried commercial pasta is generally made with hard durum wheat flour (semolina) and without eggs. Semolina pasta has a distinctive taste that combines well with both delicate and robust sauces. Such pasta, when cooked al dente, has a sturdy texture that is not gummy or starchy. We keep many different shapes and sizes of dried semolina pasta in our pantries.

**Couscous**　Couscous is a pasta product indigenous to North Africa. The tiny beads cook almost instantly, creating a light and fluffy texture. Couscous is available at any well-stocked supermarket.

## Seasonings

Numerous distinctive seasonings are used to create the region's diverse and delicious cuisines. Since ancient trade routes brought foods from every corner of the world to the various ports of the Mediterranean, some flavors have become established as essential throughout the region. Though each country has its signature dishes, there is much common ground. The seasonings discussed below are readily available and are prominent in Mediterranean cooking.

## Herbs and Spices

Fresh herbs and aromatic dried spices are at the heart of Mediterranean cuisine. Many households maintain herb gardens, if only a flourishing window box on a balcony, and we encourage you to do the same. Herbs are easy to grow and hardy. If you choose not to grow your own, look for fresh herbs in the produce section of major supermarkets, specialty food shops, or at farmers' markets.

Dried herbs and spices are readily available and have abundant uses. A good source for these culinary essentials is a natural food store that has a bulk herb section. There you may buy herbs and spices in small quantities without expensive packaging. Since dried herbs and ground spices lose their potency rather quickly, store them in dated airtight containers and replace them at least annually.

In general, the flavors and aromas of fresh herbs are more delicate than those of their dried counterparts. As a rule of thumb, dried herbs are added early in the cooking of a particular dish, while fresh herbs are added toward the end. Keep in mind that in most of our recipes, dried herbs are not interchangeable with fresh herbs.

The following Mediterranean herbs and spices are called for most frequently in this book.

**Allspice**  Indigenous to the West Indies, this aromatic berry is used to season both sweet and savory dishes. Its taste resembles a mixture of clove, cinnamon, nutmeg, and pepper—hence the name.

**Basil**  The appetizing peppery aroma and flavor of fresh basil is unsurpassed in Italian cooking. Fresh basil is typically not cooked but rather is added just before the dish is served.

**Bay leaf**   There are dozens of different varieties of bay trees, many with culinary uses. Any dried bay leaf sold as a seasoning is suitable for use in our recipes. Add whole bay leaves to dishes at the beginning of the cooking time, as they release their distinctive flavor and fragrance gradually. Remove and discard them before serving.

**Caraway**   Caraway is an ancient seasoning native to Asia and some parts of Europe. Its flavor is warm, pungent, and slightly bitter.

**Chili flakes**   Dried crushed red chilies, including the seeds, are frequently used in the bold cooking of southern Italy. Different brands or batches can vary in intensity. A good rule of thumb is to start with a very small amount and add more if a spicier dish is desired.

**Cilantro**   See Coriander.

**Cinnamon**   Savory dishes in the Mediterranean sometimes combine hot spices with sweet ones, such as cinnamon, to create wonderful depth and complexity. Cinnamon is the dried bark of a tropical tree. Its flavor is slightly woody and bittersweet.

**Coriander**   Fresh coriander leaves, best known to American cooks as cilantro, is also sometimes sold as Chinese parsley. The dried seeds of the same plant, sold as whole or ground coriander, provide a much different, more subtle, spicy/sweet flavor. Cilantro and coriander are common seasonings in eastern Mediterranean and North African dishes.

**Cumin**   Cumin's pungent, warm, somewhat smoky flavor adds depth to many eastern Mediterranean dishes. The dried seeds are sold whole or ground.

**Dill**  Feathery fresh dill leaves have a bright, refreshing flavor extensively utilized in Greek cuisine. Dill weed is available dried, and the seeds also have culinary uses.

**Fennel seed**  Fresh fennel is a much-loved vegetable in Italy. The dried seeds of the plant are also used to impart a licorice-like flavor to a dish. The seeds are usually crushed with a mortar and pestle before using.

**Herbes de Provence**  This classic blend of dried herbs and spices from the south of France lends a characteristic flavor to dishes of the region. Many variations exist. It is simple and economical to make up such a blend at home. We provide a recipe on page 38.

**Marjoram**  Marjoram is similar to oregano but is preferred in dishes where a slightly sweeter, more floral flavor and aroma are desired. Its delicacy will be overwhelmed if combined in a recipe with strong-flavored herbs and spices.

**Mint**  Many Mediterranean dishes rely on the refreshing fragrance and taste of fresh mint leaves. Any variety of mint sold as a fresh herb, such as peppermint or spearmint, is suitable for cooking purposes. Mint is particularly carefree as an herb for the home garden.

**Nutmeg**  Nutmeg has a deliciously spicy, sweet, and nutty flavor. When used with too heavy a hand, however, a bitterness develops that can overpower the dish. Freshly grated whole nutmeg is called for in our recipes. You may purchase a special nutmeg grinder, or use the fine-holed side of a standard kitchen grater. Commercially ground nutmeg may be used, but it tends to be less flavorful.

**Oregano**  Fresh oregano is mild and aromatic. When dried, its flavor intensifies and can be quite strong. Both types have their uses in Mediterranean cooking, particularly in the cuisines of Italy and Greece.

**Paprika**   Paprika is complex and robust in flavor, with both sweet and slightly hot flavor notes. It adds an appetizing color to many Spanish, eastern Mediterranean, and North African dishes.

**Parsley**   We use parsley leaves in their fresh form, never dried. The curly-leaf variety and the flat-leaf Italian variety are interchangeable in our recipes, though their raw texture is somewhat different. We prefer the flat-leaf variety because it is slightly sweeter and more aromatic.

**Rosemary**   Rosemary is another easy home garden herb. It is intensely aromatic and lends a distinctive flavor to cooked foods. It is used in Mediterranean cooking in both its fresh and dried forms. The rather spiky leaves should be chopped, if fresh, or crumbled, if dried, before using.

**Saffron**   The flavor of saffron is subtle yet pungent. It is prized as much for the lovely golden color it imparts to a dish as for its flavor. Saffron "threads" are the dried stigmas of a certain crocus flower. It is expensive because the stigmas must be harvested by hand; however, a little goes a long way. We recommend buying saffron threads rather than powdered saffron, which loses its potency very rapidly.

**Sage**   This woodsy herb is a popular seasoning in some parts of the Mediterranean. Its leaves may be utilized in fresh, "rubbed," or ground form.

**Tarragon**   Tarragon has a distinctive licorice-like flavor much appreciated by French cooks. It should be used with a light hand, since its flavor can overwhelm a dish. Both fresh and dried tarragon are useful. The dried form is particularly potent in flavor.

**Thyme**   This aromatic, versatile herb is a potent seasoning compatible with other strong flavors. Use it either fresh or dried, as specified in individual recipes.

## Capers

Capers are the unopened buds of a type of wild nasturtium common to certain regions of the Mediterranean. The buds are typically pickled in vinegar, though they sometimes come packed in salt. Salted capers should be rinsed thoroughly before being used. Large capers (*capote*) and small capers (*nonpareil*) are interchangeable in our recipes, though very large ones may require mincing before being added to a dish.

## Lemon

The flavor and aroma of lemon is central to many dishes throughout the Mediterranean basin. We prefer to use Meyer lemons, which are juicier, less tart, and have a thinner skin than other varieties. Freshly squeezed lemon juice adds a refreshing, tart note that can bring a dish to life, and minced peel or zest provides a bright, slightly bitter flavor. Purchase an inexpensive lemon zester, which will make quick work of scraping off paper-thin curls of lemon peel. As a rule of thumb, one medium Meyer lemon will yield two teaspoons of lemon zest.

Preserved lemons, a staple of North African cooking, have a unique, exotic flavor. We have provided a recipe for them on page 36.

## Vinegar

Good wine vinegar begins with good wine, so don't immediately reach for the cheapest wine vinegar on your grocer's shelf. Sample different types and you'll discover the brands you most enjoy. Choice wine vinegars appear clear, not cloudy.

In addition to white and red wine vinegars, we keep traditional Italian balsamic vinegar and sherry vinegar on hand for their distinctive, more mellow flavors.

## *Wines and Spirits*

Wine is widely used in some parts of the Mediterranean, for drinking as well as cooking. For cooking purposes, select a good wine, one that you enjoy drinking. The finished dish will be only as good as the sum of its ingredients.

We select wines from California as well as imported wines for cooking as well as drinking. We keep dry red and white varieties on hand, plus a few specialty wines for their unique flavors. Dry marsala, sherry, and Madeira appear in a few of our recipes. Again, purchase the best quality you can afford.

# Stock

Freshly made stocks have real soul that canned and powdered broths can't imitate. We have provided simple instructions for making vegetable stock at home using ingredients you probably have on hand in your kitchen (see page 32). Homemade stock can be refrigerated for several days or frozen for longer periods. In a pinch, you may prepare stock from vegetable bouillon cubes, with somewhat different but good results. Look for low-sodium or no-salt-added brands.

# Vegetables

Vegetables are central to the Mediterranean diet. Many of the best-loved vegetables of the region are also favorites in the United States, so they are readily available.

We provide information below about some of the lesser-known Mediterranean vegetables used in our recipes.

**Arugula**   The people of the Mediterranean grow and enjoy a wider variety of greens and lettuces than the typical American cook. Specialty greens are becoming more familiar sights in our markets, however, and arugula is now commonly available. Sometimes sold as rocket, it has a distinct peppery flavor.

**Fava beans**   Fava beans (*Vicia faba*), also called broad beans, have a distinctive flavor. Part of the culinary crop is eaten fresh, and the remainder is dried. Succulent fresh favas can be eaten either cooked or raw, although some people have difficulty digesting them raw. The large pods—ranging from six to twelve inches in length—host a bean that has a flavor unique among shell beans. Getting to them is an easy but time-consuming task. First the bean is removed from the pod, then it is blanched and peeled. Favas harvested while very young and tender may be eaten without peeling.

Select pods that are bright green and glossy, with well-developed, bulging seeds. Blackening at the ends of the pods is a sign that the beans will not be of good quality. Favas in their pods will stay fresh for a few days if refrigerated in a plastic bag. Since fresh fava beans are only available for a few weeks each year, you may wish to freeze some for later use. Peel and blanch several pounds of beans, then freeze them in two-cup quantities in Ziploc bags or plastic containers.

**Fennel**   Fresh fennel bears some resemblance to celery, with numerous stalks attached at their bases in overlapping layers to form a thick bulb. Its foliage, however, is feathery and the bulb is paler in color and more enlarged than that of a bunch of celery. Fennel has a pronounced licorice flavor that is unusual and delicious when raw and mellows to a delectable sweetness when cooked. Though the leaves and stalks are edible, it is the bulb portion that is sliced and used as a vegetable in Italian cooking.

Fennel is sometimes sold as sweet anise or labeled with its Italian name, *finocchio*. Buy fennel bulbs that have straight stalks protruding from a plump, tightly closed, whitish base. Wrap fennel in plastic and store in the vegetable crisper, where the bulb will stay fresh for a few days.

**Radicchio**   A member of the chicory family, radicchio adds a unique, mildly bitter accent to salads and other dishes. Though different colors are cultivated, the most common variety in American markets is mottled purple and white. Shop for small, crisp-looking leaves forming a loose, cabbage-like head. The color should be robust and glossy, with no brown spots. Wrap radicchio loosely in a plastic bag and store it in the vegetable crisper. Wash the leaves and spin them dry just before using them as called for in recipes.

**Tomatoes**   Though not an uncommon vegetable, the tomato deserves special mention. For optimum flavor, enjoy fresh tomato dishes only when vine-ripened tomatoes are available at the market. At other times, good-quality canned tomatoes are a better choice for cooked dishes than fresh. Look for brands that contain no additives.

Pear-shaped tomatoes are commonly used for cooking because they have a firmer, meatier texture and less juice than round, salad tomatoes. The latter are best used in fresh preparations.

People with an abundance of garden tomatoes on hand may substitute three pounds of fresh pear tomatoes for one twenty-eight-ounce can of pear tomatoes. Before using them, blanch, peel, and seed them according to the directions on page 28.

# Nutrition Alert

By a pleasant happenstance, the foods that dominate the Mediterranean diet are also the foods now heralded by top nutritionists. We are encouraged to eat more fruits, vegetables, and whole grains to increase our intake of antioxidants such as beta-carotene, flavonoids, and vitamin E. Research indicates that these nutrients play an important role in minimizing one's risk of developing heart disease. In addition, fruits, vegetables, and whole grains contain little or no fat, making them good choices in maintaining a lowfat diet.

In 1992, the U.S. Department of Agriculture released the Food Guide Pyramid, presenting the food groups with new and different emphasis. At the base of the pyramid are the foods from which we should get most of our calories. At the tip are the foods that should supply us with the fewest calories. (To order a brochure depicting the Food Guide Pyramid and discussing the concept in detail, order Home and Garden Bulletin #252 from USDA, Human Nutrition Information Service, 6505 Belcrest Road, Hyattsville, MD 20782.)

The basic message of the pyramid is to cut down on fats and added sugars, as well as to eat a variety of foods from the different food groups. Our chief eating goals, says the USDA, should be variety, moderation, and balance. It is the overall picture that counts—what you eat over a period of days is more important than what you eat in a single meal. A diet primarily comprised of grains and cereal products (six to eleven servings per day), vegetables (three to five servings per day), and fruits (two to four servings per day), combined with lowfat protein sources (two to three servings per day) and lowfat dairy products (two to three servings per day) conforms to the Food Guide Pyramid, creating a well-balanced mix of proteins, carbohydrates, and fats.

For some people, three to five servings of vegetables will sound like a lot, but serving sizes stipulated by the Food Guide Pyramid are moderate. A cup of leafy raw vegetables (as in a salad), one-half cup of cooked or chopped raw vegetables, three-quarters cup of vegetable juice, or one-quarter cup of dried fruit equals one serving. There is no need to measure— the serving sizes are only a guideline. Furthermore, a single dish may supply servings in more than one category: for example, a sandwich may provide a grain serving (the bread), a dairy serving (the lowfat cheese), and a vegetable serving (the lettuce, sprouts, and tomato).

The nutritional experts who designed the Food Guide Pyramid recommend eating a variety of vegetables to be sure we are getting all the nutritional benefits this vast family of foods can provide. They also recommend making sure at least one serving each day is high in vitamin A; at least one each day is high in vitamin C; at least one each day is high in fiber; and that we eat cruciferous vegetables several times each week.

Vitamins A and C are particularly important because they function in the body as antioxidants. Studies have shown that antioxidants help protect us against the development of coronary heart disease and cancer, and they may even slow down the aging process. Antioxidants are a class of nutrients that neutralize "free radicals," unstable oxygen molecules that cause cell damage over time, increasing the body's vulnerability to serious disease. Vitamin A is present in animal products or it can be manufactured as needed by the body from the beta-carotene in vegetables that are dark-green (for example, leafy greens and broccoli) or orange-yellow (for example, sweet potatoes). Vitamin C is present in some quantity in most fruits and vegetables—the best sources include citrus fruits, strawberries, tomatoes, broccoli, leafy greens, and sweet potatoes. Cruciferous vegetables contain considerable quantities of antioxidants as well as beneficial nitrogen compounds called indoles, which have been shown in recent studies to be effective cancer preventers.

The Surgeon General and the American Heart Association are proponents of what is described as a semivegetarian approach to eating, which is based primarily on grains, vegetables, and fruits. The Food Guide Pyramid and other expert recommendations support semivegetarianism as an important aspect of a healthy lifestyle. The major shift required for many Americans is to view meat, if it is to be consumed at all, as a side dish or condiment.

Many studies are being conducted to determine optimum levels of various food components in the human diet. Our intent here is to provide an introduction to basic nutrition. For further investigation, check with your local librarian or bookseller for thorough reference works.

The recipes in this book have been analyzed for calories, proteins, carbohydrates, fat, cholesterol, sodium, and fiber. We discuss below the importance of each of these components.

**Calories**  It is important to be aware of your total caloric intake in a day, but most important to note is where the calories are coming from. Calories derive from three primary sources: proteins, carbohydrates, and fats. Fats contain a greater concentration of calories than do carbohydrates or protein, and they are much harder for the body to metabolize. The U.S. Food and Drug Administration therefore suggests that the average American diet should be adjusted so that fewer calories come from fatty foods and more from carbohydrates. The American Heart Association specifically recommends that no more than 30 percent of the calories in our overall diets be derived from fat.

**Fat** The type of fat that you consume is as important as the amount. Fats are divided into three categories: monounsaturated, polyunsaturated, and saturated. Saturation refers to the number of hydrogen atoms present in the fat, with saturated fats containing the most.

The primary reason to pay attention to the saturation level of fats is because saturated fats tend to increase levels of the dangerous component of blood cholesterol in some people. Therefore, it is wise to choose polyunsaturated or monounsaturated fats over saturated fats. To assist in making this choice, remember that most saturated fats are from animal origin and are hard at room temperature (such as butter and cheese) and most unsaturated fats are of vegetable origin and are liquid at room temperature (such as olive oil).

Olive oil, which is used extensively in Mediterranean cooking, is a monounsaturated oil that helps to stimulate the body's production of HDL, a component of cholesterol that is actually beneficial. HDL helps the body limit the buildup of substances that block arteries, leading to heart disease. In recent studies, olive oil has been shown to also lower the level of LDL in cholesterol, the component that is instrumental in depositing fat on artery walls. Perhaps this begins to explain the relatively low rates of heart disease in Mediterranean countries.

Our bodies need some fat, as it is an essential component in energy production, but it is estimated that most of us consume six to eight times more fat than we need. High-fat diets are implicated not only in heart disease but also in the development of some cancers, most notably of the colon and breast. It is likely to contribute to a healthier—perhaps even longer—life to learn the basics about dietary fat.

There are 9 calories in a gram of fat. A gram of protein or carbohydrate contains only four calories. Hence, the less fat one consumes, the lower one's intake of calories and the lower one's percentage of calories from fat. Calories derived from dietary fats are more troublesome than calories from any other source, as the body is most efficient at converting fat calories into body fat.

Consider that the average tablespoon of oil contains 14 grams of fat and 120 calories, while almost no fat is contained in a half cup of steamed brown rice (206 calories) or a cup of cooked broccoli (44 calories). This illustrates the volume of food that can be eaten without increasing one's fat-to-calories ratio.

To calculate the fat-to-calories ratio for a particular dish or for one's entire daily food intake, multiply the number of fat grams by 9, then divide the resulting number by the number of total calories. The result is the percentage of calories derived from fat. It is okay to enjoy an occasional higher-fat dish as long as one's ratio averages 30 percent or less over the course of a day.

Another way of monitoring one's fat intake is by counting fat grams consumed. The nutritional analyses provided with each of our recipes facilitates this by listing fat in total grams per serving. An easy way to calculate how much fat you should consume is to divide your body weight in half. This number is an estimate of the maximum fat in grams a moderately active person should ingest over the course of a day to maintain that weight.

**Fiber** Dietary fiber—also called roughage—is the material from plant foods that cannot be completely digested by humans. It provides the bulk necessary to keep the digestive and eliminative systems functioning properly. Foods high in fiber also tend to be high in beta-carotene, low in fat, and filling enough to reduce our dependence on higher-fat foods.

In recent years, evidence demonstrating that dietary fiber promotes human health has mounted. Studies have linked high fiber intake with reduced risk of constipation; diverticulosis; colon, rectal, and breast cancer; heart disease; diabetes; and obesity. Because high-fiber diets tend to be low in fat and high in other health-promoting substances, it is difficult to prove its individual protective effects. However, the connection is compelling and studies are ongoing.

Many doctors now recommend adding fiber to the diet for optimum health. Organizations such as the USDA and the National Cancer Institute (NCI) have recently made increased fiber consumption part of their standard recommendations for a healthy diet.

The NCI recommends that we eat between 20 and 30 grams of fiber daily but that our consumption not exceed 35 grams per day. Experts estimate that most Americans now eat only about half of the recommended amount. A recent national food survey showed that diets including five servings of fruits and vegetables daily-as recommended in the Food Guide Pyramid-provided about 17 grams of fiber. When whole grains and legumes are included in the daily diet, it's easy to reach the recommended level.

Experts agree that fiber should come from foods and not supplements, which provide no nutrients. Ways to consume more fiber—along with valuable vitamins, minerals, and amino acids—include choosing whole grain rather than refined-flour products; not peeling fruits and vegetables; and eating dried peas and beans. The Mediterranean diet is centered around all of these food categories.

It is especially important for people on high-fiber diets to drink plenty of water, or the fiber can slow down or block healthy bowel functioning. Eating too much fiber can cause gastrointestinal distress in people unaccustomed to it, so fiber content should be increased gradually.

Dietary fiber encompasses both soluble and insoluble fiber. The dietary fiber value included in our nutritional analyses includes both types.

**Protein**   Since our bodies store only small amounts of protein, it needs to be replenished daily. Although protein is needed for growth and tissue repair, it is not needed in great abundance. The National Academy of Science's Food and Nutrition Board recommends 45 grams of protein per day for the average 120-pound woman and 55 grams for the average 154-pound man.

Some nutritionists think this is more protein than needed on average. Recent nutritional studies suggest, in fact, that the detrimental effects of excessive protein consumption should be of greater concern to most Americans than the threat of protein deficiency. While this debate continues, it makes sense to choose protein sources that are low in fat and, thus, calories.

Most people associate protein consumption with eating meat; however, the protein in our recipes derives from combining grains with legumes and dairy products and is quite sufficient to meet the body's protein needs.

**Carbohydrates**   There is a common misconception that carbohydrates such as pasta, grains, and potatoes are high in calories and low in nutritive value. However, starchy complex carbohydrates do not present a calorie problem; the problem is typically with the fats that are added to them.

Nutritional experts now suggest that more of our daily calories come from carbohydrates than from fats or protein, since the body provides energy more economically from carbohydrates. Carbohydrates are quickly converted into glucose, the body's main fuel.

Complex carbohydrates are low in fat and are a good source of fiber. They should comprise a large share of our daily calories.

**Cholesterol**   Numerous volumes have been written on cholesterol in recent years, and much is being discovered about its role in overall health and nutrition. Cholesterol is essential for the construction of cell walls, the transmission of nerve impulses, and the synthesis of important hormones. It plays a vital role in the healthy functioning of the body and poses no problem when present in the correct amount. Excess cholesterol, however, is considered a major risk factor in the development of heart disease. The U.S. Senate Select Committee on Nutrition and Human Needs recommends that the average person consume no more than 300 milligrams of cholesterol per day. The best course of action is to have your cholesterol level checked by your doctor and follow his or her specific guidelines.

Recent studies have shown that the total amount of fat a person eats—especially saturated fat—may be more responsible for the cholesterol level in the body than the actual cholesterol count found in food. Current evidence suggests that a high-fiber diet low in overall fat can reduce cholesterol levels, particularly the harmful LDL type. Vegetables are certainly major players in such a diet.

**Sodium** The American Heart Association recommends that sodium intake be limited to 3,000 milligrams per day (a teaspoon of salt contains 2,200 milligrams of sodium). However, the actual physiological requirement is only about 220 milligrams a day. Sodium is essential for good health, since each cell of the body must be bathed continually in a saline solution. Yet high sodium intake disrupts this balance and is associated with high blood pressure and life-threatening conditions such as heart disease, kidney disease, and stroke.

Many foods naturally contain some sodium, so you do not need to add much when cooking to achieve good flavor. Particularly if you have salt-related health concerns, dishes that taste a little bland unsalted can be seasoned with herbs or other salt-free alternatives. When our recipes call for salt, you may add less than the recommended amount, or none at all, if your doctor has advised you to drastically reduce your sodium intake.

Monitoring your intake of the above food components is important; however, unless you're under doctor's instructions, you needn't be overly rigid. It is preferable to balance your intake over the course of a day, or even several days, rather than attempting to make each meal fit the pattern recommended by nutritional experts. This rule of thumb allows you to enjoy a recipe that may be higher in fat or salt, for instance, than you would normally choose, knowing that at your next meal you can eliminate that component altogether to achieve a healthy daily balance.

The information given here is not set in stone; the science of nutrition is constantly evolving. The analyses for our recipes is provided for people on normal diets who want to plan healthier meals. If your physician has prescribed a special diet, check with a registered dietitian to see how these recipes fit into your guidelines.

We encourage you to spend some time learning about how foods break down and are used by the body as fuel. A basic understanding of the process and application of a few simple rules can contribute to a longer and—more important—a healthier life.

## *Seven Simple Guidelines for a Healthy Diet*

1. Eat a variety of foods.
2. Maintain desirable weight.
3. Avoid too much fat, saturated fat, and cholesterol.
4. Eat foods with adequate starch and fiber.
5. Avoid excessive sugar.
6. Avoid excessive sodium.
7. If you drink alcoholic beverages, do so in moderation.

SOURCE: *National Cancer Institute, U.S. Department of Health and Human Services*

# An Introduction to the Recipes

Mediterranean cooks take their inspiration from whatever is in season and fresh at the market. Their cuisine is comforting, casual, and earthy. Their cooking is an art, not a science, and relies on the best quality ingredients prepared simply and with passion. Many recipes have been passed on verbally from generation to generation, so every family has its favorite "traditional" version of classic dishes, slightly different perhaps from that of the family next door.

An introduction to each chapter provides information to familiarize you with the specific categories of Mediterranean cuisine.

You will notice that our recipes list ingredients in an unconventional format, with the name of food in the first column and the quantity required in a separate column to the right. This facilitates quick perusal of the ingredients, so you can determine whether you're in the mood for that particular dish or whether you have the required items on hand. We find this format particularly easy to use, and we hope you will agree.

# Tips for Successful Cooking from Recipes

Follow the suggestions below to ensure a smooth and enjoyable cooking experience when working from written recipes.

- Use only the freshest, finest ingredients. Your finished dish will be only as good as the individual components that go into it, so don't compromise on quality.

- Read a recipe all the way through before beginning to cook. This will allow you to take care of any preliminary steps, such as bringing ingredients to room temperature, and will give you a solid grasp of the entire process.

- Set out your ingredients and equipment on the work surface before you begin. This will save you walking from one end of the kitchen to the other to rummage in a cupboard for the long-lost nutmeg, for instance, while neglecting whatever is cooking on the stove.

- For certain ingredients, quantities are by nature approximations. When we call for a large carrot, for example, the one you use may be more or less large than the one we used. This is nothing to worry about. When using a specific amount is essential to the success of a dish, we have provided cup or pound measurements. Otherwise, exercise your own judgment about which carrot in the bin is "large."

- Garlic amounts in our recipes refer to medium-size cloves. If you are using elephant garlic or the tiny cloves in the center of a garlic bulb, adjust accordingly the number of cloves you use.

- Serve hot food on warmed serving dishes and warmed individual plates so the food stays at optimal temperature as long as possible. This is easy to accomplish by placing the dishes near the heat source as you cook; or warm your oven several minutes before dinnertime, turn off the heat, and place the dishes there until needed.

# Techniques for the Basics

Here we explain some basic techniques used in various recipes in this book. They are simple and quick procedures. Once you have mastered them, you will find them quite useful.

## *Blanching Tomatoes*

To blanch fresh tomatoes, drop them into boiling water for about one minute. With a slotted spoon, transfer the tomatoes to a bowl of cold water, then drain in a colander. When cool enough to handle, peel off the skins and cut out and discard the stems. Cut the tomatoes in half crosswise and squeeze gently to remove the juicy seed pockets. Proceed as directed in individual recipes.

## *Cooking on a Grill*

In regions where summer brings high temperatures, outdoor grilling is a great alternative to stove-top cooking, which can heat up not only the kitchen but the entire house. In California, the climate allows us to enjoy grilled foods practically year-round.

To preheat a coal grill, start the charcoal at least fifteen to twenty minutes before cooking begins so the proper temperature can be achieved in time. The coals of a high-temperature charcoal grill have a bright red glow with a small amount of visible white ash. The coals of a medium-temperature grill have an orange glow with a coating of gray ash. Gas grills are equipped with a dial for setting the appropriate temperature. Preheat a gas grill for at least ten minutes or according to the manufacturer's specific directions.

Some safety tips: Set up the grill in an open area away from the house, and never attempt to move a hot grill. Do not cook on a charcoal fire in high winds. Avoid wearing flowing garments when cooking on a grill. Never squirt charcoal lighter fluid directly into a fire. Use long-handled utensils and wear heavy-duty mitts. Make sure ashes are completely cold before discarding.

## Cooking Beans

The texture and flavor of freshly cooked dried beans are far superior to those of canned varieties, and dried beans are economical. When our recipes call for cooked beans, we strongly recommend you use freshly cooked ones. As a general rule of thumb, one cup of dried beans will yield two to two and a half cups of cooked beans.

Before cooking beans, rinse them thoroughly to remove surface dirt and sort them carefully. Often small dirt clods, pebbles, or other foreign objects will find their way through the factory sorters and into the market bin or bags. Also discard beans that are shriveled or discolored.

We usually soak dried beans for several hours before cooking. This softens them slightly and shortens the cooking time. Cover with plenty of fresh water and leave at room temperature overnight, loosely covered with a tea towel or lid. A quicker method is to cover them with boiling water and leave them to soak, loosely covered, for at least two hours. Drain off the starchy soaking liquid.

Cover the beans with fresh water and boil until tender. Depending on the type of bean and its age, this can take any-where from thirty minutes to two hours. Test frequently so as not to overcook. For most uses, beans should be boiled until they yield easily to the bite but are not mushy. If they are to be cooked further after boiling, as in a casserole, take them from the pot when barely al dente.

You may wish to add garlic, bay leaves, and/or chili flakes to the cooking water, but wait to salt the pot until the beans are tender and ready for their final seasoning, because cooking in salt can give beans a tough or rubbery texture.

Cooked beans freeze well. Cook them in larger quantities than the recipe calls for then freeze the surplus in their cooking liquid in small measured portions.

# Frequently Used Homemade Ingredients

When our recipes call for such ingredients as vegetable stock or bread crumbs, you may purchase commercial varieties. For top quality and economy, however, make your own. It's easier than you think to keep homemade "convenience" foods on hand.

## Bread Crumbs and Cubes

If you have part of a whole grain or thick-crusted loaf of bread that is slightly stale or has begun to dry out, simply break the bread into chunks and chop it in a food processor to either coarse or fine consistency. It is sometimes useful to have seasoned bread crumbs on hand, made by mixing dried herbs and granulated garlic into the crumbs before storing.

You can also prepare dried bread crumbs from fresh bread. Preheat the oven or a toaster oven to 350 degrees F. Use your hands to crumble bread onto a dry baking sheet. Place in the oven for 15 minutes, then turn off the heat, and allow the crumbs to continue drying for about half an hour. When recipes call for bread cubes, simply cut fresh or slightly stale bread into the desired size before baking.

Dried bread crumbs and cubes will keep for long periods when stored in a dry place in an airtight container.

# Homemade Vegetable Stock

*VEGAN*

*Any vegetable trimmings can be included in the stockpot. This recipe emphasizes Mediterranean seasonings and vegetables, but virtually any combination of vegetables, including fresh or dried mushrooms and herbs, will make a good stock. Don't feel compelled to measure precisely—just use about twice as much water as mixed vegetables, by volume, and don't allow a single vegetable to predominate.*

*Yield:* About 10 cups

| | |
|---|---|
| **Russet potatoes, not peeled** | 2 **medium, diced** |
| **Yellow onions** | 2 **medium, diced** |
| **Green bell pepper** | 1 **medium, diced** |
| **Celery** | 1 **rib, chopped** |
| **Button mushrooms** | ½ **pound** |
| **Assorted vegetables, chopped**\* | 2 **cups** |
| **Garlic** | 6 **cloves, chopped** |
| **Whole bay leaves** | 2 **large** |
| **Dried rosemary** | 2 **teaspoons** |
| **Dried basil** | 2 **teaspoons** |
| **Dried thyme** | ½ **teaspoon** |
| **Whole peppercorns** | ½ **teaspoon** |
| **Salt** | ¾ **teaspoon** |

Put 14 cups of water on to boil in a large stockpot over medium-high heat. Add all the vegetables, herbs, peppercorns, and salt and

---

\*Good choices for the assorted vegetables would be trimmings such as broccoli stalks, spinach or chard stems, pea pods, asparagus stems, and carrot peels. If you include broccoli or other members of the cabbage family, keep the quantity at no more than 1 cup total, as the flavors and aromas of such strong vegetables can take over the stock.

*An Introduction to the Recipes*

bring to a boil. Reduce the heat to low and simmer, uncovered, for 45 minutes. Turn off the heat and allow to steep for an additional 15 to 30 minutes before straining into glass jars. Any stock you do not use immediately may be stored for several days in the refrigerator or for several months in the freezer.

---

Each cup provides:

| | | | |
|---|---|---|---|
| 10 | Calories | 2 g | Carbohydrate |
| 1 g | Protein | 164 mg | Sodium |
| 0 g | Fat | 0 mg | Cholesterol |
| 0 g | Dietary Fiber | | |

# Crostini

*ALMOST INSTANT, VEGAN*

*Crostini are nothing more than oven-baked slices of toast, but they must be made from an excellent fresh bread. They can be served with any number of tasty toppings. Crostini can be made several hours or a day ahead and held at room temperature in a loosely closed cloth or paper bag.*

*Yield:* About 12 servings

| Thick-crusted unsliced bread | 1 one-pound loaf |
|---|---|

Preheat the oven to 375 degrees F. If the bread is a long, skinny shape (such as a baguette), cut it crosswise into ¼-inch slices. If you are using a dome-shaped loaf, cut it in half, then cut each half into ¼-inch slices. Arrange the slices in a single layer on a baking sheet and bake for about 8 to 10 minutes, until the bread is evenly browned and well crisped. You want the finished toasts to have a crunchy texture.

---

Each serving provides:

| 109 | Calories | 20 g | Carbohydrate |
|---|---|---|---|
| 3 g | Protein | 221 mg | Sodium |
| 1 g | Fat | 0 mg | Cholesterol |
| 1 g | Dietary Fiber | | |

# Basil Pesto

*ALMOST INSTANT*

*We have prepared this simple version of the classic Genovese pesto for years using aromatic basil picked fresh from our summer gardens. We enjoy pesto on pasta, as a seasoning in soups and other dishes, and as a spread on slices of bread or crostini.*

*Yield:* 1 cup

| | |
|---|---|
| **Fresh basil leaves** | **2 cups, firmly packed** |
| **Extra virgin olive oil** | **⅓ cup** |
| **Pine nuts** | **¼ cup** |
| **Garlic** | **6 cloves, chopped** |
| **Parmesan cheese, finely grated** | **¾ cup** |

Wash the basil, discard the stems, and dry thoroughly. In a food processor or blender, puree the basil with ¼ cup of the oil, the pine nuts, garlic, and Parmesan until thick and uniform. With the machine running, add the remaining oil in a thin stream to create a smooth paste.

---

Each tablespoon provides:

| | | | |
|---|---|---|---|
| 72 | Calories | 1 g | Carbohydrate |
| 2 g | Protein | 70 mg | Sodium |
| 7 g | Fat | 3 mg | Cholesterol |
| 0 g | Dietary Fiber | | |

# Preserved Lemons

*VEGAN*

*For best results, use organically grown Meyer lemons. They are juicy and have a slightly sweet flavor and thin skin. Commercially preserved lemons are available from ethnic markets.*

*Yield:* 6 preserved lemons

| | |
|---|---|
| **Meyer lemons** | 6  medium (about 1 pound) |
| **Coarse sea salt** | ¼ cup |

Place the whole lemons in a basin of cold water and use a vegetable brush to scrub the skins. Put the lemons in a bowl, fill the bowl with lukewarm water, and let the lemons soak for 1 hour. Drain the lemons and pat them dry.

Slit each lemon lengthwise in four equidistant places, cutting deep but not clear through the lemon. Do this over a glass or ceramic bowl to catch any juice. Place the lemons into the bowl and pack the slits with the salt. Place a plate on top of the lemons and weigh down the plate so the lemons are slightly squashed. Let stand at room temperature 2 to 3 days, until the juice of the lemons has been released and the lemons are almost completely submerged in their own liquid.

Use a wooden spoon to transfer the lemons to a large, sterilized glass jar that has a tight-fitting lid, packing them in tightly. Pour the released lemon juice over the lemons. Add lukewarm boiled water, if necessary, to completely submerge the lemons. Be sure not to touch the lemons or their juice with metal utensils or the metal lid of the jar.

*An Introduction to the Recipes*

Tightly cover the jar and place it in a cool place for 10 to 14 days. At this point the lemons are ready to use, or you may place the jar in the refrigerator and use the lemons over the course of 6 months. Rinse well before using as directed in individual recipes.

---

Each lemon provides:

| | | | |
|---|---|---|---|
| 17 | Calories | 7 g | Carbohydrate |
| 1 g | Protein | 1065 mg | Sodium |
| 0 g | Fat | 0 mg | Cholesterol |
| 1 g | Dietary Fiber | | |

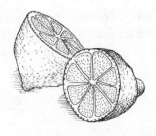

# Herbes de Provence

*ALMOST INSTANT, VEGAN*

*This classic combination of herbs typifies the cooking of the Provençal region. Added to soups, stews, and sautés, it will lend a delicious and authentic taste of southern France to your home cooking. We recommend looking for the individual dried herbs at a natural food store or other market that sells herbs in bulk. Bulk herbs are much more economical than their packaged counterparts, and you can buy them in small amounts, which minimizes waste.*

*Yield:* ¼ cup

| | |
|---|---|
| **Fennel seed** | 1 teaspoon |
| **Dried savory** | 2 teaspoons |
| **Dried oregano** | 2 teaspoons |
| **Dried marjoram** | 2 teaspoons |
| **Dried thyme** | 2 teaspoons |
| **Dried lavender flowers** | 1 teaspoon |
| **Dried rosemary** | 1 teaspoon |
| **Dried tarragon** | 1 teaspoon |
| **Ground sage** | ½ teaspoon |

Crush the fennel seeds finely with a mortar and pestle. Combine all the herbs in a small jar with a tight-fitting lid. Use as directed in recipes, or experiment on your own.

---

Each teaspoon provides:

| | | | |
|---|---|---|---|
| 4 | Calories | 1 g | Carbohydrate |
| 0 g | Protein | 1 mg | Sodium |
| 0 g | Fat | 0 mg | Cholesterol |
| 0 g | Dietary Fiber | | |

*An Introduction to the Recipes*

# Appetizers and Small Bites

Everywhere in the Mediterranean, at even the most humble taverns, small plates of snacks are brought to the table whenever drinks are ordered. Since in parts of the region the evening meal is served as late as 9:00 or 10:00 P.M., these savory snacks sustain people's energy through lively presupper gatherings with friends. This chapter offers an extensive selection of such small bites.

Each of the Mediterranean countries interprets this tradition in a unique way—Spanish *tapas,* Greek *orektiko,* Turkish *mezedes,* Italian *antipasti,* French *hors d'oeuvres.* Many of the same ingredients appear in different guises: olives and olive oil, garlic and onions, beans, breads, and the region's plentiful sun-loving vegetables, such as eggplants and peppers.

Some of these dishes are substantial enough to constitute a lunch or light dinner unto themselves, or several of them can be served together as a wonderful buffet meal to take your guests on a tour of the region's delectable flavors.

## Tips and Tools

- The marinated foods and spreads in this chapter should be prepared well in advance so the flavors have time to blend and balance. These dishes will keep well in the refrigerator, but always return them to room temperature before serving.

- A food processor is most helpful in creating vegetable or bean spreads and purees, though a blender or, in some cases, a hand masher may be used instead.

*Appetizers and Small Bites*

# Grilled Garlic Bread

*ALMOST INSTANT, VEGAN*

*Known in Italy as* bruschetta, *this simple and scrumptious snack is the classic garlic bread. Traditionally, the bread is grilled over a hot fire to give it the characteristic dark stripes. A perfectly good version, however, can be made by broiling the bread. You may use any long baguette or dome-shaped loaf with a thick crust and coarse texture.*

*Yield:* 12 appetizer servings

| | |
|---|---|
| **Extra virgin olive oil** | **6 tablespoons** |
| **Garlic** | **4 cloves, minced** |
| **Fresh, thick-crusted bread** | **1 one-pound loaf** |

Preheat a coal or gas grill to medium (see page 28) or preheat the broiler. Combine the oil and garlic in a small bowl and set aside. If the bread has a long, skinny shape (such as a baguette), cut it crosswise into ½-inch slices. If you are using a dome-shaped loaf, cut it in half, then cut each half crosswise into ½-inch slices. Arrange the slices in a single layer directly on the grill or on the broiler pan. Cook about 2 minutes per side, until the bread is lightly browned and crisp on the outside but still soft and chewy on the inside. Don't dry it out by grilling it too long. Remove the bread from the grill and immediately brush one side of each slice liberally with the oil and garlic mixture. Serve hot.

---

Each serving provides:

| | | | |
|---|---|---|---|
| 169 | Calories | 20 g | Carbohydrate |
| 3 g | Protein | 220 mg | Sodium |
| 8 g | Fat | 0 mg | Cholesterol |
| 1 g | Dietary Fiber | | |

# Garlic Marinated Green Olives

*VEGAN*

*Olives are an essential part of any Mediterranean appetizer offering.
They may be prepared well in advance and used over the course of a
month or so. The olives called for here are tree-ripened green olives
with pits. They are commonly sold in cans, packed in water.*

*Yield:* 12 appetizer servings

| | |
|---|---|
| **Unpitted green olives, water-packed** | 1 **12-ounce can (dr. wt.)** |
| **Garlic** | 8 **cloves** |
| **Extra virgin olive oil** | ¼ **cup** |
| **Sherry vinegar** | 2 **tablespoons** |

Drain the olives and place them in a glass jar that has a tight-
fitting lid. Peel the garlic cloves and lightly crush them with the
broad side of a knife, then add them to the jar. Add the oil and
vinegar, place the lid tightly on the jar, and turn the jar to coat
the olives. The marinade will not completely cover the olives,
so turn the jar several times a day, whenever you think of it.
Marinate in the refrigerate for at least 2 to 3 days for best
results. Bring the olives to room temperature before serving.

Leftover olives may continue to marinate in the refrigerate, to be enjoyed over the course of a month or two.

---

Each serving provides:

| | | | |
|---|---|---|---|
| 51 | Calories | 2 g | Carbohydrate |
| 1 g | Protein | 680 mg | Sodium |
| 6 g | Fat | 0 mg | Cholesterol |
| 1 g | Dietary Fiber | | |

*Appetizers and Small Bites*

# Black Olive Tapenade

*ALMOST INSTANT, VEGAN*

*For this spread, use a distinctive but unseasoned black olive. We recommend the oil-cured variety, the Greek calamata, or a combination of the two. It will take about ½ pound of olives with pits to yield 1 cup of pitted olives. Serve this and the following Green Olive Tapenade with a sliced baguette or crisp Crostini (page 34), and offer a bowl of pistachios and cut-up raw vegetables to complete the appetizer course.*

*Yield:* 16 appetizer servings

| | |
|---|---|
| **Black olives, pitted and coarsely chopped** | 1  **cup** |
| **Tomato juice** | 2  **tablespoons** |
| **Capers, drained** | 2  **tablespoons** |
| **Dry sherry** | 2  **tablespoons** |
| **Extra virgin olive oil** | 1  **tablespoon** |
| **Dijon mustard** | 1  **tablespoon** |
| **Garlic** | 2  **cloves, chopped** |
| **Dried red chili flakes** | ½  **teaspoon** |

Place all ingredients in a small food processor. Puree until smooth and well combined. Serve immediately or allow to age in the refrigerator for up to two weeks.

---

Each serving provides:

| | | | |
|---|---|---|---|
| 37 | Calories | 1 g | Carbohydrate |
| 0 g | Protein | 145 mg | Sodium |
| 4 g | Fat | 0 mg | Cholesterol |
| 0 g | Dietary Fiber | | |

# Green Olive Tapenade

*ALMOST INSTANT, VEGAN*

*Small green* picholines *are perfect for this recipe, but any unseasoned green olive will work. It will take about ½ pound of olives with pits to yield 1 cup of pitted olives. Buy commercially blanched almonds, or boil raw almonds for one minute, then slip them out of their skins.*

*Yield:* 16 appetizer servings

| | |
|---|---|
| **Green olives, pitted and coarsely chopped** | 1 cup |
| **Blanched unsalted almonds, chopped** | ¼ cup |
| **Extra virgin olive oil** | 2 tablespoons |
| **Fresh-squeezed lemon juice** | 2 tablespoons |
| **Dry white wine** | 2 tablespoons |
| **Garlic** | 1 clove, chopped |
| **Dried rosemary, crushed** | ½ teaspoon |
| **Fennel seed, crushed** | ½ teaspoon |
| **Salt** | A pinch |
| **Black pepper** | Several grinds |

Place all ingredients in a small food processor. Puree until smooth and well combined. Serve immediately or allow to age in the refrigerator for up to two weeks.

---

Each serving provides:

| | | | |
|---|---|---|---|
| 42 | Calories | 3 g | Carbohydrate |
| 0 g | Protein | 217 mg | Sodium |
| 4 g | Fat | 0 mg | Cholesterol |
| 1 g | Dietary Fiber | | |

# Pasta al Pesto Frittata

*This unusual egg and pasta casserole comes together quickly if you have basil pesto on hand. Serve it as a side dish or try it as a main course for six, accompanied by a tangy salad and a distinctive vegetable dish.*

*Yield:* 12 appetizer servings

| | |
|---|---|
| Olive oil | ½ teaspoon |
| Dried vermicelli | 6 ounces |
| Eggs | 6 large |
| Basil Pesto (page 35) | ¼ cup |
| Salt | A scant pinch |
| Black pepper | Several grinds |
| Part-skim mozzarella cheese, shredded | 3 ounces (¾ cup) |

Put several quarts of water on to boil for the pasta. Preheat the oven to 375 degrees F. Use the oil to rub down a heavy 10-inch skillet that can take the heat of the oven (cast iron is perfect). Cook the pasta in the boiling water until al dente and drain well. Distribute it in an even thickness over the bottom of the skillet and allow it to cool for about 10 minutes.

Meanwhile, whisk the eggs with the pesto, salt, and pepper, then stir in the cheese. Pour the egg mixture evenly over the pasta in the skillet. Bake uncovered for 20 minutes, then remove it from the oven and allow it to cool in the pan 5 minutes before serving. Cut the frittata into wedges and serve hot or at room temperature.

---

Each serving provides:

| | | | |
|---|---|---|---|
| 136 | Calories | 12 g | Carbohydrate |
| 8 g | Protein | 99 mg | Sodium |
| 6 g | Fat | 112 mg | Cholesterol |
| 1 g | Dietary Fiber | | |

# Spiced Yogurt Cheese
# with Pita Crisps

*Yogurt is a popular food in eastern Mediterranean countries, where it is put to many uses. This refreshing appetizer hails from Israel. Serve a bowl of olives along with it.*

*Yield:* 8 appetizer servings

| | |
|---|---|
| **Plain nonfat yogurt** | 2 cups |
| **Fresh mint leaves, minced** | 1 tablespoon |
| **Ground cumin** | ⅛ teaspoon |
| **Salt** | ¼ teaspoon |
| **Cayenne** | A pinch |
| **Extra virgin olive oil** | 1 tablespoon |
| **Whole wheat pita bread** | 6 rounds |

Place a sieve or fine-mesh strainer over a bowl large enough so that the bottom of the strainer is at least an inch from the bottom of the bowl. Line the strainer with 4 layers of cheesecloth or a clean tea towel, allowing several inches of cloth to hang over the edge of the bowl. Spoon the yogurt into the strainer and fold the overhanging edges of cloth over the yogurt. Place in the refrigerator for 6 to 8 hours. The liquid will drain into the bowl, and the yogurt will thicken. (The liquid whey can be used in smoothies or baked goods, or you may simply discard it.)

Meanwhile, combine the mint, cumin, salt, and cayenne in a small bowl. When the yogurt has drained, remove the resulting "cheese" from the strainer and place it in a shallow bowl, swirling it slightly to make several depressions. Sprinkle with the spice mixture, then drizzle the oil over the top.

Just before serving, preheat a toaster oven or conventional oven to 350 degrees F. Cut each pita bread round into quarters, then separate the layers to create 8 triangles per round. Place the triangles in a single layer on a baking sheet and toast for 10 to 12 minutes, until lightly browned and quite crisp. (If you are using a toaster oven, you may need to toast the pieces in more than one batch.) Place the toasted triangles in a serving basket and serve them with the yogurt cheese.

---

Each serving provides:

| 153 | Calories | 22 g | Carbohydrate |
| 8 g | Protein | 309 mg | Sodium |
| 3 g | Fat | 1 mg | Cholesterol |
| 2 g | Dietary Fiber | | |

# Sesame Eggplant Spread

*VEGAN*

*Anyone who is fond of both eggplant and garlic will become addicted to this eastern Mediterranean eggplant spread, called* baba ghanouj. *It is easy to prepare from readily available ingredients, and it makes a healthy snack or light lunch when served with pita bread, whole wheat bread, or sesame crackers. Standard globe eggplants are most convenient to use for this dish.*

*Yield:* 12 appetizer servings

| | |
|---|---|
| **Eggplant** | 2 **pounds** **(2 medium)** |
| **Extra virgin olive oil** | 1 **tablespoon plus** 1 **teaspoon** |
| **Sesame tahini, raw or toasted** | 2 **tablespoons** |
| **Fresh-squeezed lemon juice** | 1 **tablespoon** |
| **Garlic** | 2 **cloves, minced** |
| **Salt** | ½ **teaspoon** |
| **Ground cumin** | ½ **teaspoon** |
| **Cayenne** | **A pinch** |

Preheat the broiler while you cut the eggplants in half lengthwise and rub the cut sides scantily with 1 teaspoon of the oil. Place the eggplant halves cut side down on the broiler pan and broil 4 inches from the heat source for 20 minutes. The skin should be blackened and crisp and the eggplants perfectly soft. Turn them over and broil 5 minutes longer to brown the tops slightly. Set the eggplants aside on a plate to cool for up to a few hours.

When the eggplants are cool enough to handle, drain off any liquid that has collected on the plate. Scrape the eggplant pulp out of the charred skin into a bowl, being careful to include the thin layer of eggplant that tends to stick to the skin. It is fine if a few bits of charred skin end up in the bowl with the eggplant.

Add the remaining 1 tablespoon oil, tahini, lemon juice, garlic, salt, cumin, and cayenne and whip with a fork until well combined. Serve immediately or allow the flavors to blend for a few hours at room temperature (or overnight in the refrigerator) before serving at room temperature.

---

Each serving provides:

| | | | |
|---|---|---|---|
| 50 | Calories | 6 g | Carbohydrate |
| 1 g | Protein | 94 mg | Sodium |
| 3 g | Fat | 0 mg | Cholesterol |
| 1 g | Dietary Fiber | | |

# Caponata

*VEGAN*

*Versions of this famous dish have been made for centuries in Sicily, where all of the main ingredients are abundant during the hot summer months. We like to serve caponata on a bed of colorful greens with cheese and Crostini (page 34). This recipe makes a lot—enough for a crowd. Any leftovers will stay fresh if stored in a covered jar in the refrigerator and can be enjoyed over the course of the next few days.*

*Yield:* 18 appetizer servings

| | |
|---|---|
| **Whole pear tomatoes*** | 1 14½-ounce can |
| **Eggplant** | 3 pounds (3 medium) |
| **Salt** | 1 tablespoon |
| **Extra virgin olive oil** | ¼ cup |
| **Yellow onion** | 1 medium, chopped |
| **Celery** | 2 ribs, chopped |
| **Garlic** | 2 cloves, minced |
| **Dried red chili flakes** | ¼ teaspoon |
| **Pitted green olives, water-packed** | 1 7¾-ounce can (dr. wt.) |
| **Capers, drained** | 2 tablespoons |
| **Fresh Italian parsley leaves, minced** | ¼ cup |
| **Fresh-squeezed lemon juice** | ¼ cup |

*You may substitute 1½ pounds fresh pear tomatoes—blanched, peeled, and seeded—for the canned variety. See the directions on page 28.

Drain the tomatoes, reserving the juice for another use. Chop the tomatoes and set them aside in a bowl. Wash and dry the eggplants and trim off and discard the stem ends. Without peeling them, chop the eggplants into ¾-inch cubes. Place the cubes in a colander and sprinkle with the salt. Set aside in the sink or over a bowl and allow to drain for 1 hour. Rinse briefly and dry thoroughly with a clean tea towel or paper towels.

Heat the oil in a large, heavy-bottomed sauté pan or skillet over medium heat. Add the onion, celery, garlic, and chili flakes. Sauté for about 5 minutes, stirring occasionally, then mix in the eggplant and sauté 5 more minutes, stirring frequently. Add the tomatoes and bring the mixture to a simmer over medium-high heat. Reduce the heat to low, cover, and simmer 10 minutes. Stir in the olives and capers and continue to cook 20 to 25 minutes, until the eggplant is tender but not mushy. Stir in the parsley and lemon juice until well combined. Serve at room temperature.

---

Each serving provides:

| | | | |
|---|---|---|---|
| 72 | Calories | 9 g | Carbohydrate |
| 1 g | Protein | 415 mg | Sodium |
| 4 g | Fat | 0 mg | Cholesterol |
| 2 g | Dietary Fiber | | |

# Greek Eggplant Puree

*VEGAN*

*This wonderful chunky eggplant concoction is a superb appetizer,
spread on Crostini (page 34), crusty bread, or crackers. It is best to
serve it soon after you have prepared it, because the eggplant will
release some liquid over time, which may ruin the texture of the dish.
It can also be served in a leaf of butter lettuce as a refreshing side dish.*

*Yield:* 12 appetizer servings

| | |
|---|---|
| **Eggplant** | **2 pounds (2 medium)** |
| **Extra virgin olive oil** | **¼ cup plus 1 teaspoon** |
| **White onion, diced** | **¼ cup** |
| **Garlic** | **2 cloves, chopped** |
| **Fresh Italian parsley, minced** | **¼ cup** |
| **Dried oregano** | **2 teaspoons** |
| **Salt** | **¼ teaspoon** |
| **Black pepper** | **Several grinds** |
| **Fresh-squeezed lemon juice** | **3 tablespoons** |

Preheat the broiler while you cut the eggplants in half lengthwise and rub the cut sides scantily with 1 teaspoon of the oil.
Place the eggplant halves cut side down on the broiler pan and
broil 4 inches from the heat source for 20 minutes. The skin
should be blackened and crisp and the eggplants perfectly soft.
Turn them over and broil 5 minutes longer to brown the tops
slightly. Set the eggplants aside on a plate to cool for up to a
few hours.

   When the eggplants are cool enough to handle, drain off
any liquid that has collected on the plate. Scrape the eggplant
pulp out of the charred skin into a food processor, being careful

to include the thin layer of eggplant that tends to stick to the skin. It is fine if a few bits of charred skin end up in the bowl with the eggplant.

Add the onion, garlic, parsley, oregano, salt, and pepper to the eggplant and pulse a few times to coarsely chop everything. Don't overprocess, because you do not want a pureed texture. Add the lemon juice and briefly pulse again. Finally, add the remaining ¼ cup of oil and pulse a time or two more, until the mixture is well combined but retains a chunky texture. Serve immediately or allow the flavors to blend at room temperature for an hour or so.

---

Each serving provides:

| 67 | Calories | 6 g | Carbohydrate |
|---|---|---|---|
| 1 g | Protein | 13 mg | Sodium |
| 5 g | Fat | 0 mg | Cholesterol |
| 1 g | Dietary Fiber | | |

# Spiced Carrot Spread

*ALMOST INSTANT, VEGAN*

*In Tunisia, spiced vegetable spreads called* ajloukes *are favorite appetizers. There are countless variations on the theme. In this one, the sweetness of the carrots combines well with the spices, and the color of the resulting puree is bright and appetizing. It can be made a day or two ahead. Serve the puree chilled or at room temperature with crisp crackers or baguette slices.*

*Yield:* 12 appetizer servings

| | |
|---|---|
| **Carrots** | 1 pound |
| **Russet potato** | ½ pound (1 medium) |
| **Extra virgin olive oil** | 2 tablespoons |
| **Fresh-squeezed lemon juice** | 2 tablespoons |
| **Garlic** | 2 cloves, minced |
| **Ground cumin** | 2 teaspoons |
| **Paprika** | 2 teaspoons |
| **Ground coriander** | 1 teaspoon |
| **Salt** | ¼ teaspoon |
| **Cayenne** | ⅛ teaspoon |

Put a few cups of water on to boil in a saucepan. Scrub the carrots and dice them. Peel the potato and dice it. Place the diced vegetables in the boiling water and cook 10 to 15 minutes, until both carrot and potato are very tender.

Drain the vegetables well and transfer them to a food processor. Add the oil, lemon juice, garlic, cumin, paprika, coriander, salt, and cayenne and process briefly to achieve a coarse but not whipped texture. Transfer the *ajlouke* to a pretty bowl and serve immediately or place it in the refrigerator. You may serve the puree cold or remove it from the refrigerator ahead of time and allow it to come to room temperature before serving.

---

Each serving provides:

| | | | |
|---|---|---|---|
| 57 | Calories | 8 g | Carbohydrate |
| 1 g | Protein | 59 mg | Sodium |
| 3 g | Fat | 0 mg | Cholesterol |
| 2 g | Dietary Fiber | | |

# Sour and Sweet Herb Sauce

*ALMOST INSTANT, VEGAN*

*This Italian* agrodolce *(sour and sweet) herb concoction has a pesto-like texture and makes a wonderful spread for Crostini (page 34) or a delicious topping for boiled, roasted, or baked potatoes. The classic recipe includes anchovies, but this vegan version is unbeatable. The sauce will stay fresh and delicious for several days. Store it in a tightly closed container in the refrigerator but return it to room temperature before serving, thinned with a drizzle of water if it has become too thick.*

*Yield:* 12 appetizer servings

| | |
|---|---|
| **Thick-crusted unsliced bread** | **2 ounces** |
| **Fresh Italian parsley leaves** | **1 cup** |
| **Fresh basil and/or mint leaves, chopped*** | **⅓ cup** |
| **Extra virgin olive oil** | **½ cup** |
| **Red wine vinegar** | **¼ cup** |
| **Dry red or white wine** | **¼ cup** |
| **Capers, drained** | **2 tablespoons** |
| **Garlic** | **3 cloves, minced** |
| **Granulated sugar** | **1 tablespoon** |
| **Dried rosemary** | **1 teaspoon** |
| **Salt** | **½ teaspoon** |
| **Black pepper** | **Several grinds** |

*Use a combination, if possible, or you may use basil or mint exclusively. The results, of course, will vary slightly.

Remove the crust from the bread and tear it into several pieces. Place the bread in a food processor and add the parsley, basil and/or mint, oil, vinegar, wine, capers, garlic, sugar, rosemary, salt, and pepper. Puree to a thick, uniform consistency. Serve immediately or store in the refrigerator for up to several days, but return the sauce to room temperature before serving.

---

Each serving provides:

| | | | |
|---|---|---|---|
| 106 | Calories | 5 g | Carbohydrate |
| 1 g | Protein | 153 mg | Sodium |
| 9 g | Fat | 0 mg | Cholesterol |
| 1 g | Dietary Fiber | | |

# Hummus

*ALMOST INSTANT, VEGAN*

*This well-seasoned garbanzo bean and tahini dip has been enjoyed in eastern Mediterranean countries since ancient times. We like it served with pita bread, sesame crackers, or fresh vegetables.*

*Yield:* 18 appetizer servings

| | |
|---|---|
| **Cooked garbanzo beans, drained\*** | **2 cups** |
| **Fresh-squeezed lemon juice** | **⅓ cup** |
| **Sesame tahini, raw or toasted** | **¼ cup** |
| **Green onions** | **2, minced** |
| **Garlic** | **2 cloves, minced** |
| **Salt** | **½ teaspoon** |
| **Paprika** | **¼ teaspoon** |

Place the beans, lemon juice, tahini, oil, and ¼ cup cold water in a blender or food processor and puree until smooth. If the mixture seems too thick, add an additional tablespoon or two of water. Add the onions, garlic, and salt and pulse to combine.

\*Cook 1 cup of dried beans according to the directions on page 29, or use canned beans that do not contain additives.

Transfer to a serving dish and dust with the paprika. Serve immediately, or refrigerate for up to several days, but return it to room temperature before serving.

---

Each serving provides:

| | | | |
|---|---|---|---|
| 51 | Calories | 6 g | Carbohydrate |
| 2 g | Protein | 64 mg | Sodium |
| 2 g | Fat | 0 mg | Cholesterol |
| 1 g | Dietary Fiber | | |

# Cannellini Bean Spread
# with Cumin, Oregano, and Cayenne

*ALMOST INSTANT, VEGAN*

*This spread makes a wonderful addition to any* tapas *platter. Serve it with crackers or crusty bread.*

*Yield:* 8 appetizer servings

| | |
|---|---|
| **Cooked cannellini beans, drained**\* | **2 cups** |
| **Bean cooking liquid or water** | **2 tablespoons** |
| **Extra virgin olive oil** | **1 tablespoon** |
| **Fresh-squeezed lemon juice** | **1 tablespoon** |
| **Ground cumin** | **½ teaspoon** |
| **Dried oregano** | **1 teaspoon, crushed** |
| **Cayenne** | **⅛ teaspoon** |
| **Salt** | **¼ teaspoon** |

Place the beans in a food processor along with the bean cooking liquid, oil, lemon juice, cumin, oregano, cayenne, and salt. Puree until smooth. If the mixture is too thick, add an

\*Cook ¾ cup of dried beans according to the directions on page 29, or use canned beans that do not contain additives.

additional tablespoon or two of bean cooking liquid or water. Serve immediately, or refrigerate for up to several days, but return it to room temperature before serving.

---

Each serving provides:

| 80 | Calories | 12 g | Carbohydrate |
|---|---|---|---|
| 4 g | Protein | 70 mg | Sodium |
| 2 g | Fat | 0 mg | Cholesterol |
| 2 g | Dietary Fiber | | |

# Pureed Yellow Split Peas with Feta and Capers

*Spreads like this pretty yellow one are popular in the Greek isles. Serve it with a good crusty bread or pita bread, additional feta cheese, Greek olives, and chilled ouzo for an authentic Greek appetizer. This recipe makes enough for a big party, but any leftovers will stay fresh in the refrigerator to be enjoyed over the course of a few days. You may also freeze part of the batch in sealed containers. Thaw the spread at room temperature when you are ready to use it.*

*Yield:* 32 appetizer servings

| | |
|---|---|
| Olive oil | 2 tablespoons |
| White onion, chopped | 1 cup |
| Homemade Vegetable Stock* | 4 cups |
| Uncooked yellow split peas | 2 cups |
| Dried oregano | 2 teaspoons, crushed |
| Salt | ½ teaspoon |
| Black pepper | Several grinds |
| Feta cheese, crumbled | 4 ounces (1 cup) |
| Capers, drained | 4 tablespoons |

Heat the oil over medium heat in a heavy-bottomed sauté pan or skillet. Add the onion and sauté for 3 to 4 minutes, until it is translucent. Add the stock, split peas, oregano, salt, and pepper and increase the heat to high. Bring to a boil, stirring occasionally, then cover the pan and reduce the heat to low. Simmer for

---

*If you do not have Homemade Vegetable Stock on hand, make some according to the directions on page 32 or dissolve 2 large low-sodium vegetable broth cubes in 4 cups of hot water.

about 50 minutes, until the peas are very tender and falling apart. Watch the pot carefully during the last 10 minutes of cooking time and turn the heat down, if necessary, to prevent scorching.

Transfer the pea mixture to a food processor and puree in several batches until smooth. Place in shallow serving bowls and top with equal amounts of the feta and capers. Serve warm or at room temperature.

---

Each serving provides:

| | | | |
|---|---|---|---|
| 63 | Calories | 9 g | Carbohydrate |
| 4 g | Protein | 120 mg | Sodium |
| 2 g | Fat | 3 mg | Cholesterol |
| 1 g | Dietary Fiber | | |

# Pearl Onions Pickled
# in Sherry Vinegar

*VEGAN*

*The combination of hot and pickled dishes appears frequently throughout the Mediterranean. This recipe makes at least 18 servings, but not all of the onions need to be eaten at one sitting. They store very well in the refrigerator for several weeks and improve with age. Be sure to begin the preparation of this dish at least 3 days before you wish to serve them.*

*Yield:* 18 appetizer servings

| | | |
|---|---|---|
| **Pearl or boiling onions** | **1½** | **pounds** |
| **Salt** | **¼** | **cup** |
| **White wine vinegar** | **1½** | **cups** |
| **Sherry vinegar** | **1** | **cup** |
| **Honey** | **1** | **tablespoon** |
| **Extra virgin olive oil** | **2** | **tablespoons** |
| **Dried oregano** | **1** | **teaspoon** |
| **Dried red chili flakes** | **¼** | **teaspoon** |
| **Whole peppercorns** | **½** | **teaspoon** |

Bring a few quarts of water to a boil and blanch the unpeeled onions by immersing them in the boiling water for about a minute. Immediately plunge them into ice water for a moment or two and drain in a colander. Trim a very small bit off the root end and peel the onions. Place them in a deep glass bowl or a small crock.

Bring 4 cups of water to a boil and add the salt; stir until dissolved. Remove from the heat, allow to cool slightly, then pour over the onions. Place a plate over the onions and weigh it down to keep the onions completely submerged in the brine. Allow to cure in the brine at room temperature for 48 hours.

Drain the onions in a colander and rinse with cold water to remove the salt. Place them in a bowl or pack into quart jars.

Pour the vinegars into a nonaluminum saucepan and add the honey, oil, oregano, chili flakes, and peppercorns. Bring to a boil over high heat, then reduce the heat to medium-low and simmer for 5 minutes. Pour the vinegar mixture over the onions, cover, and cool to room temperature before storing in the refrigerator. Allow to marinate for at least a day before serving. They will keep for at least 2 months in a tightly closed container in the refrigerator.

---

Each serving provides:

| 20 | Calories | 4 g | Carbohydrate |
|-----|----------|-----|--------------|
| 1 g | Protein | 355 mg | Sodium |
| 1 g | Fat | 0 mg | Cholesterol |
| 1 g | Dietary Fiber | | |

# Fresh Fava Beans
# in Basil Marinade

*VEGAN*

*This dish can only be prepared during the fava bean's short season, which makes it quite a special treat. During spring and early summer, look for fresh fava beans in an Italian grocery or at a local farmers' market. These large tender beans melt in your mouth.*

*Yield:* 12 appetizer servings

| | |
|---|---|
| **Fresh fava beans, in pods** | **3 pounds** |
| **Extra virgin olive oil** | **¼ cup** |
| **Fresh-squeezed lemon juice** | **3 tablespoons** |
| **Garlic** | **1 clove, minced** |
| **Salt** | **¼ teaspoon** |
| **Black pepper** | **Several grinds** |
| **Fresh basil leaves, minced** | **¼ cup** |

Bring several cups of water to a boil for the favas. Shell the beans, discarding the pods, and add them to the boiling water. Return to a boil and blanch 2 to 4 minutes, until the skins have loosened, then transfer to a colander and rinse well with cold water to stop the cooking. When the beans are cool enough to handle, pop them out of their skins. Discard the skins and place the beans in a serving bowl.

Whisk together the oil, lemon juice, garlic, salt, and pepper. Pour this mixture over the beans, then add the basil and toss to combine. Allow to marinate at room temperature for about an hour before serving. This dish may be kept overnight in the refrigerator, but return it to room temperature before serving.

---

Each serving provides:

| 27 | Calories | 2 g | Carbohydrate |
|---|---|---|---|
| 2 g | Protein | 27 mg | Sodium |
| 1 g | Fat | 0 mg | Cholesterol |
| 0 g | Dietary Fiber | | |

# Roasted Peppers in Spicy Marinade

*ALMOST INSTANT, VEGAN*

*Here is a well-spiced vegetable appetizer based on Tunisian* mushwiya.
*It combines wonderfully with the Spiced Carrot Spread (page 54) to
prepare the palate for any strongly seasoned entrée, such as Cabbage
Stuffed with Rice and Gorgonzola (page 214). You may use peppers
of any color, but red and yellow ones yield the prettiest color and
sweetest flavor.*

*Yield:* 8 appetizer servings

| | |
|---|---|
| **Fresh bell peppers** | 4  medium |
| **Whole pear tomatoes, canned** | 4, chopped |
| **Garlic** | 2  cloves, minced |
| **Ground cumin** | 1  teaspoon |
| **Salt** | ¼ teaspoon |
| **Cayenne** | ⅛ teaspoon |
| **Extra virgin olive oil** | 2  tablespoons |
| **Fresh-squeezed lemon juice** | 1  tablespoon |

Preheat the broiler or a coal or gas grill (see page 28). Place the
whole peppers on the grill or under the broiler and cook for
several minutes, until the skin is charred black on one side.
Turn the peppers over and cook several more minutes to
blacken the other side. Continue to turn and cook until the
entire skin of the peppers is almost uniformly black. Transfer
the peppers to a paper or plastic bag, close the bag tightly, and
set aside for 10 minutes or so. The steam inside the bag will finish cooking the peppers. When the peppers are cool enough to
handle, remove them from the bag and peel off and discard
their blackened skin. Discard the seeds, stems, and membranes
and dice the peppers into ½-inch pieces.

*Appetizers and Small Bites*

Combine the pepper pieces in a small bowl with the tomatoes, garlic, cumin, salt, and cayenne and toss to combine well. Add the oil and lemon juice and toss again. Serve immediately or allow the flavors to ripen at room temperature for a few hours before serving.

---

Each serving provides:

| | | | |
|---|---|---|---|
| 55 | Calories | 6 g | Carbohydrate |
| 1 g | Protein | 73 mg | Sodium |
| 4 g | Fat | 0 mg | Cholesterol |
| 1 g | Dietary Fiber | | |

# Peppery Potatoes with Vinegar

*VEGAN*

*This simple-to-prepare dish is another of Spain's classic tapas. It is a popular snack with everyone who loves potatoes, and who doesn't?*

*Yield:* 6 appetizer servings

| | | |
|---|---|---|
| New potatoes, red, yellow, or white | 1¼ | pounds |
| Canola oil | 2 | tablespoons |
| Salt | ½ | teaspoon |
| Tomato juice | 3 | tablespoons |
| Red wine vinegar | 1 | tablespoon |
| Paprika | ½ | teaspoon |
| Freshly ground black pepper | ¼ | teaspoon |
| White onion, minced | 2 | tablespoons |
| Dried oregano | ½ | teaspoon, crushed |

If the potatoes are tiny, leave them whole. Otherwise, cut them into halves or quarters to create bite-size wedges. Bring 1 inch of water to a boil in a large saucepan with a steaming tray inserted in it. When the water is boiling, place the potatoes in the tray and steam them for 5 minutes. Remove the potatoes from the steaming tray and set them aside for a few minutes to cool down a bit.

Heat the oil in a heavy-bottomed skillet over medium heat. Place the steamed potatoes into the hot oil and sprinkle them with ¼ teaspoon of the salt. Sauté until they are nicely browned and fork-tender, 12 to 15 minutes, scraping the pan occasionally with a metal spatula to prevent the potatoes from sticking to the bottom. The cooking time will vary, depending on the size of the potatoes.

*Appetizers and Small Bites*

Meanwhile, stir together the tomato juice, vinegar, paprika, remaining ¼ teaspoon salt, and pepper. When the potatoes are done, combine them in a serving bowl with the tomato sauce and allow them to cool for at least 30 minutes or up to several hours at room temperature, stirring occasionally. Just before serving, distribute the onion and oregano evenly over the potatoes. Serve warm or at room temperature.

---

Each serving provides:

| 128 | Calories | 20 g | Carbohydrate |
|-----|----------|------|--------------|
| 2 g | Protein | 208 mg | Sodium |
| 5 g | Fat | 0 mg | Cholesterol |
| 4 g | Dietary Fiber | | |

# Grilled Eggplant with Spiced Yogurt Topping

*An authentic version of this Lebanese snack would probably include lamb and would call for the eggplant to be deep-fried. We use grilled eggplant instead to create a variation that is just as flavorful. It begins any Middle Eastern feast with exotic flair.*

*Yield:* 6 appetizer servings

| | |
|---|---|
| Eggplant | 1¼ pounds (1 large) |
| Olive oil | 2 tablespoons |
| Plain nonfat yogurt | ¾ cup |
| Fresh mint leaves, minced | 2 tablespoons, lightly packed |
| Fresh cilantro leaves, minced | 2 tablespoons, lightly packed |
| Garlic | 1 clove, minced |
| Honey | 1 teaspoon |
| Paprika | ¾ teaspoon |
| Salt | ⅛ teaspoon |
| Black pepper | Several grinds |
| Raw, unsalted pine nuts | 2 tablespoons |
| Whole wheat pita bread | 4 rounds |

Preheat the broiler. Wash and dry the eggplant and cut it crosswise into ½-inch slices. Very lightly brush the cut sides of the slices with the oil. Place the eggplant slices on the broiler pan and broil 4 inches from the heat about 5 minutes, then turn them over and broil an additional 3 to 5 minutes, until the eggplant is nicely browned and fairly soft. Set it aside to cool for a few minutes.

Stir together the yogurt, mint, cilantro, garlic, honey, paprika, salt, and pepper. Set aside. To toast the pine nuts, place them in a dry, heavy-bottomed skillet in a single layer over medium heat. Stir or shake the pan frequently until the nuts are lightly browned. Immediately remove them from the pan and set aside. When they have cooled for a few minutes, finely mince them.

Coarsely chop the eggplant slices and heap them in the center of a pretty, shallow serving dish. Pour the yogurt sauce over the top and then sprinkle on the pine nuts.

Just before serving, preheat a toaster oven or conventional oven to 350 degrees F. Cut each pita bread round into quarters, then separate the layers to create 8 triangles per round. Place the triangles in a single layer on a baking sheet and toast for 10 to 12 minutes, until lightly browned and quite crisp. (If you are using a toaster oven, you may need to toast the pieces in more than one batch.) Arrange the toasted bread triangles around the dish, or serve them in a separate basket. Garnish the dish with a few sprigs of mint or cilantro and serve at room temperature.

---

Each serving provides:

| | | | |
|---|---|---|---|
| 197 | Calories | 26 g | Carbohydrate |
| 8 g | Protein | 248 mg | Sodium |
| 8 g | Fat | 0 mg | Cholesterol |
| 3 g | Dietary Fiber | | |

# Beets with Potato Garlic Sauce

*VEGAN*

*This succulent sauce, a version of Greek skordalia, is delicious on bread, potatoes, or steamed vegetables. We find the sweetness of fresh cooked beets to be a wonderful counterpoint to the pungent flavors of the sauce. If you are especially fond of beets, you could make a main dish out of this—it is that delicious and satisfying. A pilaf would be the perfect accompaniment. Or serve it alone or with other small bites for a classic Mediterranean snack.*

*Yield:* 12 appetizer servings

| | | |
|---|---|---|
| Fresh beets, without greens | 1½ | pounds (6 medium) |
| Russet potato | ½ | pound (1 large) |
| Garlic | 2 | cloves, minced |
| Salt | ¼ | teaspoon |
| Dried red chili flakes | ⅛ | teaspoon |
| Extra virgin olive oil | ¼ | cup |
| Red wine vinegar | 1 | tablespoon |
| Fresh-squeezed lemon juice | 1 | tablespoon |
| Fresh Italian parsley, minced | ¼ | cup |

Place the unpeeled beets in a saucepan and cover them with water. Bring to a boil over high heat, then reduce heat to medium and cook 20 to 25 minutes, depending on their size, until you can easily pierce each beet clear through to the middle with a sharp skewer or knife. Transfer the cooked beets to a colander and rinse with cold water. When they are cool enough to handle, use your hands to rub off the skins. Cut the beets into about 8 wedges each and arrange the wedges in a single layer on a serving platter.

Meanwhile, bring a few cups of water to a boil and boil the whole potato until it is very tender but not falling apart, about 15 minutes. Remove it from the water and allow it to cool a bit, then peel it and cut it into a few pieces. Place the potato in a food processor along with the garlic, salt, and chili flakes. Process briefly to mash the potato and combine it with the other ingredients. With the machine running, slowly add the oil, then the vinegar, lemon juice, and ½ cup cold water. Process for only about 30 seconds. If the texture of the sauce is gooey rather than pourable, add more water a tablespoon at a time until a smooth, moderately thick consistency has been achieved. Drizzle the sauce evenly over the beets on the platter, garnish with the parsley, and serve immediately.

---

Each serving provides:

| 82 | Calories | 10 g | Carbohydrate |
|---|---|---|---|
| 1 g | Protein | 90 mg | Sodium |
| 5 g | Fat | 0 mg | Cholesterol |
| 1 g | Dietary Fiber | | |

# Tortilla of Potatoes, Artichokes, and Red Bell Pepper

*One of the classic* tapas *of Spain, the* tortilla *is similar in character to the Italian* frittata. *This version uses some favorite vegetables of the sunny Mediterranean.*

*Yield:* 12 appetizer servings

| | |
|---|---|
| **Russet potato** | **½ pound (1 large)** |
| **Extra virgin olive oil** | **2 tablespoons** |
| **Yellow onion** | **½ medium, diced** |
| **Red bell pepper** | **½ medium, diced** |
| **Fresh or frozen artichoke hearts, sliced** | **1 cup** |
| **Eggs** | **6 large** |
| **Salt** | **½ teaspoon** |
| **Black pepper** | **Several grinds** |
| **Fresh Italian parsley, minced** | **2 tablespoons** |

Scrub the potato and cut it crosswise into ¼-inch slices. Bring 1 inch of water to a boil in a large suacepan with a steaming tray inserted in it. Steam the slices for about 5 minutes or until barely fork-tender. Remove them from the pan and set aside.

Meanwhile, heat 1 tablespoon of the oil in a heavy-bottomed, ovenproof skillet (such as cast iron) over medium heat. Add the onion, bell pepper, and artichoke hearts and sauté about 5 minutes, stirring frequently, until the onion and pepper are softening.

Stir together the eggs, salt, pepper, and parsley in a large bowl. When the vegetables are done, scrape them out of the pan into the egg mixture and stir to combine. Heat the remaining 1 tablespoon oil in the same skillet over medium heat, then add the egg and vegetable mixture. Add the potatoes, distributing them evenly in a single layer and pushing them down a little into the eggs. Reduce the heat to medium-low and cook for 7 to 10 minutes, until the bottom is well browned (use a metal spatula to lift one side of the tortilla to check for browning).

Meanwhile, preheat the broiler. When the tortilla is well browned on the bottom, place the skillet under the broiler for 3 to 5 minutes to finish cooking. The tortilla is done when the eggs are set and the top of the tortilla is barely browned. Remove the pan from the oven and cool for five minutes, then run a spatula around the edges and under the bottom of the tortilla to loosen it from the pan. Turn the tortilla out onto a serving dish and cut it into 12 wedges. Serve hot or at room temperature, garnished with a few parsley sprigs and/or strips of red bell pepper.

---

Each serving provides:

| 86 | Calories | 7 g | Carbohydrate |
|----|----------|-----|--------------|
| 4 g | Protein | 109 mg | Sodium |
| 5 g | Fat | 0 mg | Cholesterol |
| 2 g | Dietary Fiber | | |

# Grape Leaves Stuffed with Rice and Herbs

*VEGAN*

*Here is our vegetarian version of* dolmas, *the stuffed grape leaves of Greek cuisine. Traditional fillings include lamb or another meat mixed with the rice. Our dolmas include no meat but plenty of flavor. They are labor-intensive morsels, so whenever we make them the meal becomes a special occasion.*

*Yield:* 12 appetizer servings

| | | |
|---|---|---|
| Uncooked long-grain brown rice | 2 | cups |
| Salt | ¾ | teaspoon plus a pinch |
| Eggplant | 1 | pound (1 medium) |
| Olive oil | ¼ | cup plus ½ teaspoon |
| Yellow onion | 1 | medium, diced |
| Fresh-squeezed lemon juice | 2 | tablespoons |
| Dried dill weed | 1½ | teaspoons |
| Dried oregano | 1 | tablespoon plus 1½ teaspoons |
| Garlic | 4 | cloves, minced |
| Black pepper | | Several grinds |
| Prepared grape leaves | 1 | 8-ounce jar |
| Whole pear tomatoes* | 1 | 28-ounce can |

*You may substitute 3 pounds fresh pear tomatoes—blanched, peeled, and seeded—for the canned variety. See the directions on page 28.

Bring 4 cups of water to a boil in a large saucepan. Add the rice and the pinch of salt, stir, and return to a boil over high heat. Cover, reduce the heat to very low, and simmer 45 minutes. Turn the heat off and allow the pan to stand 5 minutes without disturbing the lid.

While you're cooking the rice, peel and dice the eggplant. Heat ¼ cup of the oil in a large skillet over medium-low heat and add the onion, eggplant, lemon juice, dill, 1½ teaspoons of the oregano, and 3 cloves of the garlic. Stir until well combined, then add 1¼ cups hot water, ½ teaspoon of the salt, and several grinds of pepper. Simmer over low heat, uncovered, for 40 minutes, stirring frequently, until the eggplant is very tender and the liquid has nearly evaporated. (More water can be added, 2 tablespoons at a time, if the mixture dries out before the eggplant is finished cooking.) Transfer the eggplant mixture to a large bowl and stir in the rice until well combined.

Rinse the grape leaves, being careful not to tear them, and place them in a colander to drain. Preheat the oven to 350 degrees F.

In a large saucepan, combine the tomatoes and their juice, the remaining 1 tablespoon of oregano, 1 clove of garlic, and ¼ teaspoon salt; and a few grinds of pepper. Cook over medium heat for 15 minutes, mashing the tomatoes into a thick sauce with the back of a wooden spoon as they cook. Set aside.

Use the remaining ½ teaspoon oil to rub down a large baking dish. Place a spoonful of the eggplant mixture near the stem end of each leaf and roll it up, starting at the stem end and folding the sides in as you roll to create tightly closed little bundles. As you stuff the leaves, place them snugly in the baking dish, seam side down. Pour the tomato sauce evenly over the stuffed grape leaves, cover, and bake 20 minutes. Serve hot or at room temperature.

---

Each serving provides:

| 192 | Calories | 31 g | Carbohydrate |
|-----|----------|------|--------------|
| 4 g | Protein | 251 mg | Sodium |
| 6 g | Fat | 0 mg | Cholesterol |
| 2 g | Dietary Fiber | | |

# Mushrooms with Cumin and Sherry Vinegar

*ALMOST INSTANT, VEGAN*

*Picture yourself and several friends at a public house in Spain, sipping a glass of wine from the Rioja Valley as you enjoy a plate of tapas—appetizers, Spanish style. This one is especially succulent.*

*Yield:* 6 appetizer servings

| | |
|---|---|
| **Button mushrooms** | **1 pound** |
| **Olive oil** | **1 tablespoon** |
| **Sherry vinegar** | **2 tablespoons** |
| **Garlic** | **2 cloves, minced** |
| **Ground cumin** | **½ teaspoon** |

Brush or wipe any loose dirt from the mushrooms, then trim off the tough tips of the stems.

Place the oil and vinegar in a large sauté pan or skillet over medium heat. Add the garlic and cook for about a minute, then stir in the cumin and mushrooms. Cover the skillet and continue to cook for 20 minutes, removing the lid to stir occasionally. The mushrooms will release their liquid and become limp. Remove the lid, increase the heat to medium-high, and continue to cook for 2 to 3 minutes, until almost all of the liquid has evaporated. Serve hot or at room temperature.

---

Each serving provides:

| | | | |
|---|---|---|---|
| 45 | Calories | 5 g | Carbohydrate |
| 2 g | Protein | 4 mg | Sodium |
| 3 g | Fat | 0 mg | Cholesterol |
| 1 g | Dietary Fiber | | |

# Salads and Cold Vegetables

Vegetables grow in glorious abundance in the Mediterranean climate, and they are prepared with care and creativity throughout the region. Since balmy weather makes cold food appealing during much of the year, salads and cold vegetable dishes are quite popular.

Green salads in the Mediterranean are typically made with a variety of crisp greens, including at least one that lends a tart or bitter flavor. Dressings frequently begin with robust extra virgin olive oil, enlivened by good-quality vinegar or fresh-squeezed lemon juice, and they might include any number of fresh or dried herbs.

Cooked or raw chopped vegetables, perhaps assembled with grains, beans, or potatoes, are delicious seasonal favorites.

These heartier combinations can be served as the main course of a refreshing summer lunch. On Mediterranean tables, crusty, fresh-baked bread and a locally made cheese would almost certainly accompany these dishes.

## Tips and Tools

- Take time to wash salad greens carefully, since dirt or sand are frequently lodged among the leaves. Be sure to dry greens well, so the water that clings to them doesn't dilute the dressing.
- We prefer leafy salads chilled but toss them with room-temperature dressing just before serving. Most non-leafy vegetable, grain, or pasta salads are most flavorful if served at room temperature.
- Large bowls and tongs or salad utensils are essential for mixing and serving salads. You may serve individual salads on plates or in bowls.
- A wire whisk makes quick work of dressings. We also depend on a manual juicer or lemon reamer for extracting citrus juices.

# Spinach and Radicchio Salad with Tomato Balsamic Vinaigrette

*ALMOST INSTANT, VEGAN*

*This simple salad is a wonderful accompaniment to any Italian entrée. The dressing is a favorite of ours that takes almost no time to prepare and dresses any leafy salad with pizzazz. The tomato juice called for in this recipe could be the juice from canned tomatoes, with the seeds strained out.*

*Yield:* 6 side-dish servings

| | |
|---|---|
| Tomato juice | 3 tablespoons |
| Balsamic vinegar | 3 tablespoons |
| Garlic | 2 cloves, minced |
| Salt | ¼ teaspoon |
| Black pepper | Several grinds |
| Extra virgin olive oil | 2 tablespoons |
| Fresh spinach leaves, chopped or torn | 5 cups |
| Radicchio, chopped or torn | 2 cups |
| Whole pear tomatoes, canned | 6, chopped |

In a small bowl, whisk together the tomato juice, vinegar, garlic, salt, and pepper, then add the oil and whisk until well combined, about 1 minute. Set aside at room temperature.

Toss the spinach, radicchio, and tomatoes together in a chilled serving bowl. Just before serving, pour the dressing over the salad and toss to combine.

---

Each serving provides:

| | | | | |
|---|---|---|---|---|
| 69 | Calories | 6 g | Carbohydrate |
| 2 g | Protein | 231 mg | Sodium |
| 5 g | Fat | 0 mg | Cholesterol |
| 1 g | Dietary Fiber | | |

# Salade Niçoise

*ALMOST INSTANT*

*Some purists argue that a true niçoise salad would never contain cooked vegetables, but we like the taste and texture of steamed green beans so well that we can't resist including them. Though anchovies and/or tuna are traditionally added, they are not missed here. Of course, those on a vegan diet may simply omit the eggs. This salad is so hearty and satisfying, it makes a wonderful summer main course with fresh, crusty bread and perhaps a fine French cheese on the side.*

*Yield:* 4 main-course servings

| | |
|---|---|
| Eggs | 2 large |
| Fresh-squeezed lemon juice | 2 tablespoons |
| Red wine vinegar | 2 tablespoons |
| Dijon mustard | 2 teaspoons |
| Garlic | 1 clove, minced |
| Salt | ½ teaspoon |
| Black pepper | Several grinds |
| Extra virgin olive oil | 2 tablespoons |
| Plain nonfat yogurt | 2 tablespoons |
| Fresh basil leaves, chiffonade* | ¼ cup |
| Green beans | ½ pound |
| Cucumber | 1 medium |
| Red or yellow bell pepper | 1 medium |
| Butter lettuce | 1 medium head |
| Cherry tomatoes | 12 medium |
| Green onions | 2 |
| Niçoise olives, unpitted | ½ cup |

*Chiffonade is the French term for a particular method of preparing fresh herbs. Stack the herb leaves on top of each other and roll slightly so you can hold them tightly in place, then use a sharp knife to slice the stack crosswise into paper-thin shreds.

Put the eggs into a pan and cover with cold water. Bring to a boil over medium-high heat, then reduce the heat to medium and boil 10 minutes. Immediately transfer the eggs to a bowl of ice water to cool for 10 minutes.

Whisk together the lemon juice, vinegar, mustard, garlic, salt, and pepper in a small bowl. Add the olive oil and yogurt and whisk until well combined, about 1 minute. Stir in the basil and set aside while you prepare the vegetables.

Pinch the stems off the green beans and string them if necessary. Bring 1 inch of water to a boil in a large saucepan with a steaming tray inserted in it. When the water is boiling, place the beans in the tray, cover, and steam 7 to 10 minutes, until the beans are fork-tender but still have a bit of crunch. Transfer them to a colander and rinse well with cold water to stop the cooking. Drain well.

If the cucumber is waxed or if the skin tastes bitter, peel it. Cut the cucumber crosswise into thin slices. Cut the bell pepper in half lengthwise and remove and discard the stem, seeds, and white membrane. Slice the pepper into very thin slivers. Wash and dry the lettuce leaves and tear them into bite-size pieces. Wash and dry the cherry tomatoes and cut them in half. Trim off the root end of the onions and about 2 inches of the green portion. Thinly slice the onions. Peel and quarter the cooled eggs.

In a pretty serving bowl, toss the lettuce with the cucumber, bell pepper strips, beans, and onions. Pour on the dressing and toss, then distribute the salad among 4 chilled serving plates. Distribute the cherry tomatoes and olives among the salads, and place 2 egg quarters alongside each serving.

---

Each serving provides:

| | | | |
|---|---|---|---|
| 210 | Calories | 15 g | Carbohydrate |
| 7 g | Protein | 470 mg | Sodium |
| 13 g | Fat | 107 mg | Cholesterol |
| 4 g | Dietary Fiber | | |

# Arugula and Pepper Salad with Mustard Fennel Seed Vinaigrette

*ALMOST INSTANT, VEGAN*

*Arugula is a peppery tasting salad green also known as rocket. It is complemented here by the sweetness of fennel seeds, ripe bell pepper, and a honey-laced vinaigrette. If you are making this salad when fresh basil is not available at the market, you may substitute 1 teaspoon of dried basil, whisked into the dressing.*

*Yield:* 4 side-dish servings

| | |
|---|---|
| Fresh-squeezed lemon juice | 3 tablespoons |
| Dijon mustard | 2 teaspoons |
| Honey | 1 teaspoon |
| Fennel seed | 1 teaspoon, crushed |
| Salt | ⅛ teaspoon |
| Black pepper | Several grinds |
| Extra virgin olive oil | 2 tablespoons |
| Fresh arugula leaves | 6 cups, lightly packed |
| Yellow or red bell pepper | 1 medium |
| Red onion, thinly sliced | ½ cup |
| Fresh basil leaves, chiffonade* | ¼ cup, lightly packed |

*Chiffonade is the French term for a particular method of preparing fresh herbs. Stack the herb leaves on top of each other and roll slightly so you can hold them tightly in place, then use a sharp knife to slice the stack crosswise into paper-thin shreds.

In a small bowl, whisk together the lemon juice, mustard, honey, fennel seed, salt, and a few grinds of pepper, then add the oil and whisk until well combined, about 1 minute. Set aside at room temperature.

Wash and dry the arugula and set it aside in a pretty serving bowl. Slice the bell pepper in half lengthwise. Remove and discard the seeds, stem, and white membrane and cut the pepper halves lengthwise into ¼-inch strips. Cut the strips in half crosswise. Toss the arugula with the bell pepper and onion until well combined. Just before serving, pour on the dressing and toss to combine. Mound the salad on 4 chilled serving plates and top each salad with a portion of the basil. Grind on a bit more pepper and serve immediately.

---

Each serving provides:

| 101 | Calories | 9 g | Carbohydrate |
|-----|----------|-----|--------------|
| 2 g | Protein | 145 mg | Sodium |
| 8 g | Fat | 0 mg | Cholesterol |
| 2 g | Dietary Fiber | | |

# Mesclun and Radish Salad
# with Mustard Lemon Dressing

*ALMOST INSTANT, VEGAN*

Mesclun—*a mixture of tender, young salad greens—is popular in the south of France. Market vendors offer their own special combinations, varied in color, texture, and flavor. Many supermarkets and gourmet food shops in the United States now carry such a salad mix. Seeds for specialty salad greens are also widely available and are easy to grow in the home garden.*

*Yield:* 4 side-dish servings

| | |
|---|---|
| **Mixed salad greens** | **4 cups, lightly packed** |
| **Red radishes** | **4 medium, thinly sliced** |
| **Fresh-squeezed lemon juice** | **1 tablespoon** |
| **Dijon mustard** | **1 teaspoon** |
| **Salt** | **Scant ⅛ teaspoon** |
| **Black pepper** | **Several grinds** |
| **Extra virgin olive oil** | **2 tablespoons** |

Wash the greens and dry them thoroughly. Place them in a large bowl, add the radishes, and toss to combine. In a small bowl, whisk together the lemon juice, mustard, salt, and pepper, then add the oil and whisk until well combined, about 1 minute. Just before serving, drizzle the dressing over the salad and toss to combine.

---

Each serving provides:

| | | | |
|---|---|---|---|
| 72 | Calories | 2 g | Carbohydrate |
| 1 g | Protein | 105 mg | Sodium |
| 7 g | Fat | 0 mg | Cholesterol |
| 1 g | Dietary Fiber | | |

# Garlic Cucumber Salad

*ALMOST INSTANT*

*In Greece this simple salad is known as* tzatziki, *but slightly different variations of it turn up throughout the eastern Mediterranean. It makes a refreshing and cooling salad or condiment.*

*Yield:* 4 side-dish servings

| | |
|---|---|
| **Cucumber** | **1 large** |
| **Salt** | **½ teaspoon** |
| **Plain nonfat yogurt** | **½ cup** |
| **Garlic** | **2 cloves, minced** |
| **White wine vinegar** | **1 teaspoon** |
| **Black pepper** | **Several grinds** |

Peel the cucumber and cut it in half lengthwise. Use a spoon to scrape out and discard the seeds. Cut the cucumber halves crosswise into ¼-inch slices. Place the slices in a colander and sprinkle evenly with the salt. Allow to stand 20 minutes.

Rinse the cucumber thoroughly with cold water. Allow it to drain for a few moments, then wrap it in a clean tea towel and squeeze gently to dry thoroughly. Place the cucumber in a bowl. Whisk together the yogurt, garlic, vinegar, and pepper. Pour over the cucumber and toss to combine, then grind on some more black pepper. Serve plain or on top of lettuce leaves. This mixture will stay fresh in the refrigerator for up to several days and may be served cold or at room temperature.

---

Each serving provides:

| | | | |
|---|---|---|---|
| 30 | Calories | 6 g | Carbohydrate |
| 2 g | Protein | 291 mg | Sodium |
| 0 g | Fat | 1 mg | Cholesterol |
| 1 g | Dietary Fiber | | |

# Classic Greek Salad

*ALMOST INSTANT*

*This simple salad is world-renowned as a feast of summertime Greece. Be sure to use tomatoes that are perfectly ripe and juicy. A crusty loaf of bread is an essential accompaniment.*

*Yield:* 8 side-dish servings

| | |
|---|---|
| **Fresh tomatoes** | **2 pounds (4 large)** |
| **Cucumber** | **1 large** |
| **Green bell peppers** | **2 medium** |
| **Red onion** | **1 medium** |
| **Calamata olives, unpitted** | **1 cup** |
| **Feta cheese** | **4 ounces** |
| **Extra virgin olive oil** | **¼ cup** |
| **Red wine vinegar** | **2 tablespoons** |
| **Capers, drained** | **2 tablespoons** |
| **Fresh Italian parsley leaves** | **½ cup** |
| **Black pepper** | **Several grinds** |

Cut out and discard the stem ends of the tomatoes and cut them into thick wedges. If the cucumber is waxed or if the skin tastes bitter, peel it, then cut it in half lengthwise. Cut each half crosswise into thick slices. Slice the bell pepper in half lengthwise. Remove and discard the stem, seeds, and white membrane of the peppers, then cut them into large cubes. Slice the red onion into ¼-inch rings. Place the vegetables, including the whole olives, in a large bowl and toss to combine. Cut the cheese into ¼-inch cubes and add it to the vegetables. Whisk together the oil and vinegar until well combined, about 1 minute, and pour over the vegetables. Add the capers, parsley, and pepper, toss to combine, and serve immediately.

---

Each serving provides:

| | | | |
|---|---|---|---|
| 198 | Calories | 14 g | Carbohydrate |
| 4 g | Protein | 682 mg | Sodium |
| 16 g | Fat | 13 mg | Cholesterol |
| 3 g | Dietary Fiber | | |

# Summary Bread Salad

# Summer Bread Salad

*ALMOST INSTANT, VEGAN*

*This wonderful version of Tuscan* panzanella *requires a really fine, rustic bread. Supermarket "French bread" just won't do. The quality of the tomatoes is important too—vine-ripened tomatoes from a back-yard garden or farmers' market will yield the best results. We like to toast the bread for crispness, but the salad is also delicious using slightly stale (but not hard) bread cubes, which will soak up the dressing and soften to an appealing chewy texture. This salad makes a refreshing, light meal unto itself, or it can serve as the first course at an Italian-inspired dinner party.*

*Yield:* 6 side-dish servings

| | |
|---|---|
| **Thick-crusted unsliced bread, cut into ¾-inch cubes** | **4 cups** |
| **Red wine vinegar** | **¼ cup** |
| **Garlic** | **2 cloves, minced** |
| **Salt** | **¼ teaspoon** |
| **Black pepper** | **Several grinds** |
| **Extra virgin olive oil** | **¼ cup** |
| **Cucumber** | **1 medium** |
| **Fresh pear tomatoes** | **1 pound** |
| **Red onion, minced** | **¼ cup** |
| **Fresh basil leaves, whole** | **¼ cup, firmly packed** |
| **Capers, drained** | **2 tablespoons** |
| **Butter lettuce leaves** | **6 large** |

Preheat a toaster oven or conventional oven to 350 degrees F. Spread the bread cubes in a single layer on a baking sheet and toast in the oven until crisp and lightly browned, 8 to 10 minutes. Set aside to cool.

Meanwhile, whisk together the vinegar, garlic, salt, and pepper, then add the oil and whisk until well combined, about 1 minute. Set the dressing aside.

If the cucumber is waxed or if the skin tastes bitter, peel it. Cut the cucumber in half lengthwise and use a spoon to scrape out and discard the seeds. Cut the cucumber halves crosswise into ¼-inch slices and set them aside in a large bowl. Cut the tomatoes in half crosswise and squeeze them gently over the sink to remove the juicy seed pockets. Cut out and discard the stem ends, then dice the tomatoes and add them to the cucumber. Add the onion, basil, capers, and dressing and toss to combine. (This much can be done ahead of time and held at room temperature for up to several hours.)

Just before serving, add the bread cubes to the salad and toss to distribute evenly. Place a lettuce leaf on each plate and mound a portion of the salad into it. Serve at room temperature.

---

Each serving provides:

| | | | |
|---|---|---|---|
| 184 | Calories | 20 g | Carbohydrate |
| 3 g | Protein | 301 mg | Sodium |
| 11 g | Fat | 0 mg | Cholesterol |
| 3 g | Dietary Fiber | | |

# Rice Salad with Eggplant, Tomatoes, Olives, and Fresh Basil

*VEGAN*

*This scrumptious salad was inspired by the traditional Sicilian dish called* caponata. *The rice takes on the piquant flavors of the dressing and provides satisfying body. We like to take this dish to potlucks or on picnics. This recipe makes a lot, but the salad keeps well in the refrigerator and can be enjoyed over the course of a few days.*

*Yield:* 10 side-dish servings

| | | |
|---|---|---|
| Uncooked long-grain white rice | 1 | cup |
| Fresh pear tomatoes | 1½ | pounds |
| Eggplant | 1 | pound (1 medium) |
| Extra virgin olive oil | 4 | tablespoons |
| White onion | 1 | medium, diced |
| Dry sherry | 2 | tablespoons |
| Garlic | 2 | cloves, minced |
| Balsamic vinegar | 3 | tablespoons |
| Salt | ¼ | teaspoon |
| Dried red chili flakes | ¼ | teaspoon |
| Capers, drained | 2 | tablespoons |
| Water-packed green olives, chopped | ¾ | cup |
| Fresh basil leaves, chopped | ¼ | cup |
| Fresh parsley leaves, minced | ¼ | cup |

Bring 2 cups of water to a boil in a medium saucepan that has a tight-fitting lid. Add the rice, cover the pan, reduce the heat to very low, and cook for 20 minutes. Remove from the heat and set aside with the lid in place for at least 5 minutes. Transfer the rice to a shallow serving bowl, fluffing it with a fork, and set aside to cool a bit while you prepare the rest of the salad.

Cut the tomatoes in half crosswise and squeeze them gently over the sink to remove the juicy seed pockets. Cut out and discard the stem ends and dice the tomatoes. Set them aside in a bowl.

Remove and discard the stem end of the eggplant and cut it into ½-inch cubes. In a large skillet, heat 1 tablespoon of the oil over medium-high heat. Add the onion and sauté 3 minutes. Stir in 1 tablespoon of the remaining oil, the sherry, eggplant, and garlic. Cook, stirring frequently, until the eggplant is tender, about 10 minutes.

In a small bowl, whisk together the remaining 2 tablespoons oil, vinegar, salt, and chili flakes until well combined, about 1 minute.

Toss the dressing with the rice, then add the eggplant mixture, tomatoes, capers, olives, basil, and parsley. Toss to combine well, then set the salad aside at room temperature for about 30 minutes so its flavor can develop.

This salad may be made ahead of time and refrigerated for up to 2 days, but return it to room temperature before serving.

---

Each serving provides:

| 193 | Calories | 30 g | Carbohydrate |
|-----|----------|------|--------------|
| 3 g | Protein | 368 mg | Sodium |
| 7 g | Fat | 0 mg | Cholesterol |
| 3 g | Dietary Fiber | | |

# Saffron Rice Salad
# with Olives and Grapes

*VEGAN*

*As unconventional as this combination of ingredients may sound, the resulting salad is full of bright, fresh flavors. It is another popular potluck offering.*

*Yield:* 10 side-dish servings

| | |
|---|---|
| **Saffron threads** | ½ teaspoon |
| **Uncooked basmati rice** | 1 cup |
| **Fresh tomatoes** | 1 pound (2 medium) |
| **Seedless green grapes, halved** | 1 cup |
| **Calamata olives, chopped** | 1 cup |
| **Fresh Italian parsley, minced** | ½ cup |
| **Fresh-squeezed lemon juice** | 2 tablespoons |
| **Garlic** | 2 cloves, minced |
| **Paprika** | 1 teaspoon |
| **Ground black pepper** | 1 teaspoon |
| **Salt** | ½ teaspoon |
| **Extra virgin olive oil** | 2 tablespoons |

Bring 2 cups of water to a boil in a medium saucepan. Use your fingers to crumble the saffron threads into the water, then stir in the rice. Cover the pan, reduce the heat to very low, and cook 20 minutes. Remove the pan from the heat and set aside with the lid in place for at least 5 minutes.

While the rice is cooking, cut the tomatoes in half crosswise and squeeze them gently over the sink to remove the juicy seed pockets. Cut out and discard the stem ends, then finely dice the tomatoes and place them in a large bowl. Add the grapes, olives, and parsley and toss to combine.

In a small bowl, whisk together the lemon juice, garlic, paprika, pepper, and salt, then add the oil and whisk until well combined, about 1 minute. Pour this over the tomato mixture and toss to combine. Fluff the rice with a fork, then add it to the tomato mixture and toss to combine. Serve immediately, or refrigerate for up to several hours, but return the salad to room temperature before serving.

---

Each serving provides:

| | | | |
|---|---|---|---|
| 174 | Calories | 24 g | Carbohydrate |
| 3 g | Protein | 562 mg | Sodium |
| 8 g | Fat | 0 mg | Cholesterol |
| 1 g | Dietary Fiber | | |

# Bulgur Salad with Parsley, Mint, and Tomatoes

*ALMOST INSTANT, VEGAN*

*This satisfying summer salad bears a strong resemblance to traditional Middle Eastern* tabbouleh *but is enlivened by the addition of fresh mint and a mustard-laced dressing.*

*Yield:* 6 side-dish servings

| | | |
|---|---|---|
| **Dried bulgur wheat** | 1¾ | **cups** |
| **Fresh tomatoes** | 1 | **pound** |
| | | **(2 medium)** |
| **Fresh-squeezed lemon juice** | 3 | **tablespoons** |
| **Dijon mustard** | 1 | **tablespoon** |
| **Garlic** | 1 | **clove, minced** |
| **Salt** | ½ | **teaspoon** |
| **Black pepper** | **Several grinds** | |
| **Extra virgin olive oil** | 2 | **tablespoons** |
| **Fresh Italian parsley, minced** | ½ | **cup** |
| **Fresh mint leaves, minced** | ½ | **cup** |
| **Green onions** | 4, | **minced** |
| **Butter lettuce leaves** | 6 | **large** |
| **Calamata olives, unpitted** | 18 | |
| **Lemon wedges** | 1 | **per serving** |

Bring 3 cups of water to a boil. Place the bulgur in a large bowl and pour the boiling water over it. Cover the bowl and allow to soak for 20 minutes. Drain off any remaining water and squeeze the bulgur gently in a clean tea towel to thoroughly dry it. Transfer it to a bowl.

Meanwhile, cut the tomatoes in half crosswise and squeeze them gently over the sink to remove the juicy seed pockets. Cut out and discard the stem ends and finely dice the tomatoes. Add them to the bulgur.

In a small bowl, whisk the lemon juice with the mustard, garlic, salt, and pepper, then add the oil and whisk until well combined, about 1 minute.

Add the parsley, mint, and green onions to the bulgur and toss to combine, then add the dressing and toss again. Line 6 chilled salad bowls with one lettuce leaf each and spoon a portion of the salad into each one. Garnish each serving with 3 olives and a wedge of lemon and serve immediately.

---

Each serving provides:

| 231  | Calories      | 38 g   | Carbohydrate |
|------|---------------|--------|--------------|
| 7 g  | Protein       | 455 mg | Sodium       |
| 8 g  | Fat           | 0 mg   | Cholesterol  |
| 7 g  | Dietary Fiber |        |              |

# Garbanzo Bean Salad with Roasted Red Peppers

*VEGAN*

*Garbanzo beans, red bell peppers, and capers are three common ingredients in Spanish cooking. Here they are combined with a mint-laced dressing to create a delicious salad.*

*Yield:* 6 side-dish servings

| | |
|---|---|
| **Red bell peppers** | **2 large** |
| **Extra virgin olive oil** | **2 tablespoons** |
| **Fresh-squeezed lemon juice** | **1 tablespoon** |
| **Salt** | **⅛ teaspoon** |
| **Black pepper** | **Several grinds** |
| **Fresh mint leaves, minced** | **¼ cup** |
| **Capers, drained** | **3 tablespoons** |
| **Garlic** | **3 cloves, minced** |
| **Cooked garbanzo beans, drained\*** | **2 cups** |

Preheat the broiler or a coal or gas grill (see page 28). Place the whole peppers under the broiler or on the grill and cook for several minutes, until the skin is charred black on one side. Turn the peppers and cook several more minutes to blacken the other side. Continue to turn and cook until the entire skin of the peppers is almost uniformly black. Transfer the peppers to a paper or plastic bag, close the bag tightly, and set aside for 10 minutes or so. The steam inside the bag will finish cooking the peppers. When the peppers are cool enough to handle,

\*Cook 1 cup of presoaked dried beans as directed on page 29, or use canned beans that do not contain additives.

remove them from the bag and peel off and discard their blackened skin. Discard the seeds, stems, and membranes and coarsely chop the peppers. Set them aside in a bowl.

Meanwhile, in a small bowl, whisk together the oil, lemon juice, salt, and pepper until well combined, about 1 minute. Stir in the mint, capers, and garlic. Set this dressing aside.

Add the garbanzo beans to the peppers and toss to combine. Add the dressing and toss again. Serve the salad immediately, or set it aside at room temperature for up to a few hours or in the refrigerator for up to a day, but return the salad to room temperature before serving.

---

Each serving provides:

| 150 | Calories | 20 g | Carbohydrate |
|-----|----------|------|--------------|
| 5 g | Protein | 150 mg | Sodium |
| 7 g | Fat | 0 mg | Cholesterol |
| 3 g | Dietary Fiber | | |

# Fava Beans with Eggs and Olives

Ful medamis, *on which this dish is based, is an age-old Egyptian preparation. It typically appears on the breakfast table but is also a popular street food, enjoyed for lunch at open-air food stalls. As with many traditional dishes, this one uses humble ingredients and prepares them in a simple way to create something delicious and nourishing. For a satisfying lunch, serve the ful with sliced fresh tomatoes and tahini-smeared bread.*

*Yield:* 4 side-dish servings

| | |
|---|---|
| **Dried fava beans** | 1 **cup** |
| **Egg** | 1 **large** |
| **Extra virgin olive oil** | 3 **tablespoons** |
| **Fresh-squeezed lemon juice** | 2 **tablespoons** |
| **Salt** | ½ **teaspoon** |
| **Fresh Italian parsley, minced** | ½ **cup** |
| **Calamata olives** | 8, **pitted** |

Sort through the fava beans, discarding any foreign objects you may find. Thoroughly rinse them and set them aside in a colander. Bring 4 cups of water to a boil in a medium stockpot over high heat. Add the beans, reduce the heat to low, and partially cover the pot, leaving the lid slightly ajar. Gently simmer the beans for about 4 hours, until almost all of the liquid has been absorbed and the beans are tender. Watch the pot carefully toward the end of the cooking time, adding several tablespoons of hot water, if necessary, to prevent scorching. During the last 30 minutes of cooking, stir the beans frequently. Some of them will break apart, creating a thick sauce. When the beans are tender, transfer them to a bowl, along with the remaining bit of liquid, and allow to cool.

Meanwhile, place the eggs in a saucepan with several cups of cold water and bring to a boil over high heat. Reduce the heat to medium and boil 10 minutes, then transfer the egg to a bowl of ice water to cool for 10 minutes. Remove it from the ice water, peel, and chop it coarsely. Set aside in a bowl.

In a small bowl, whisk the oil with the lemon juice and salt until well combined, about 1 minute, then stir in the parsley. Pour this over the beans and stir to combine. Transfer the beans to a serving platter and sprinkle with the chopped egg. Arrange the olives on top and serve.

---

Each serving provides:

| 253 | Calories | 23 g | Carbohydrate |
| 12 g | Protein | 417 mg | Sodium |
| 13 g | Fat | 53 mg | Cholesterol |
| 6 g | Dietary Fiber | | |

# French Lentil Salad
# with Fresh Basil and Mint

*VEGAN*

*French lentils are small, dark green lentils that have a slightly pep-
pery flavor. Here they are the foundation for a colorful and delicious
salad. Use basil-flavored red wine vinegar for this recipe if you have
some on hand.*

*Yield:* 6 side-dish servings

| | |
|---|---|
| **Uncooked French lentils** | 1 **cup** |
| **Red bell pepper** | 1 **medium, diced** |
| **Yellow onion, diced** | ½ **cup** |
| **Fresh basil leaves, chiffonade\*** | ½ **cup** |
| **Fresh mint leaves, chiffonade\*** | ½ **cup** |
| **Extra virgin olive oil** | ¼ **cup** |
| **Red wine vinegar** | 2 **tablespoons** |
| **Garlic** | 2 **cloves, minced** |
| **Salt** | ¼ **teaspoon** |
| **Black pepper** | **Several grinds** |

Wash and sort the lentils, discarding any foreign objects you
may find. Place them in a saucepan and cover with 4 cups of
water. Bring to a boil over high heat, then reduce the heat to
medium-high and simmer rapidly for 12 to 14 minutes, until
the lentils are tender but not mushy. Drain thoroughly in a

---

*Chiffonade is the French term for a particular method of preparing fresh
herbs. Stack the herb leaves on top of each other and roll slightly so you can
hold them tightly in place, then use a sharp knife to slice the stack crosswise
into paper-thin shreds.

colander, rinsing well with cold water to stop the cooking, then transfer the lentils to a large bowl and set aside to cool for at least 30 minutes.

Add the bell pepper, onion, basil, and mint to the lentils and toss to combine. In a small bowl, whisk together the oil, vinegar, garlic, salt, and pepper until well combined, about 1 minute. Pour this dressing over the lentils and toss to combine. Set aside at room temperature for up to a few hours so the flavors can blend, or refrigerate for up to a day, but bring the salad to room temperature before serving.

---

Each serving provides:

| | | | |
|---|---|---|---|
| 203 | Calories | 22 g | Carbohydrate |
| 10 g | Protein | 95 mg | Sodium |
| 9 g | Fat | 0 mg | Cholesterol |
| 4 g | Dietary Fiber | | |

# Tomato and Mint Salad with Feta Cheese

*ALMOST INSTANT*

*Fresh mint is used extensively in Turkish cuisine. During the hot summer months, vine-ripened tomatoes are often seasoned with it, creating a refreshing salad. Use a combination of red and yellow tomatoes, if possible, to create a particularly colorful salad.*

*Yield:* 8 side-dish servings

| | | |
|---|---|---|
| **Fresh tomatoes** | 1½ | **pounds** |
| | | **(3 medium)** |
| **White onion** | 1 | **small** |
| **Green bell pepper** | 1 | **large** |
| **Cucumber** | 1 | **medium** |
| **Fresh mint leaves, minced** | ½ | **cup** |
| **Extra virgin olive oil** | 3 | **tablespoons** |
| **Fresh-squeezed lemon juice** | 2 | **tablespoons** |
| **Black pepper** | | **Several grinds** |
| **Feta cheese, crumbled** | 2 | **ounces (½ cup)** |

Cut the tomatoes in half crosswise and squeeze them gently over the sink to remove the juicy seed pockets. Cut out and discard the stem ends, then finely dice the tomatoes and transfer them to a large bowl. Peel the onion and thinly slice it. Add the onion to the bowl. Slice the bell pepper in half lengthwise. Remove and discard the stem, seeds, and white membrane. Coarsely chop the pepper and add it to the bowl. If the cucumber is waxed or if its skin tastes bitter, peel the cucumber and cut it in half lengthwise. Use a spoon to scrape out and discard the seeds, then cut the cucumber halves crosswise into ¼-inch slices. Add the cucumber to the bowl. Sprinkle the mint over the vegetables and toss to combine.

In a small bowl, whisk together the oil, lemon juice, and pepper until well combined, about 1 minute. Drizzle this dressing over the tomato mixture and toss to combine. Add the cheese and toss again. Serve immediately, or refrigerate for several hours, but return the salad to room temperature before serving.

---

Each serving provides:

| 104 | Calories | 9 g | Carbohydrate |
|-----|----------|-----|--------------|
| 3 g | Protein | 89 mg | Sodium |
| 7 g | Fat | 6 mg | Cholesterol |
| 2 g | Dietary Fiber | | |

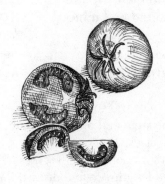

# Salad of Grilled Eggplant, Peppers, and Mushrooms

*VEGAN*

*This warm salad is composed of a delightful combination of grilled vegetables. In Spain, the vegetables would be bathed with much more olive oil than we call for here, but this lower-fat version doesn't scrimp at all on flavor.*

*Yield:* 4 side-dish servings

| | |
|---|---|
| **Eggplant** | 1  pound (1 medium) |
| **Portobello mushrooms** | ½ pound (2 medium) |
| **Red bell pepper** | 1  large |
| **Olive oil** | 2  tablespoons plus ½ teaspoon |
| **Fresh-squeezed lemon juice** | 1  tablespoon |
| **Fresh oregano leaves, minced** | 1  tablespoon |
| **Capers, drained and minced** | 2  teaspoons |
| **Salt** | ⅛ teaspoon |
| **Black pepper** | Several grinds |
| **Red leaf lettuce** | 4  large leaves |

Preheat a coal or gas grill to medium-high (see page 28). Cut off and discard the stem end of the eggplant, then cut it lengthwise into ½-inch slices. Remove the stems of the mushrooms and reserve them for another use, such as soup stock. Slice the bell pepper in half lengthwise and discard the stem, seeds, and white membrane. Cut each half into 4 lengthwise strips. Use ½ teaspoon of the oil to lightly coat the vegetables, or use an olive oil spray.

Place all of the vegetables on the preheated grill. Cook the eggplant and mushrooms for about 5 minutes, then turn and cook for another 5 minutes. The eggplant should be tender and slightly charred and the mushrooms tender and juicy. (Depending on the thickness of the mushrooms, they may need to cook for an additional 3 to 4 minutes.) Cook the pepper strips for about 5 minutes, turning once, until they are slightly limp and lightly charred.

Meanwhile, combine the remaining 2 tablespoons oil, lemon juice, oregano, capers, salt, and pepper in a blender and puree until smooth.

Line each of 4 salad plates or bowls with a red lettuce leaf. Cut the grilled eggplant and mushrooms into long strips and arrange them on top of the lettuce. Garnish with the pepper strips. Drizzle evenly with the dressing and serve.

---

Each serving provides:

| 132 | Calories | 15 g | Carbohydrate |
|-----|----------|------|--------------|
| 3 g | Protein | 107 mg | Sodium |
| 8 g | Fat | 0 mg | Cholesterol |
| 3 g | Dietary Fiber | | |

# Spiced Beet, Tomato, and Radish Salad

*This eastern Mediterranean vegetable salad explodes on the tongue with hot and sweet flavors. Its colors, too, are exciting—a study in red.*

*Yield:* 6 side-dish servings

| | | |
|---|---|---|
| **Fresh beets, without greens** | 1¼ | pounds (5 medium) |
| **Fresh tomatoes** | 1 | pound (2 medium) |
| **Red radishes** | 6 | medium, thinly sliced |
| **Plain nonfat yogurt** | ¼ | cup |
| **Fresh-squeezed lemon juice** | 2 | tablespoons |
| **Extra virgin olive oil** | 1 | tablespoon |
| **Garlic** | 1 | clove, minced |
| **Paprika** | 1 | teaspoon |
| **Ground cumin** | 1 | teaspoon |
| **Ground cinnamon** | ½ | teaspoon |
| **Honey** | ½ | teaspoon |
| **Cayenne** | ¼ | teaspoon |
| **Salt** | ¼ | teaspoon |
| **Fresh mint, chiffonade\*** | ¼ | cup |

\*Chiffonade is the French term for a particular method of preparing fresh herbs. Stack the herb leaves on top of each other and roll slightly so you can hold them tightly in place, then use a sharp knife to slice the stack crosswise into paper-thin shreds.

Place the unpeeled beets in a saucepan, cover with cold water, and bring to a boil over high heat. Reduce the heat to medium and boil 20 to 25 minutes, until a knife or sharp skewer can be easily inserted through the middle of each beet. Drain the beets and set them aside to cool. (The beets can be cooked a day or two ahead of time, if desired, and stored in the refrigerator until you are ready to use them.)

Use your hands to rub off and discard the skins of the beets. Dice the beets and place them in a bowl. Cut the tomatoes in half crosswise and gently squeeze them over the sink to remove their juicy seed pockets. Cut out and discard the stem ends. Slice the tomatoes into thin wedges and add them to the beets. Add the sliced radishes and toss.

In a small bowl, whisk together the yogurt, lemon juice, oil, garlic, paprika, cumin, cinnamon, honey, cayenne, and salt. Pour this mixture over the vegetables and toss to combine. Mound onto a serving plate, top with the mint, and serve immediately.

---

Each serving provides:

| | | | |
|---|---|---|---|
| 85 | Calories | 14 g | Carbohydrate |
| 3 g | Protein | 169 mg | Sodium |
| 3 g | Fat | 0 mg | Cholesterol |
| 2 g | Dietary Fiber | | |

# Potato Salad with Spanish Olives

*Here is an irresistible potato salad with flavors reminiscent of Spain. It makes a scrumptious picnic or potluck offering, or it can be served as part of a buffet supper. A crusty bread is one essential accompaniment, to soak up the delicious dressing.*

*Yield:* 6 side-dish servings

| | | |
|---|---|---|
| Red bell pepper | 1 | medium |
| Red potatoes | 2 | pounds |
| Fresh-squeezed lemon juice | 2 | tablespoons |
| Red wine vinegar | 2 | tablespoons |
| Reduced-fat mayonnaise | 2 | tablespoons |
| Paprika | 1½ | teaspoons |
| Ground cumin | 1½ | teaspoons |
| Garlic | 2 | cloves, minced |
| Salt | ½ | teaspoon |
| Black pepper | Several grinds | |
| Extra virgin olive oil | 2 | tablespoons |
| Red onion, finely diced | ½ | cup |
| Fresh Italian parsley, minced | ½ | cup |
| Pimiento-stuffed olives, sliced | ½ | cup |

Preheat the broiler or a coal or gas grill (see page 28). Place the whole pepper on the grill or under the broiler and cook for several minutes, until the skin is charred black on one side. Turn the pepper over and cook several more minutes to blacken the other side. Continue to turn and cook until the entire skin of the pepper is almost uniformly black. Transfer the pepper to a paper or plastic bag, close the bag tightly, and set aside for 10 minutes or so. The steam inside the bag will finish cooking the pepper. When the pepper is cool enough to handle, remove it from the bag and peel off and discard the blackened skin. Discard the seeds, stem, and membrane and dice the pepper. Set aside in a bowl.

Meanwhile, put a few quarts of water on to boil in a large saucepan or stockpot. Peel the potatoes and cut them into fairly uniform 1-inch pieces. Add them to the boiling water, return to a boil, and cook 3 to 5 minutes, until they are fork-tender but not soft enough to fall apart. Transfer the potatoes to a colander and rinse gently under cold water to stop the cooking.

In a small bowl, whisk together the lemon juice, vinegar, mayonnaise, paprika, cumin, garlic, salt, and pepper. Add the oil and whisk until well combined, about 1 minute. Set aside at room temperature.

When the potatoes are cooled somewhat, toss them gently in a large serving bowl with the diced pepper, onion, parsley, and olives. Add the dressing and toss again. Serve immediately.

---

Each serving provides:

| 212 | Calories | 25 g | Carbohydrate |
|---|---|---|---|
| 3 g | Protein | 560 mg | Sodium |
| 7 g | Fat | 0 mg | Cholesterol |
| 3 g | Dietary Fiber | | |

# Cold Pasta with Tomatoes, Artichokes, and Capers

*ALMOST INSTANT*

*Bright Mediterranean flavors and colors combine beautifully in this simple-to-prepare pasta dish. Serve it at a picnic or potluck, or serve larger portions for a wonderful light supper entrée in summer.*

*Yield:* 12 side-dish servings

| | | |
|---|---|---|
| Dried penne pasta | 1 | pound |
| Extra virgin olive oil | ⅓ | cup plus 1 teaspoon |
| Fresh tomatoes | 1½ | pounds (3 large) |
| Marinated artichoke hearts | 2 | 6-ounce jars, drained |
| Calamata olives, pitted and chopped | ⅓ | cup |
| Capers, drained | ¼ | cup |
| Fresh-squeezed lemon juice | ¼ | cup |
| Red wine vinegar | 2 | tablespoons |
| Fresh oregano leaves, minced | 2 | tablespoons |
| Garlic | 3 | cloves, minced |
| Salt | ¼ | teaspoon |
| Cayenne | ⅛ | teaspoon |
| Feta cheese, crumbled | 4 | ounces (1 cup) |

Bring several quarts of water to a boil in a large stockpot and cook the pasta until al dente. Transfer to a colander and rinse with cold water to stop the cooking. Drain thoroughly. Transfer the pasta to a large bowl. If the pasta is done before the rest of the ingredients are ready, toss it with 1 teaspoon of the oil to prevent it from sticking together and set aside at room temperature.

While the pasta is cooking, cut the tomatoes in half cross-wise and squeeze them gently over the sink to remove their juicy seed pockets. Cut out and discard the stem ends of the tomatoes. Chop the tomatoes and place them in a large serving bowl. Add the artichokes, olives, and capers.

In a separate bowl, whisk together the lemon juice, vinegar, oregano, garlic, salt, and cayenne. Add the remaining ⅓ cup oil and whisk until well combined, about 1 minute. Pour the dressing over the tomato mixture and toss to combine. Add the pasta and feta cheese and toss again. If time permits, allow the salad to sit at room temperature for an hour or so, so its flavors can develop. You may store any leftovers in the refrigerator to be enjoyed over the next day or two.

---

Each serving provides:

| 290 | Calories | 36 g | Carbohydrate |
|-----|----------|------|--------------|
| 7 g | Protein | 426 mg | Sodium |
| 14 g | Fat | 8 mg | Cholesterol |
| 3 g | Dietary Fiber | | |

# Soups and Stews

The Mediterranean cook's imagination and skill with fresh ingredients is expressed in countless delicious soups and stews. Classics such as chunky Italian *minestrone,* pungent Spanish *gazpacho,* and tangy Greek *avgolemono* are some world-renowned soups of the region, but they are only the start. This chapter explores the vast range of Mediterranean soup possibilities.

Combining beans or grains with seasonal vegetables in a good homemade stock, we have created a few Mediterranean-inspired stews satisfying enough to make a meal in a bowl. Good crusty bread, cheese, and wine would round out such a meal in authentic fashion.

On a lighter note, excellent broth is the foundation of some delicious first course soups, and exquisitely smooth pureed soups deliver the essence of some of our favorite vegetables.

Most of the soups presented here are to be served hot, but we have included Creamed Tomato and Fennel Soup with Pine Nuts, which can be served at room temperature. Cream of Zucchini and Fresh Basil Soup and an innovative Green Gazpacho are best served chilled. Any of the latter three could launch a Mediterranean-inspired summer dinner party, served on a garden patio or deck, with refreshing flair.

## Tips and Tools

- Homemade stock is a great soup enhancer. We provide a simple recipe on page 32. We strongly encourage you to keep a batch on hand in the refrigerator or freezer. However, for those times when the real thing isn't available, our recipes provide alternative instructions for making stock from vegetable bouillon cubes.

- When a recipe calls for pureeing a soup, do so in small batches to avoid splattering the hot liquid.

- Most soups maintain their quality, or may even improve in flavor, over the course of a day or two when held in the refrigerator. Reheat soups over low heat, or use a double boiler in the case of cream soups to prevent scorching. Of course, soups can also be reheated in a microwave oven, following the manufacturer's instructions.

- Since pasta, beans, and grains may continue to absorb liquid after a soup is cooked, leftover soups that contain these ingredients may need to have broth added when they are reheated to achieve an appealing consistency.

- The only tools essential to wonderful soup making are a heavy-bottomed stockpot or large saucepan, a long-handled wooden spoon for stirring, and a ladle for serving. Pureed soups, of course, also require a blender or food processor.

# Spinach Soup with Oregano and Calamata Olives

*VEGAN*

*This soup is decidedly Greek in origin, though its character is lighter than most Greek cuisine. Its preparation is simple—washing the spinach is the most time-consuming part. Serve this soup as a delightful early spring starter course or as a light summer meal along with good bread and a salad.*

*Yield:* 4 first-course servings

| | | |
|---|---|---|
| **Spinach** | 1½ | **pounds (2 bunches)** |
| **Olive oil** | 2 | **tablespoons** |
| **Yellow onion, diced** | ½ | **cup** |
| **Garlic** | 3 | **cloves, minced** |
| **Dried oregano** | 1 | **teaspoon** |
| **Homemade Vegetable Stock*** | 4 | **cups** |
| **Salt** | ¼ | **teaspoon** |
| **Black pepper** | | **Several grinds** |
| **Fresh-squeezed lemon juice** | ¼ | **cup** |
| **Calamata olives, pitted and diced** | ¼ | **cup** |
| **Fresh oregano leaves** | 1 | **tablespoon** |

*If you do not have Homemade Vegetable Stock on hand, make some according to the directions on page 32 or dissolve 2 large low-sodium vegetable broth cubes in 4 cups of hot water.

Carefully wash the spinach, discarding the thick stems. You don't need to dry the spinach. Stack several leaves on top of each other and cut them crosswise into ½-inch strips. Repeat until all the spinach is sliced and set aside in a colander.

Place the oil in a stockpot or large saucepan over medium heat. Add the onion, garlic, and dried oregano. Sauté for about 2 minutes, stirring frequently, then add the stock. Bring to a boil over high heat and add the spinach. Return to a boil, reduce the heat to medium, cover, and cook 5 minutes. Stir in the salt, pepper, lemon juice, olives, and fresh oregano and simmer about 3 minutes longer. Serve immediately.

---

Each serving provides:

| 143 | Calories | 12 g | Carbohydrate |
| 6 g | Protein | 627 mg | Sodium |
| 10 g | Fat | 0 mg | Cholesterol |
| 5 g | Dietary Fiber | | |

# Egg-Lemon Soup
# with Spinach and Rice

*ALMOST INSTANT*

*This is our favorite variation on the beloved Greek* avgolemono. *It comes together in a flash if you have cooked brown rice on hand. Enjoy it with thick country bread for lunch or as the first course of a Mediterranean feast. We like to use the sweeter Meyer lemons here, but you can substitute other varieties as long as they are fully ripe. Unripe lemon juice will lend an unpleasant bitter quality to the soup.*

*Yield:* 6 first-course servings

| | | |
|---|---|---|
| **Olive oil** | 1 | **tablespoon** |
| **White onion** | 1 | **medium, diced** |
| **Homemade Vegetable Stock***  | 5 | **cups** |
| **Garlic** | 1 | **clove, minced** |
| **Cooked brown rice** | 1½ | **cups** |
| **Eggs****  | 2 | **large** |
| **Fresh-squeezed lemon juice** | ⅓ | **cup** |
| **Salt** | ½ | **teaspoon** |
| **Black pepper** | | **Several grinds** |
| **Fresh spinach leaves, chopped** | 3 | **cups, lightly packed** |
| **Fresh mint leaves, chiffonade*****  | ¼ | **cup** |

*If you do not have Homemade Vegetable Stock on hand, make some according to the directions on page 32 or dissolve 2½ large low-sodium vegetable broth cubes in 5 cups of hot water.

**Some authorities suggest avoiding dishes made with raw eggs, due to the remote possibility of salmonella contamination. People with compromised immune systems may wish to heed this advice. For more information, contact your local office of the U.S. Department of Agriculture.

***Chiffonade is the French term for a particular method of preparing fresh herbs. Stack the herb leaves on top of each other and roll slightly so you can hold them tightly in place, then use a sharp knife to slice the stack crosswise into paper-thin shreds.

Heat the oil over medium heat in a stockpot or large saucepan and sauté the onion until nicely browned, about 10 minutes. Add the stock, garlic, and rice and bring to a simmer over high heat.

Meanwhile, place the eggs and lemon juice in a large bowl and beat lightly with a fork. Slowly beat about 1 cup of the hot soup into the egg mixture, then beat in another cup. (This will warm the egg mixture slowly so that it doesn't curdle when added to the soup.)

Turn off the heat under the soup and stir the egg mixture gently into it. Stir in the salt, pepper, and spinach and allow the soup to stand in the pan for 5 minutes before serving. Ladle into warmed bowls and top each serving with a portion of the mint.

---

Each serving provides:

| 134 | Calories | 19 g | Carbohydrate |
|------|----------|------|--------------|
| 5 g | Protein | 359 mg | Sodium |
| 4 g | Fat | 70 mg | Cholesterol |
| 2 g | Dietary Fiber | | |

# Garlic Broth with Vegetables and Crostini

*ALMOST INSTANT*

*Various versions of garlic soup are enjoyed throughout the Mediterranean. This one adds some finely chopped vegetable to the broth for textural interest. It is warming and nourishing, as all good soups should be.*

*Yield:* 4 first-course servings

| | | |
|---|---|---|
| Homemade Vegetable Stock* | 4½ | cups |
| Garlic | 8 | cloves, minced |
| Whole bay leaf | 1 | large |
| Green cabbage, minced | 1 | cup |
| Carrot | 1 | medium, finely diced |
| Paprika | 1 | teaspoon |
| Ground sage | ¼ | teaspoon |
| Salt | ¼ | teaspoon |
| Black pepper | Several grinds | |
| Thick-crusted unsliced bread | 4 | half-inch slices |
| Egg yolk** | 1 | large |
| Extra virgin olive oil | 1 | tablespoon |
| Tomato paste | 2 | tablespoons |
| Parmesan cheese, finely grated | ¼ | cup |
| Fresh Italian parsley, minced | 1 | tablespoon |

*If you do not have Homemade Vegetable Stock on hand, make some according to the directions on page 32 or dissolve 2 large low-sodium vegetable broth cubes in 4½ cups of hot water.

**Some authorities suggest avoiding dishes made with raw eggs, due to the remote possibility of salmonella contamination. People with compromised immune systems may wish to heed this advice. For more information, contact your local office of the U.S. Department of Agriculture.

In a stockpot or large saucepan, combine the stock, garlic, and bay leaf and bring to a boil over high heat. Add the cabbage, carrot, paprika, sage, salt, and pepper, reduce the heat to medium, and simmer 20 minutes.

Meanwhile, toast the bread slices until crisped and lightly browned. Set them aside. In a small bowl, beat the egg yolk and oil together with a fork until well combined. When the soup is finished simmering, remove the pan from the heat and slowly add about 2 tablespoons of the hot broth to the egg, beating it in with the fork. Add another 2 tablespoons of broth and beat again. Now slowly pour the egg mixture into the soup, stirring it in with a wooden spoon. Stir in the tomato paste until it is dissolved.

Place one slice of toasted bread in each of 4 warmed shallow serving bowls. Ladle a portion of the soup over the bread in each bowl, making sure to portion out the broth and vegetables as evenly as possible. Garnish each serving with a tablespoon of the Parmesan and a bit of parsley and serve immediately.

---

Each serving provides:

| 158 | Calories | 18 g | Carbohydrate |
|---|---|---|---|
| 6 g | Protein | 591 mg | Sodium |
| 7 g | Fat | 57 mg | Cholesterol |
| 2 g | Dietary Fiber | | |

# Cauliflower and Potato Soup
# with Paprika, Cilantro, and Lemon

*ALMOST INSTANT, VEGAN*

*Here is a simple soup that combines two of our favorite vegetables
with the seasonings of the eastern Mediterranean. It is quite delicious
and wonderfully nourishing. For a light but satisfying cool weather
meal, serve it with crusty bread and Hummus (page 58).*

*Yield:* 6 main-course servings

| | |
|---|---|
| Olive oil | 1 tablespoon |
| White onion | 1 medium, diced |
| Dried red chili flakes | ½ teaspoon |
| Homemade Vegetable Stock* | 6 cups |
| Red potatoes | ½ pound, diced |
| Uncooked short-grain white rice | ½ cup |
| Cauliflower, diced | 4 cups |
| Garlic | 2 cloves, minced |
| Paprika | 2 teaspoons |
| Ground coriander | 2 teaspoons |
| Ground cumin | 1 teaspoon |
| Salt | ½ teaspoon |
| Fresh tomatoes | ½ pound, diced |
| Fresh-squeezed lemon juice | 2 tablespoons |
| Fresh cilantro leaves, minced | ¼ cup |

*If you do not have Homemade Vegetable Stock on hand, make some accord-
ing to the directions on page 32 or dissolve 3 large low-sodium vegetable
broth cubes in 6 cups of hot water.

Heat the oil in a stockpot or large saucepan over medium heat and sauté the onion with the chili flakes for 5 minutes, stirring frequently. Add the stock, potatoes, and rice, increase the heat to medium-high, and bring the soup to a simmer. When it is bubbling, add the cauliflower, garlic, paprika, coriander, cumin, and salt and continue to simmer for 10 minutes, stirring occasionally. Stir in the tomatoes and cook an additional 10 minutes. Stir in the lemon juice and cilantro and serve immediately.

---

Each serving provides:

| 177 | Calories | 34 g | Carbohydrate |
|---|---|---|---|
| 5 g | Protein | 359 mg | Sodium |
| 3 g | Fat | 0 mg | Cholesterol |
| 4 g | Dietary Fiber | | |

# Vegetable Soup with Capers and Garlic Croutons

*ALMOST INSTANT, VEGAN*

*This recipe combines some of the classic flavors of the Mediterranean basin to create a marvelous, full-bodied soup. The savory crunch of the croutons provides just the right textural contrast to the cooked vegetables and broth. For an extra pretty touch, you may top off the soup with a sprinkling of minced parsley or a simple sprig. A sprinkling of grated Parmesan or crumbled feta cheese would also be delicious.*

*Yield:* 4 main-course servings

| | | |
|---|---|---|
| Whole pear tomatoes* | 1 | 28-ounce can |
| Turnip | 1 | medium |
| Carrot | 1 | medium |
| White onion | 1 | medium |
| Olive oil | 2 | tablespoons |
| Fresh Italian parsley, minced | ¼ | cup |
| Homemade Vegetable Stock** | 2½ | cups |
| Capers, drained | 2 | tablespoons |
| Garlic | 1 | clove, minced |
| Dried marjoram | ½ | teaspoon |
| Salt | ¼ | teaspoon |
| Black pepper | Several grinds | |
| Bay leaf | 1 | large |

*You may substitute 3 pounds fresh pear tomatoes—blanched, peeled, and seeded—for the canned variety. See the directions on page 28.

**If you do not have Homemade Vegetable Stock on hand, make some according to the directions on page 32 or dissolve 1 large low-sodium vegetable broth cube in 2½ cups of hot water.

| | | | |
|---|---|---|---|
| **Thick-crusted unsliced bread, cut into ¾-inch cubes** | **2** | **cups** |
| **Granulated garlic** | **½** | **teaspoon** |

Drain the juice from the canned tomatoes and reserve it for another use. Chop the tomatoes coarsely and set them aside in a bowl. Peel the turnip, carrot, and onion and finely dice them.

Heat 1 tablespoon of the oil in a stockpot or large saucepan over medium heat and sauté the turnip, carrot, onion, and parsley for about 7 minutes, stirring frequently, until the vegetables are beginning to brown. Add the tomatoes, stock, capers, garlic, marjoram, salt, pepper, and bay leaf and bring to a boil over medium-high heat. Reduce the heat to medium and simmer 10 to 15 minutes, until the turnips are tender.

Meanwhile, make the croutons. Preheat a toaster oven or conventional oven to 400 degrees F. Place the bread cubes in a bowl and drizzle the remaining 1 tablespoon oil evenly over them. Toss to distribute the oil, then add the granulated garlic and toss again. Place the cubes on a baking sheet and bake for 5 to 10 minutes, stirring occasionally, until lightly browned and crisp.

When the soup is ready, transfer half of it to a blender or food processor and puree until smooth, then stir the puree back into the pot. Ladle the soup into warmed individual serving bowls and top each serving with ½ cup of the garlic croutons. Serve very hot.

---

Each serving provides:

| | | | |
|---|---|---|---|
| 163 | Calories | 2 g | Carbohydrate |
| 4 g | Protein | 886 mg | Sodium |
| 8 g | Fat | 0 mg | Cholesterol |
| 4 g | Dietary Fiber | | |

# Spiced Carrot Soup with Yogurt and Couscous

*ALMOST INSTANT*

*This soup has a light quality but is full flavored. Be sure to dice the vegetables very finely to achieve the proper delicate consistency.*

*Yield:* 6 first-course servings

| | |
|---|---|
| **Unsalted butter** | 2 **tablespoons** |
| **Yellow onion** | 1 **small, finely diced** |
| **Carrots** | 3 **medium, finely diced** |
| **Red bell pepper** | 1 **medium, finely diced** |
| **Salt** | ¼ **teaspoon** |
| **Ground cumin** | 1 **teaspoon** |
| **Ground coriander** | 1 **teaspoon** |
| **Paprika** | 1 **teaspoon** |
| **Ground cinnamon** | ¼ **teaspoon** |
| **Cayenne** | ¼ **teaspoon** |
| **Homemade Vegetable Stock\*** | 6 **cups** |
| **Dried couscous** | ½ **cup** |
| **Plain nonfat yogurt** | 1 **cup** |
| **Lowfat milk** | 1 **cup** |
| **Fresh cilantro leaves, minced** | 2 **tablespoons** |

\*If you do not have Homemade Vegetable Stock on hand, make some according to the directions on page 32 or dissolve 3 large low-sodium vegetable broth cubes in 6 cups of hot water.

Melt the butter in a large stockpot. Add the onion, carrots, bell pepper, and salt and sauté over very low heat 3 to 4 minutes. Stir in the cumin, coriander, paprika, cinnamon, and cayenne and cook for a minute, then add the stock and bring to a boil over high heat. Reduce the heat to medium, cover, and simmer 10 minutes. Stir in the couscous, cover, and cook 6 minutes.

Meanwhile, whisk together the yogurt and milk in a bowl. Add a few tablespoons of the hot soup to the yogurt mixture and stir it in. Add a little more hot soup and stir again. This will gradually heat the yogurt so it does not curdle when added to the soup. When a warm, thin consistency is achieved, stir the yogurt mixture into the soup and heat through briefly, but do not allow the soup to come back to a simmer. Stir in the cilantro and serve very hot.

---

Each serving provides:

| | | | |
|---|---|---|---|
| 176 | Calories | 26 g | Carbohydrate |
| 7 g | Protein | 320 mg | Sodium |
| 5 g | Fat | 15 mg | Cholesterol |
| 2 g | Dietary Fiber | | |

# Potato, Garlic, and Thyme Soup

*VEGAN*

*This thick and creamy yet dairy-free soup is a variation of Provençal aiigo bouido. The fresh thyme seasons the potatoes to perfection.*

*Yield:* 4 main-course servings

| | |
|---|---|
| **Olive oil** | 1 **tablespoon** |
| **Dry sherry** | 1 **tablespoon** |
| **Yellow onion** | 1 **medium, chopped** |
| **Russet potatoes** | 2 **pounds (4 large)** |
| **Homemade Vegetable Stock**\* | 5 **cups** |
| **Garlic** | 6 **cloves** |
| **Whole bay leaves** | 2 **large** |
| **Fresh thyme leaves** | 1 **tablespoon** |
| **Salt** | ½ **teaspoon** |
| **Black pepper** | **Several grinds** |
| **Green onions** | 2, **minced** |

Heat the oil and sherry in a stockpot or large saucepan over medium heat. Add the onion and sauté, stirring occasionally, for 7 minutes. Meanwhile, peel the potatoes and chop them into ½-inch cubes. Add the potatoes, stock, garlic, and bay leaves to the onion in the pan. Increase the heat to high and bring to a boil, then stir and cover. Reduce the heat to medium and simmer for 25 to 30 minutes, until the potatoes are very tender. Add the thyme during the last 5 minutes of cooking.

\*If you do not have Homemade Vegetable Stock on hand, make up a batch using the recipe on page 32, or dissolve 2½ large low-sodium vegetable broth cubes in 5 cups of hot water.

emove and discard the bay leaves. Place the soup in a
er, one third at a time, and puree several seconds until
mooth. Return the puree to the pan, add the salt and pep-
and heat through for a minute or two. Serve in warmed
ls, topped with the minced onions.

---

Each serving provides:

| | | | |
|---|---|---|---|
| 271 | Calories | 55 g | Carbohydrate |
| 6 g | Protein | 485 mg | Sodium |
| 4 g | Fat | 0 mg | Cholesterol |
| 5 g | Dietary Fiber | | |

# Pumpkin Rice Soup
# with Sage and Allspice

*ALMOST INSTANT*

*Pumpkin soup is enjoyed in many countries throughout the Mediterranean region. In this recipe it is paired with rice to create a satisfying main-course soup. For a vegan version, use rice milk in place of the lowfat milk. During pumpkin season you may use 4 cups cooked and pureed fresh pumpkin, rather than canned.*

*Yield:* 4 main-course servings

| | |
|---|---|
| **Homemade Vegetable Stock*** | 5 cups |
| **Pumpkin** | 1 29-ounce can |
| **Garlic** | 3 cloves, minced |
| **Uncooked long-grain white rice** | ⅓ cup |
| **Dried sage** | 1 teaspoon, crushed |
| **Salt** | ¼ teaspoon |
| **Allspice** | Scant ⅛ teaspoon |
| **Black pepper** | Several grinds |
| **Lowfat milk** | 1 cup |
| **Fresh Italian parsley, minced** | ¼ cup |
| **Raw walnuts, chopped** | ¼ cup |

*If you do not have Homemade Vegetable Stock on hand, make some according to the directions on page 32 or dissolve 2½ large low-sodium vegetable broth cubes in 5 cups of hot water.

In a stockpot or large saucepan, combine the stock, pumpkin, and garlic. Bring to a boil over high heat, then stir in the rice, sage, salt, allspice, and pepper. Reduce the heat to medium-low and simmer for about 20 minutes, until the rice is tender. Add the milk and parsley and heat through for a minute or two.

Meanwhile, toast the walnuts by placing them in a dry, heavy-bottomed skillet over medium heat. Stir or shake the pan frequently until the nuts are lightly browned and immediately remove them from the pan. Serve the soup in warm bowls with a sprinkling of nuts on top.

---

Each serving provides:

| 228 | Calories | 38 g | Carbohydrate |
|---|---|---|---|
| 8 g | Protein | 383 mg | Sodium |
| 7 g | Fat | 5 mg | Cholesterol |
| 4 g | Dietary Fiber | | |

# Creamed Pea and Lettuce Soup

*Lettuce with peas is a subtle but delicious Provençal flavor combination, especially when enriched by a bit of butter and cream and a distinctive touch of nutmeg. It makes a wonderful spring luncheon entrée, along with crusty bread and a hearty salad like the Salade Niçoise on page 84. Use fresh shelled peas, if possible—you will need to purchase about 1½ pounds of plump pods to yield 2½ cups shelled peas.*

Yield: 4 main-dish servings

| | |
|---|---|
| **Russet potato** | ½ pound (1 medium) |
| **Yellow onion** | ½ medium |
| **Unsalted butter** | 2 tablespoons |
| **Romaine lettuce leaves, chopped** | 4 cups, lightly packed |
| **Shelled peas, fresh or frozen** | 2½ cups |
| **Garlic** | 1 clove, minced |
| **Herbes de Provence (page 38)** | 1 teaspoon |
| **Salt** | ½ teaspoon |
| **Black pepper** | Several grinds |
| **Lowfat milk** | 1½ cups |
| **Half-and-half** | ⅓ cup |
| **Freshly grated nutmeg** | ½ teaspoon |

Peel and dice the potato and onion. Melt the butter in a heavy-bottomed stockpot or large saucepan over medium heat. Sauté the potato and onion for 5 to 7 minutes, stirring frequently, until they are beginning to brown a bit. Add the lettuce, peas, garlic, herbes de Provence, salt, and pepper and stir and sauté for 2 to 3 minutes, until the lettuce wilts and is well combined with the other ingredients. Add the milk and 2 cups of water and bring to a simmer. Reduce the heat to medium-low and simmer for 20 minutes, until the potatoes and peas are very tender.

In a food processor, puree the mixture in small batches until smooth, then return the puree to the pot. Add the half-and-half in a thin stream and stir in the nutmeg. If the soup seems too thick, thin it by adding a tablespoon or two of water. Heat through over medium-low heat until steaming, but don't allow the soup to boil again or the cream may curdle. Serve hot.

---

Each serving provides:

| 282 | Calories | 37 g | Carbohydrate |
|---|---|---|---|
| 11 g | Protein | 331 mg | Sodium |
| 11 g | Fat | 30 mg | Cholesterol |
| 5 g | Dietary Fiber | | |

# Cannellini Bean and Lentil Soup with Tomatoes and Fresh Basil

*VEGAN*

*This satisfying bean soup is inspired by the flavors of Tuscany. A soup such as this might appear on the table in the fall, made with the last of the fresh garden basil.*

*Yield:* 4 main-course servings

| | |
|---|---|
| **Dried cannellini beans** | 1 cup |
| **Whole pear tomatoes*** | 1 28-ounce can |
| **Homemade Vegetable Stock**** | 5 cups |
| **White onion** | 1 medium, chopped |
| **Garlic** | 4 cloves, minced |
| **Dried red chili flakes** | ¼ teaspoon |
| **Dried brown lentils** | ½ cup |
| **Fresh basil leaves, minced** | ¼ cup |
| **Fresh Italian parsley, minced** | ¼ cup |
| **Salt** | ¼ teaspoon |
| **Black pepper** | Several grinds |

*You may substitute 3 pounds fresh pear tomatoes—blanched, peeled, and seeded—for the canned variety. See the directions on page 28.

**If you do not have Homemade Vegetable Stock on hand, make some according to the directions on page 32 or dissolve 2½ large low-sodium vegetable broth cubes in 5 cups of hot water.

Rinse and sort the cannellini beans, discarding any foreign objects you may find, and place them in a large pot. Cover them with boiling water to a depth of about 2 inches, put a lid on the pot, and soak for several hours, then drain the beans in a colander and set aside.

Coarsely chop the tomatoes and place them, along with their juice, in a stockpot or large saucepan. Add the soaked cannellini beans, stock, onion, garlic, and chili flakes and bring to a boil over high heat, stirring occasionally. Reduce the heat to medium-high and simmer, stirring occasionally, for 30 to 45 minutes, until the beans are tender. In a blender or food processor, puree the bean mixture in small batches. Return the pureed beans to the pot and briefly set aside.

Meanwhile, rinse and sort the lentils, discarding any foreign objects you may find. Bring 2 cups of water to a boil in a small pot and add the lentils. Reduce the heat to medium-high and simmer 15 to 20 minutes, until the lentils are tender but not falling apart. Drain them in a colander. Add them to the pureed soup, along with the basil, parsley, salt, and pepper and heat through over medium-low heat. Serve immediately.

---

Each serving provides:

| | | | |
|---|---|---|---|
| 339 | Calories | 63 g | Carbohydrate |
| 22 g | Protein | 874 mg | Sodium |
| 1 g | Fat | 0 mg | Cholesterol |
| 8 g | Dietary Fiber | | |

# Garbanzo Bean and Tomato Stew with Olives and Preserved Lemons

*VEGAN*

*This Morocco-inspired dish calls for Preserved Lemon (page 36). The tart and salty yet sweet flavor gives this soup a deliciously unique flavor.*

*Yield:* 4 main-course servings

| | | |
|---|---|---|
| **Whole pear tomatoes\*** | 1 | 28-ounce can |
| **Preserved Lemon (page 36)** | 1 | lemon |
| **Olive oil** | 1 | tablespoon |
| **White onion** | 1 | medium, diced |
| **Garlic** | 3 | cloves, minced |
| **Fresh ginger, grated** | 2 | teaspoons |
| **Ground cinnamon** | ½ | teaspoon |
| **Saffron threads** | ½ | teaspoon, crushed |
| **Homemade Vegetable Stock\*\*** | 4 | cups |
| **Cooked garbanzo beans, drained\*\*\*** | 2 | cups |
| **Fresh Italian parsley, minced** | 1 | cup |
| **Fresh cilantro leaves, minced** | ¼ | cup |
| **Calamata olives, chopped** | ½ | cup |

\*You may substitute 3 pounds fresh pear tomatoes—blanched, peeled, and seeded—for the canned variety. See the directions on page 28.

\*\*If you do not have Homemade Vegetable Stock on hand, make some according to the directions on page 32 or dissolve 2 large low-sodium vegetable broth cubes in 4 cups of hot water.

\*\*\*Cook 1 cup dried garbanzo beans according to the directions on page 29, or use canned beans that do not contain additives.

Chop the tomatoes and set them aside in a bowl, along with their juice. Separate the preserved lemon into quarters, discarding the pulp. Finely chop the peel and set it aside.

Heat the oil over medium heat in a stockpot or large saucepan and add the onion, garlic, ginger, cinnamon, and saffron. Sauté for 1 to 2 minutes, then add the tomatoes, stock, and garbanzo beans. Increase the heat to high to bring the soup to a rapid simmer, then reduce the heat to medium-high and simmer for about 10 minutes. Stir in the parsley, cilantro, olives, and lemon peel. Heat through for a minute or two and serve.

---

Each serving provides:

| | | | |
|---|---|---|---|
| 298 | Calories | 41 g | Carbohydrate |
| 11 g | Protein | 1326 mg | Sodium |
| 12 g | Fat | 0 mg | Cholesterol |
| 5 g | Dietary Fiber | | |

# Tomato Soup with Garbanzo Beans, Fava Beans, and Caraway

*VEGAN*

*This hearty and distinctively seasoned dish is inspired by a traditional Moroccan soup called* harira. *Plan to make it in the spring when fresh fava beans appear at the markets.*

*Yield:* 4 main-course servings

| | |
|---|---|
| **Dried garbanzo beans** | ½ **cup** |
| **Olive oil** | 2 **tablespoons** |
| **Yellow onions** | 2 **medium, diced** |
| **Celery** | 2 **medium ribs, diced** |
| **Ground cinnamon** | ½ **teaspoon** |
| **Fresh ginger, grated** | 1 **teaspoon** |
| **Paprika** | 1 **teaspoon** |
| **Ground cumin** | 1 **teaspoon** |
| **Ground turmeric** | 1 **teaspoon** |
| **Ground allspice** | ½ **teaspoon** |
| **Crushed tomatoes** | 2 **28-ounce cans** |
| **Fresh fava beans, in pods** | 2 **pounds** |
| **Caraway seeds** | 2 **teaspoons** |
| **Fresh Italian parsley, minced** | ½ **cup** |
| **Salt** | ½ **teaspoon** |
| **Black pepper** | **Several grinds** |

Rinse and sort the garbanzo beans, discarding any foreign objects you may find, then place them in a large pot. Cover them with boiling water to a depth of about 2 inches, put a lid on the pot, and soak for several hours, then drain the beans in a colander and set aside.

When the beans have finished soaking, heat the oil over medium heat in a stockpot or large saucepan and add the onions, celery, cinnamon, ginger, paprika, cumin, turmeric, and allspice. Sauté for about 5 minutes, until the onions are tender, then stir in the tomatoes and their juice. Add the drained garbanzo beans to the stockpot along with 2 cups of water. Increase the heat to high to bring the soup to a boil, then reduce the heat to medium and simmer for 45 to 50 minutes, until they are tender but not mushy.

Meanwhile, bring several cups of water to a boil for the favas. Shell the beans, discarding the pods, and add them to the boiling water. Return to a boil and blanch 2 to 4 minutes, until the skins are loosened, then transfer to a colander and rinse well with cold water to stop the cooking. When the beans are cool enough to handle, pop them out of their skins. Discard the skins and set the beans aside in a bowl.

Place the caraway seeds in a dry heavy-bottomed skillet over medium-high heat and stir them around until they begin to pop. Immediately remove them from the pan and set aside.

When the garbanzo beans are tender, add the fava beans, caraway seeds, parsley, salt, and pepper. Heat through for about 5 minutes and serve very hot.

---

Each serving provides:

| | | | |
|---|---|---|---|
| 302 | Calories | 45 g | Carbohydrate |
| 12 g | Protein | 1352 mg | Sodium |
| 10 g | Fat | 0 mg | Cholesterol |
| 6 g | Dietary Fiber | | |

# Mushroom and Lima Bean Stew with Cabbage and Fresh Mint

*VEGAN*

*Hearty and delicious, this stew pulls together many of the favorite flavors of the Mediterranean. It is true comfort food.*

*Yield:* 6 main-course servings

| | |
|---|---|
| Dried baby lima beans | 1 cup |
| Garlic | 2 cloves, minced |
| Whole bay leaf | 1 large |
| Button mushrooms | ½ pound |
| Olive oil | 2 tablespoons |
| White onion | 1 medium, diced |
| Carrot | 1 medium, diced |
| Celery, finely diced | 1 cup |
| Fresh Italian parsley, minced | ¼ cup |
| Dried rosemary | 1 teaspoon |
| Unbleached white flour | 2 tablespoons |
| Tomato paste | ¼ cup |
| Homemade Vegetable Stock* | 3 cups |
| Salt | ½ teaspoon |
| Black pepper | Several grinds |
| Green cabbage, diced | 3 cups |
| Fresh mint leaves, chiffonade** | ¼ cup |
| Fresh basil leaves, chiffonade** | ¼ cup |

*If you do not have Homemade Vegetable Stock on hand, make some according to the directions on page 32 or dissolve 1½ large low-sodium vegetable broth cubes in 3 cups of hot water.

**Chiffonade is the French term for a particular method of preparing fresh herbs. Stack the herb leaves on top of each other and roll slightly so you can hold them tightly in place, then use a sharp knife to slice the stack crosswise into paper-thin shreds.

Sort the beans, discarding any foreign objects you may find. Rinse and drain the beans, then put them in a large saucepan with 3½ cups of water, 1 of the minced garlic cloves, and the bay leaf. Bring to a boil over high heat, then reduce the heat to medium-low and simmer gently for 40 minutes.

Meanwhile, wipe any visible dirt from the button mushrooms and quarter them. Set aside. In a stockpot, heat the oil over medium heat and sauté the onion, carrot, celery, parsley, rosemary, and remaining 1 clove garlic for 3 minutes. Stir in the flour, then add the tomato paste, stock, salt, and pepper. Bring to a simmer and add the hot lima beans with their cooking water, the button mushrooms, and cabbage. Return to a simmer over medium-high heat, then reduce the heat to medium-low and cook, uncovered, about 30 minutes, stirring frequently, until the cabbage and lima beans are tender. Add a few tablespoons of hot water, if necessary, to keep the beans and vegetables submerged throughout the cooking time. Stir in the mint and basil and serve very hot.

---

Each serving provides:

| 209 | Calories | 34 g | Carbohydrate |
|-----|----------|------|--------------|
| 9 g | Protein | 382 mg | Sodium |
| 5 g | Fat | 0 mg | Cholesterol |
| 9 g | Dietary Fiber | | |

# Stewed Fava Beans with Tomatoes, Garlic, and Oregano

*VEGAN*

*Here is another classic Greek dish—aromatic, warming, and scrumptious. Serve it with fruity red wine, an excellent thick-crusted bread, and a fresh tomato and cucumber salad, such as the Classic Greek Salad on page 90. What could be better on a summer evening? The dried favas may take some seeking out, but many natural food stores and ethnic markets carry them.*

*Yield:* 4 main-course servings

| | |
|---|---|
| Dried fava beans | 2 cups |
| Whole bay leaf | 1 large |
| Dried red chili flakes | ½ teaspoon |
| Whole pear tomatoes* | 1 28-ounce can |
| Garlic | 6 cloves, minced |
| Dried oregano | 2 teaspoons |
| Salt | ½ teaspoon |
| Fresh-squeezed lemon juice | 3 tablespoons |
| Extra virgin olive oil | 2 tablespoons |
| Black pepper | Several grinds |
| Fresh Italian parsley, minced | ½ cup |

Sort the beans, discarding any foreign objects you may find. Rinse and drain the beans and place them in a large bowl or pot. Cover them with water to a depth of about 2 inches and leave them to soak several hours or overnight.

---

*You may substitute 3 pounds fresh pear tomatoes—blanched, peeled, and seeded—for the canned variety. See the directions on page 28.

Drain the beans and peel off their outer skins. Place the beans in a large saucepan or stockpot with 6 cups of fresh water, bay leaf, and chili flakes and bring to a boil over high heat. Reduce the heat to medium and simmer 40 minutes. Add a few tablespoons of hot water, if necessary, to keep the beans submerged throughout the cooking time.

Drain the juice from the canned tomatoes, reserving the juice. Chop the tomatoes. Add the tomatoes, garlic, oregano, and salt to the beans, along with ½ cup of the reserved tomato juice, and cook, stirring occasionally, 15 to 20 minutes longer, until the beans are tender and the liquid has reduced to a thick sauce consistency. Remove from the heat and stir in the lemon juice and oil. Remove the bay leaf. Serve hot, with a grind of black pepper and a portion of the parsley sprinkled on each serving.

---

Each serving provides:

| | | | |
|---|---|---|---|
| 368 | Calories | 56 g | Carbohydrate |
| 22 g | Protein | 605 mg | Sodium |
| 9 g | Fat | 0 mg | Cholesterol |
| 12 g | Dietary Fiber | | |

# Provençal Bean and Vegetable Stew

*VEGAN*

*This delicious and nourishing dish is similar in character to a classic cassoulet, but it is simpler to prepare. If you cook the beans ahead of time, you will find it comes together quickly. Serve it with a good crusty bread or with polenta or rice on the side.*

*Yield:* 8 main-course servings

| | |
|---|---|
| White onion | 1 large |
| Turnip | 1 medium |
| Carrot | 1 large |
| Button mushrooms | ½ pound |
| Olive oil | 2 tablespoons |
| Dry white wine | 1 cup |
| Tomato paste | 2 tablespoons |
| Garlic | 2 cloves, minced |
| Herbes de Provence (page 38) | 2 teaspoons |
| Unbleached white flour | 2 tablespoons |
| Cauliflower, chopped | 2 cups |
| Salt | ½ teaspoon |
| Black pepper | Several grinds |
| Cooked flageolet beans or small white beans, drained* | 2 cups |
| Fresh Italian parsley, minced | ¼ cup |
| Shelled peas, fresh or frozen | 1 cup |

*Cook 1 cup of dried beans according to the directions on page 29, or use canned beans that do not contain additives.

Peel and dice the onion and turnip and set them aside separately. Scrub the carrot and cut it crosswise into ¼-inch slices. Set aside in a colander. Wipe any loose dirt from the mushrooms and quarter them. Add them to the sliced carrots in the colander.

Heat the oil in a stockpot or large saucepan over medium heat and sauté the onion, stirring frequently, until it is nicely browned, 7 to 10 minutes. Stir in the wine, tomato paste, garlic, and herbes de Provence and cook 5 minutes over medium heat, stirring frequently. Sprinkle the flour into the pan and stir it in, then add 2 cups of water and the turnip and bring the mixture to a boil over medium-high heat. Add the carrot, mushrooms, cauliflower, salt, and pepper and stir to combine well. Bring to a simmer, then cover the pan, reduce the heat to medium-low, and cook for 5 minutes. Remove the lid and stir the vegetables, then cover and cook 3 more minutes.

Stir in the cooked beans and parsley. If using fresh peas, also add them at this point. Cover and cook 5 more minutes, until everything is heated through. If using frozen peas, add them to the pot for only the last minute of cooking time. Serve very hot.

---

Each serving provides:

| | | | |
|---|---|---|---|
| 167 | Calories | 25 g | Carbohydrate |
| 8 g | Protein | 190 mg | Sodium |
| 4 g | Fat | 0 mg | Cholesterol |
| 5 g | Dietary Fiber | | |

# Creamed Tomato and Fennel Soup with Pine Nuts

*Sautéed fresh fennel bulb adds a subtle yet distinctive flavor to this delicious and easy-to-prepare soup. It makes a delightful first course on a Tuscan or Provençal menu or a wonderful light main course when served with a hearty salad, bread, and cheese. The soup is good hot or at room temperature. If you wish to make it ahead of time, you may hold it in the refrigerator for a few hours, then return it to room temperature or reheat it over low heat. Ladle it into bowls and top it with the garnishes just before serving.*

*Yield:* 8 first-course servings

| | |
|---|---|
| **Fresh fennel bulbs** | 2 **medium** |
| **Whole pear tomatoes*** | 2 **28-ounce cans** |
| **Unsalted butter** | 1 **tablespoon** |
| **White onion** | 1 **medium, diced** |
| **Garlic** | 2 **cloves, minced** |
| **Homemade Vegetable Stock**** | 1 **cup** |
| **Dry white wine** | 1 **cup** |
| **Salt** | ½ **teaspoon** |
| **Black pepper** | **Several grinds** |
| **Pine nuts** | 3 **tablespoons** |
| **Half-and-half** | ¼ **cup** |

*You may substitute 6 pounds fresh pear tomatoes—blanched, peeled, and seeded—for the canned variety. See the directions on page 28.

**If you do not have Homemade Vegetable Stock on hand, make some according to the directions on page 32 or dissolve ½ of a large low-sodium vegetable broth cube in 1 cup of hot water.

Trim the stalks from the fennel bulb and discard them. Reserve the feathery fennel leaves. Slice off and discard the root end of the bulbs and coarsely chop the remaining fennel. Drain the juice from the canned tomatoes and reserve it for another use. Gently squeeze each tomato over the sink to remove as many seeds as possible. Coarsely chop the tomatoes and set them aside in a bowl.

Melt the butter over medium heat in a heavy-bottomed stockpot and sauté the onion, fennel, and garlic for 10 minutes, stirring very frequently. Add the tomatoes, stock, wine, salt, and pepper. Bring the soup to a simmer and cook, stirring occasionally, for 10 minutes.

Meanwhile, place the pine nuts in a dry, heavy-bottomed skillet in a single layer over medium heat. Stir or shake the pan frequently until the nuts are lightly browned. Immediately remove them from the pan and set aside. When they have cooled for a few minutes, finely mince them and set aside. Mince the feathery fennel leaves to measure about 3 tablespoons and set aside.

In a blender or food processor, puree the tomato mixture in small batches. Return the puree to the pot and stir constantly as you add the cream in a slow stream. Reheat over medium-low heat until steaming hot, but do not allow the soup to simmer or the cream may curdle. Ladle the soup into shallow bowls and top each serving with a portion of the pine nuts and a sprinkling of the fennel leaves.

---

Each serving provides:

| | | | |
|---|---|---|---|
| 130 | Calories | 16 g | Carbohydrate |
| 4 g | Protein | 513 mg | Sodium |
| 5 g | Fat | 7 mg | Cholesterol |
| 2 g | Dietary Fiber | | |

# Cream of Zucchini and Fresh Basil Soup

*ALMOST INSTANT*

*This wonderful soup makes good use of two of the garden's abundant summer crops—zucchini and basil. For the best texture, use zucchini that are on the small side, not the huge late-season ones. This soup comes together quickly and is delicious hot, or it can be chilled for several hours before serving. A sprinkling of nutmeg and a whole basil leaf make a nice garnish. For a delicious vegan version, simply replace the butter with olive oil and omit the cream, thinning the soup if necessary with a little additional stock.*

*Yield:* 8 first-course servings

| | |
|---|---|
| Zucchini | 2 pounds |
| Unsalted butter | 1 tablespoon |
| White onion | 1 large, diced |
| Homemade Vegetable Stock* | 3 cups |
| Garlic | 3 cloves, minced |
| Fresh basil leaves, chopped | ½ cup, lightly packed |
| Salt | ½ teaspoon |
| Freshly grated nutmeg | ¼ teaspoon |
| Black pepper | Several grinds |
| Half-and-half | ⅓ cup |

*If you do not have Homemade Vegetable Stock on hand, make some according to the directions on page 32 or dissolve 1½ large low-sodium vegetable broth cube in 3 cups of hot water.

Trim off and discard the root and stem ends of the zucchini. Dice the zucchini. Melt the butter in a stockpot or large saucepan over medium heat and sauté the onion for 5 minutes, stirring frequently. Add the zucchini, stock, garlic, basil, salt, nutmeg, and pepper and bring to a boil over medium-high heat. Reduce the heat to medium-low, cover the pot, and simmer about 10 minutes, until the zucchini is very tender.

In a blender or food processor, puree the soup in small batches. Return the puree to the pot and add the half-and-half. Heat through briefly, but do not allow the soup to return to the boil. Serve hot or chill the soup for several hours and serve cold.

---

Each serving provides:

| | | | |
|---|---|---|---|
| 62 | Calories | 8 g | Carbohydrate |
| 2 g | Protein | 203 mg | Sodium |
| 3 g | Fat | 8 mg | Cholesterol |
| 2 g | Dietary Fiber | | |

# Green Gazpacho

*ALMOST INSTANT, VEGAN*

*There are hundreds of different versions of gazpacho, all designed to provide cooling nourishment when temperatures are scorching. Our variation on the theme uses only green vegetables for an unusual twist on tradition. Serve this gazpacho with the Tortilla of Potatoes, Artichokes, and Red Bell Pepper (page 76) and a good crusty bread to create a wonderful Spanish luncheon or light supper.*

*Yield:* 4 first-course servings

| | |
|---|---|
| Fresh tomatillos | 1 pound |
| Cucumber | 1 large |
| Green bell pepper | 1 medium |
| Serrano chile pepper | 1 medium |
| Green onions | 3, chopped |
| Fresh mint leaves, minced | ¼ cup plus 2 tablespoons |
| Thick-crusted unsliced bread, cut into ¾-inch cubes | 1 cup |
| Extra virgin olive oil | 2 tablespoons |
| Red wine vinegar | 1 tablespoon |
| Garlic | 1 clove, chopped |
| Salt | ½ teaspoon |
| Granulated sugar | ½ teaspoon |
| Red bell pepper, finely diced | ¼ cup |
| Red radishes, finely diced | ¼ cup |
| Lime wedges | 1 per serving |

Bring 2 cups of water to a boil in a saucepan while you peel off and discard the paper husks of the tomatillos. Place the whole tomatillos in the boiling water and cook about 8 minutes, until the tomatillos are quite soft. Drain well and transfer them to a blender. Puree thoroughly, then strain the puree through a fine mesh strainer into the bowl of a food processor (press the tomatillos through the strainer with a rubber spatula or the back of a wooden spoon to force as much pulp and juice as possible through).

Peel the cucumber and cut it in half lengthwise. Use a spoon to scrape out and discard the seeds. Coarsely chop the cucumber and add it to the food processor. Cut the bell pepper in half and discard the seeds, stem, and white membrane. Coarsely chop the bell pepper and add it to the food processor. Discard the stem of the chile pepper and scrape out the seeds for a milder dish. Chop it into a few pieces. Add the chopped green onions to the food processor along with ¼ cup of the mint, the chile, bread, oil, vinegar, garlic, salt, and sugar. Pour in ¾ cup of cold water and puree the mixture thoroughly to achieve a thick, uniform texture. Taste the mixture. If it is too tart, add a bit more sugar. Set the pureed soup aside in the refrigerator.

In a small bowl, combine the red bell pepper, radishes, and the remaining 2 tablespoons mint. When ready to serve the soup, thin it if necessary to achieve a thick but not viscous texture by stirring in cold water a tablespoon at a time. Ladle the soup into chilled shallow bowls and top with a portion of the bell pepper, radish, and mint mixture. Serve immediately with lime wedges on the side.

---

Each serving provides:

| | | | |
|---|---|---|---|
| 155 | Calories | 19 g | Carbohydrate |
| 3 g | Protein | 327 mg | Sodium |
| 9 g | Fat | 0 mg | Cholesterol |
| 4 g | Dietary Fiber | | |

# Pasta and Couscous

Though Italy is known as the pasta capital of the world, this versatile food is enjoyed in other Mediterranean countries as well. Semolina pasta in Europe typically takes the shape of ribbons, strands, tubes, and twists. In North Africa, on the other hand, semolina flour is transformed into the tiny beads called couscous, which are delectably light and delicate.

The sauce or topping is what transforms this simple flour and water concoction into a truly special dish. Our recipes draw on seasonal vegetables, herbs, tomatoes, olives, and other classic ingredients to create memorable dishes that deliver tantalizing Mediterranean aromas and flavors. They are likely to become favorite family fare, and they are delicious enough for company.

Scrumptious, satisfying, versatile, and quick-to-prepare—it is no wonder pasta is featured at many a meatless Mediterranean meal. These dishes give you a taste of the delightful possibilities.

# Tips and Tools

- We find that salting and oiling pasta cooking water is unnecessary. To prevent sticking, cook pasta in plenty of water (6 to 8 quarts per pound of pasta) that has been brought to a strong, rolling boil. Stir the pasta immediately after adding it to the pot, and stir again, vigorously, a few times during cooking.

- Dried Italian-style pasta should always be cooked to the *al dente* stage. This Italian phrase literally means "to the tooth," suggesting that the tooth should meet a little resistance when biting into the pasta. The manufacturer usually provides the recommended cooking time on the pasta package. Set your timer a couple of minutes less than the recommended time and when it goes off, remove a noodle from the pot. If it is undercooked, it will stick to your teeth when you bite into it. Continue cooking, testing again every minute or so until the pasta is tender all the way through but not mushy. This is the sought-after al dente stage.

- Drain the al dente pasta immediately in a large, footed colander. Shake the colander to remove excess water, but do not rinse the pasta.

- If your sauce is not ready when the pasta is done, toss the cooked pasta with a drizzle of olive oil to prevent sticking and return it to the hot pot in which it was cooked. Cover and set aside in a warm place.

- The most essential investment for successful pasta cooking is a large stockpot that holds plenty of water so the pasta can move around while it cooks. A long-handled wooden spoon is ideal for stirring pasta.

- Metal tongs or wooden forks are perfect implements for tossing pasta with the sauce.

- A medium-sized saucepan with a tight-fitting lid is all that is required for cooking couscous.

# Orzo with Onions and Olives

*ALMOST INSTANT, VEGAN*

*The flavors of green onions, olives, and red chili flakes turn simple
boiled orzo into a sensational side dish that will complement any
Mediterranean entrée. For a nonspicy version, simply leave out the
chili flakes.*

*Yield:* 6 side-dish servings

| | | |
|---|---|---|
| **Dried orzo** | 1½ | **cups** |
| **Extra virgin olive oil** | 1 | **tablespoon** |
| **Garlic** | 1 | **clove, minced** |
| **Dried red chili flakes** | ½ | **teaspoon** |
| **Fresh-squeezed lemon juice** | 1 | **tablespoon** |
| **Green onions** | 4, | **thinly sliced** |
| **Calamata olives, slivered** | ¼ | **cup** |
| **Fresh lemon peel, minced** | ½ | **teaspoon** |
| **Salt** | ¼ | **teaspoon** |

Bring 8 cups of water to a boil over high heat. Add the orzo and
cook until al dente, 5 to 7 minutes. Do not overcook.

Meanwhile, heat the oil in a small saucepan over medium-
low heat and sauté the garlic and chili flakes for 1 to 2 minutes,
until the garlic just begins to turn golden. Transfer to a warmed
serving bowl, scraping the pan well to retrieve all the flavorful
oil. Add the lemon juice.

When the orzo is done, immediately add 1 cup cold water to the pan to stop the cooking, then drain the orzo very well in a wire-mesh strainer. Put the orzo in the bowl with the oil mixture. Add the green onions, olives, lemon peel, and salt and toss until well combined. Serve hot.

---

Each serving provides:

| 253 | Calories | 43 g | Carbohydrate |
|---|---|---|---|
| 7 g | Protein | 274 mg | Sodium |
| 5 g | Fat | 0 mg | Cholesterol |
| 2 g | Dietary Fiber | | |

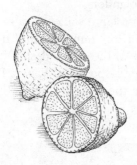

# Orecchiette with Sautéed Greens

*ALMOST INSTANT, VEGAN*

*Orecchiette—"little ears"—is a chewy pasta that is a hallmark of the cooking of the Apulia region of Italy. The pasta's disk shape makes it perfect for collecting sauce or for pairing with sautéed greens or broccoli rabe. Here pungent mustard greens are used to create a simple pasta dish.*

*Yield:* 8 side-dish servings

| | | |
|---|---|---|
| **Mustard greens** | 1½ | **pounds** |
| **Extra virgin olive oil** | 2 | **tablespoons** |
| **Garlic** | 4 | **cloves, minced** |
| **Salt** | ½ | **teaspoon** |
| **Dried red chili flakes** | ¼ | **teaspoon** |
| **Dried orecchiette** | 1 | **pound** |

Bring several quarts of water to a boil for the pasta. Wash the mustard greens and coarsely chop them. Without drying them, set aside in a large colander.

Place the oil in a large skillet over medium heat and add the garlic. Sauté for 1 to 2 minutes, until the garlic is just turning golden, then stir in the salt and chili flakes. Add the mustard greens and 2 tablespoons of water. Increase the heat to medium-high, cover the pan, and cook the greens until they wilt, about 7 minutes.

Meanwhile, cook the pasta until al dente. Drain it well and transfer it to a large warmed bowl. Distribute the greens over the pasta and toss to combine. Serve immediately, passing Parmesan cheese if desired.

---

Each serving provides:

| 276 | Calories | 50 g | Carbohydrate |
|------|----------|------|--------------|
| 10 g | Protein | 156 mg | Sodium |
| 5 g | Fat | 0 mg | Cholesterol |
| 5 g | Dietary Fiber | | |

# Fusilli with Sage
# and Grilled Tomatoes

*VEGAN*

*The sage in this dish enhances the smoky quality of the grilled tomatoes, and the balsamic vinegar adds a bright and deep flavor note.*

*Yield:* 6 main-course servings

| | | |
|---|---|---|
| Fresh pear tomatoes | 1½ | pounds |
| Dried fusilli | 1 | pound |
| Fresh sage leaves, minced | 2 | tablespoons |
| Extra virgin olive oil | 2 | tablespoons |
| Balsamic vinegar | 2 | tablespoons |
| Salt | ⅛ | teaspoon |
| Black pepper | Several grinds | |

Preheat a coal or gas grill to medium (see page 28). Cut out the stem ends of the tomatoes, but leave them whole. Place the tomatoes on the grill and cook for about 30 minutes, turning occasionally. They will be soft and slightly charred.

Meanwhile, bring several quarts of water to a boil for the pasta. When the tomatoes are almost cooked, add the pasta to the boiling water and cook until al dente.

Place the unpeeled grilled tomatoes in a food processor, along with the sage, oil, vinegar, salt, and pepper. Puree a minute or two until a thick sauce develops. Drain the pasta well and transfer it to a large, warmed serving bowl. Top with the sauce, toss to combine, and serve immediately.

---

Each serving provides:

| | | | |
|---|---|---|---|
| 331 | Calories | 59 g | Carbohydrate |
| 10 g | Protein | 56 mg | Sodium |
| 6 g | Fat | 0 mg | Cholesterol |
| 5 g | Dietary Fiber | | |

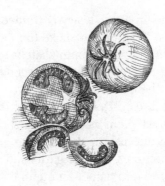

# Fusilli with Tomatoes, Fennel, Raisins, and Pine Nuts

*VEGAN*

*This pasta combines ingredients common to the island of Sicily to create a slightly hot, slightly sweet pasta with just a hint of anise flavor from the fennel.*

*Yield:* 4 main-course servings

| | | |
|---|---|---|
| **Pine nuts** | 2 | **tablespoons** |
| **Fresh pear tomatoes** | 1½ | **pounds** |
| **Marsala** | ¼ | **cup** |
| **Olive oil** | 1 | **tablespoon** |
| **Garlic** | 2 | **cloves, minced** |
| **Fresh fennel, chopped** | 1 | **cup** |
| **Dried fusilli** | 8 | **ounces** |
| **Golden raisins** | ½ | **cup** |
| **Dried red chili flakes** | ¼ | **teaspoon** |

Place the pine nuts in a dry, heavy-bottomed skillet in a single layer over medium heat. Stir or shake the pan frequently until the nuts are lightly browned. Immediately remove them from the pan and set aside. When they have cooled for a few minutes, finely mince them and set aside.

Cut out and discard the stem ends of the tomatoes. Dice the tomatoes and set them aside in a bowl. Place the marsala and oil in a large sauté pan or skillet over medium heat. When the mixture is simmering, add the garlic and cook for a minute or two, then stir in the tomatoes and fennel. Sauté for 15 to 20 minutes, stirring occasionally, until the fennel is tender and a thick sauce has formed.

Meanwhile, bring several quarts of water to a boil for the pasta and cook the fusilli until al dente. While the pasta is cooking, cover the raisins with boiling water and set them aside for about 5 minutes to plump. (Alternately, you may plump the raisins by covering them with water and heating them for 1 minute in a microwave oven.) Drain the raisins well, then stir them into the sauce, along with the chili flakes, and continue to cook for several minutes.

Drain the pasta well and place it in a warmed serving bowl. Toss with the sauce and distribute the pine nuts evenly over the top. Serve immediately.

---

Each serving provides:

| | | | |
|---|---|---|---|
| 363 | Calories | 66 g | Carbohydrate |
| 10 g | Protein | 31 mg | Sodium |
| 8 g | Fat | 0 mg | Cholesterol |
| 6 g | Dietary Fiber | | |

# Rigatoni with Ouzo and Roasted Pepper Sauce

*ALMOST INSTANT*

*The smoky flavor of the roasted peppers combines beautifully with dill and ouzo, a traditional Greek anise liqueur. If you include anchovies in your diet, garnish this dish with four to six of them for an authentic touch.*

*Yield:* 6 side-dish servings

| | | |
|---|---|---|
| Red bell peppers | 2 | large |
| Red onion, minced | ¼ | cup |
| Extra virgin olive oil | 1 | tablespoon |
| Ouzo | 1 | tablespoon |
| Fresh dill, minced | 1 | tablespoon |
| Garlic | 1 | clove, minced |
| Dried red chili flakes | ⅛ | teaspoon |
| Salt | ¼ | teaspoon |
| Dried rigatoni | 12 | ounces |
| Feta cheese, crumbled | 4 | ounces (1 cup) |

Preheat the broiler or a coal or gas grill (see page 28). Place the whole peppers under the broiler or on the grill and cook for several minutes, until the skin is charred black on one side. Turn the peppers and cook several more minutes to blacken the other side. Continue to turn and cook until the entire skin of the peppers is almost uniformly black. Transfer the peppers to a paper or plastic bag, close the bag tightly, and set aside for 10 minutes or so. The steam inside the bag will finish cooking the peppers. When the peppers are cool enough to handle, peel them, discarding the stems, seeds, and white membranes, and place them in a food processor with the onion, oil, ouzo, dill, garlic, chili flakes, and salt. Puree until smooth. Set aside at room temperature.

Bring several quarts of water to a boil in a large stockpot and cook the pasta until al dente. Drain well and transfer to a warmed serving dish. Pour the sauce over the rigatoni and toss well to combine. Sprinkle with the feta cheese and serve immediately.

---

Each serving provides:

| | | | |
|---|---|---|---|
| 295 | Calories | 45 g | Carbohydrate |
| 10 g | Protein | 303 mg | Sodium |
| 7 g | Fat | 17 mg | Cholesterol |
| 3 g | Dietary Fiber | | |

# Penne with Peas, Tarragon, Walnuts, and Goat Cheese

*ALMOST INSTANT*

*This wonderful little pasta dish makes frequent appearances on our dinner table, since it is simple to prepare and the ingredients are easy to come by year-round. Of course, you may use fresh peas in the springtime in place of the frozen variety. Simply cook them for 3 or 4 minutes longer than called for here, or until they are tender but not mushy. Also, if you have tarragon growing outside your back door, you may substitute 1½ tablespoons fresh for the dried amount specified below.*

*Yield:* 6 main-course servings

| | | |
|---|---|---|
| **Soft goat cheese (chèvre)** | 2 | **ounces** |
| **Dried penne** | 8 | **ounces** |
| **Dry white wine** | ½ | **cup** |
| **Garlic** | 2 | **cloves, minced** |
| **Dried tarragon** | 2 | **teaspoons** |
| **Frozen shelled peas** | 1½ | **cups** |
| **Salt** | ¼ | **teaspoon** |
| **Black pepper** | | **Several grinds** |
| **Green onions** | 3, | **chopped** |
| **Raw, unsalted walnuts, chopped** | ⅓ | **cup** |

Cut or crumble the chèvre into small pieces (it is easier to handle when cold). Set aside in the refrigerator. Bring several quarts of water to a boil for the pasta.

Cook the penne in the boiling water until al dente. Meanwhile, place the wine, garlic, and tarragon in a skillet and bring to a simmer over medium heat. Add the peas, salt, and pepper and cover the pan. Cook 2 minutes, stir, then cover the pan again and turn off the heat. Allow to stand in the covered pan until the peas are tender, about 2 to 3 minutes, then transfer the mixture to a warmed serving bowl.

When the pasta is done, reserve ½ cup of the cooking water, then drain the pasta thoroughly. Add the pasta to the peas in the bowl, along with the chèvre, green onions, and ¼ cup of the reserved pasta cooking water. Toss to combine. Add the walnuts and toss again. Add the rest of the reserved pasta cooking water if necessary to achieve a smooth rather than gooey texture. Serve very hot.

---

Each serving provides:

| | | | |
|---|---|---|---|
| 246 | Calories | 35 g | Carbohydrate |
| 10 g | Protein | 128 mg | Sodium |
| 7 g | Fat | 4 mg | Cholesterol |
| 3 g | Dietary Fiber | | |

# Linguine with Carrots, Cilantro, and Spiced Yogurt Sauce

*This colorful pasta transports us to the eastern Mediterranean. It is distinctively delicious and quite nutritious.*

*Yield:* 4 main-course servings

| | | |
|---|---|---|
| Plain nonfat yogurt | 1 | cup |
| Carrots | 2 | medium |
| Unsalted butter | 2 | tablespoons |
| Red onion | 1 | medium, diced |
| Salt | ½ | teaspoon |
| Garlic | 2 | cloves, minced |
| Paprika | 2 | teaspoons |
| Ground cumin | 1 | teaspoon |
| Cayenne | ⅛ | teaspoon |
| Honey | 1½ | teaspoons |
| Dried linguine | 12 | ounces |
| Fresh cilantro leaves | ¼ | cup, lightly packed |

Line a sieve or fine-mesh strainer with 4 layers of cheesecloth or a clean tea towel, allowing several inches of cloth to hang over the edge of the strainer. Place the sieve over a bowl large enough so that the bottom of the strainer is at least one inch from the bottom of the bowl. Spoon the yogurt into the sieve, folding the cloth over the top. Set aside at room temperature for 1 hour. (A good quantity of liquid will have drained off. This whey can be used in smoothies or baked goods, or you may simply discard it.) Set the yogurt aside.

When the yogurt has finished draining, put several quarts of water on to boil for the pasta. Peel the carrots and slice them in half lengthwise, then cut the halves crosswise into ¼-inch slices. Melt the butter in a heavy-bottomed sauté pan or skillet over medium-high heat and sauté the onion and carrots with the salt for 10 minutes, stirring frequently. The vegetables should be browning nicely. Add the garlic, paprika, cumin, cayenne, and ⅓ cup water. Bring to a simmer and cook 1 minute, then remove the pan from the heat and stir in the yogurt and honey. Heat over very low heat, stirring very frequently, until heated through, about 3 minutes, but don't allow the yogurt to simmer or it will curdle. Stir in the cilantro, cover, and set aside briefly if the pasta is not yet done.

Meanwhile, cook the pasta in the boiling water until al dente, adding the carrot slices for the final 2 minutes of cooking time. Drain well and toss with the sauce in a warmed serving bowl. Top with a dusting of paprika.

------------

Each serving provides:

| 421 | Calories | 73 g | Carbohydrate |
|---|---|---|---|
| 13 g | Protein | 293 mg | Sodium |
| 8 g | Fat | 18 mg | Cholesterol |
| 6 g | Dietary Fiber | | |

# Linguine with Eggplant Tomato Sauce

*VEGAN*

*Eggplant sautéed in olive oil, then braised in tomato sauce and wine, makes a succulent and delicious sauce for pasta, reminiscent of southern Italy. Baby eggplants are best for this dish if you can find them, though the thin Japanese variety also works well. Select the smallest and freshest ones you can find.*

*Yield:* 6 main-course servings

| | | |
|---|---|---|
| Japanese eggplants | 1 | pound |
| Olive oil | 2 | tablespoons |
| Dried red chili flakes | ½ | teaspoon |
| Fennel seed | 1 | teaspoon |
| Dried rosemary | 1 | teaspoon |
| Whole pear tomatoes* | 1 | 28-ounce can |
| Dry red wine | ¾ | cup |
| Garlic | 4 | cloves, minced |
| Salt | ½ | teaspoon |
| Tomato paste | 3 | tablespoons |
| Dried linguine | 12 | ounces |
| Black pepper | | Several grinds |

Put several quarts of water on to boil for the pasta. Wash and dry the eggplants and trim off the stem ends. Cut them crosswise at a slant into 1-inch pieces. Heat the oil in a large high-walled skillet over medium heat and add the eggplant. Sauté,

*You may substitute 3 pounds fresh pear tomatoes—blanched, peeled, and seeded—for the canned variety. See the directions on page 28.

stirring occasionally, for 10 minutes. Meanwhile, use a mortar and pestle or a spice grinder to lightly crush the chili flakes, fennel seed, and rosemary. Set aside.

Add the canned tomatoes with their juice to the eggplant, along with the wine, chili flakes, fennel seed, rosemary, garlic, and salt. Increase the heat to medium-high and simmer the sauce for 20 minutes, stirring frequently and breaking up the tomatoes as they cook with the back of a wooden spoon. Add the tomato paste and stir to incorporate it into the sauce.

Meanwhile, cook the linguine in the boiling water until al dente. Drain well and toss with the sauce in a warmed serving bowl. Grind on the black pepper and serve.

---

Each serving provides:

| 301 | Calories | 53 g | Carbohydrate |
| 9 g | Protein | 461 mg | Sodium |
| 6 g | Fat | 0 mg | Cholesterol |
| 4 g | Dietary Fiber | | |

# Linguine with Red Peppers, Broccoli, Basil, and Romano Cheese

*ALMOST INSTANT*

*Here is a simple, earthy, and satisfying combination of flavors. It is one of our standby pasta dishes for evenings when we want dinner on the table fast.*

*Yield:* 6 main-course servings

| | | |
|---|---|---|
| Red bell peppers | 2 | medium |
| Broccoli | 1 | pound |
| Unsalted butter | 1 | tablespoon |
| Dried red chili flakes | ½ | teaspoon |
| Salt | ½ | teaspoon |
| Dry white wine | ⅔ | cup |
| Garlic | 2 | cloves, minced |
| Fresh basil leaves, chiffonade* | ½ | cup |
| Dried linguine | 12 | ounces |
| Extra virgin olive oil | 2 | tablespoons |
| Romano cheese, coarsely grated | ½ | cup |
| Black pepper | A few grinds | |

*Chiffonade is the French term for a particular method of preparing fresh herbs. Stack the herb leaves on top of each other and roll slightly so you can hold them tightly in place, then use a sharp knife to slice the stack crosswise into paper-thin shreds.

Bring several quarts of water to a boil for the pasta. Meanwhile, cut the bell peppers in half, discard the seeds, stems, and white membranes, and cut them into 1-inch-square pieces. Set aside. Cut the broccoli into spears, peeling the stems if they have tough skins. Set aside.

Melt the butter in a heavy-bottomed skillet over medium heat and sauté the peppers with the chili flakes and salt for 10 minutes, stirring occasionally. The peppers should be browning nicely. Add the wine and garlic and cook 1 minute, then transfer the mixture to a warmed serving bowl, scraping the skillet well. Add the basil to the bell pepper mixture and stir to combine.

Meanwhile, cook the linguine in the boiling water for 6 minutes, then add the broccoli and cook until the linguine is al dente, about 3 to 5 minutes. When the pasta is done, reserve ½ cup of the cooking water and drain the pasta and broccoli well. Add the reserved cooking water to the pepper mixture and stir, then add the drained pasta and broccoli.

Drizzle the oil evenly over the pasta and sprinkle on half of the cheese. Toss to distribute everything evenly, then top the dish with the remaining cheese and the pepper. Serve very hot, passing additional cheese, if you wish.

------

Each serving provides:

| 325 | Calories | 46 g | Carbohydrate |
|-----|----------|------|--------------|
| 12 g | Protein | 281 mg | Sodium |
| 10 g | Fat | 12 mg | Cholesterol |
| 5 g | Dietary Fiber | | |

# Fettuccine with Potatoes, Zucchini, and Blue Cheese

*Here is a hearty and strongly seasoned pasta dish for the blue cheese fans among us. Only a tart, leafy salad is needed to complete the meal, and perhaps a fruity red wine.*

*Yield:* 4 main-course servings

| | |
|---|---|
| **Red potatoes** | **¾ pound** |
| **Zucchini** | **1 pound** |
| **Olive oil** | **1 tablespoon** |
| **Dried red chili flakes** | **1 teaspoon** |
| **Dried rosemary** | **½ teaspoon** |
| **Garlic** | **3 cloves, minced** |
| **Salt** | **¼ teaspoon** |
| **Fresh Italian parsley, minced** | **¼ cup** |
| **Dry white wine** | **⅓ cup** |
| **Dried fettuccine** | **8 ounces** |
| **Blue cheese, crumbled** | **6 ounces (¾ cup)** |

Bring several cups of water to a boil in a large saucepan. Peel and cut the potatoes into 1-inch cubes. Add them to the boiling water. Cook 6 to 8 minutes, until barely tender. Place the potatoes in a colander and rinse with cold water to stop the cooking. Drain well and set aside.

Bring several quarts of water to a boil for the pasta. Meanwhile, trim off the ends of the zucchini and quarter them lengthwise. Cut the quarters crosswise into ½-inch pieces and set aside.

Heat the oil in a large sauté pan or skillet over medium heat and sauté the chili flakes and rosemary 1 minute. Add the garlic, zucchini, and salt. Reduce the heat to medium-low and sauté, stirring frequently, until the zucchini is beginning to soften and brown, 6 to 8 minutes. Add the potatoes, parsley, and wine to the pan and sauté, stirring frequently, for 5 minutes. Cover the pan and remove from the heat.

Meanwhile, cook the fettuccine in the boiling water until al dente. Reserve ½ cup of the cooking water, then drain well and transfer the pasta to a warmed serving bowl. Top with the potato mixture and cheese and toss until well combined. If the mixture seems too dry or gooey, add the reserved pasta cooking water a tablespoon at a time until the right texture is achieved. Serve very hot.

---

Each serving provides:

| | | | |
|---|---|---|---|
| 480 | Calories | 62 g | Carbohydrate |
| 19 g | Protein | 740 mg | Sodium |
| 17 g | Fat | 32 mg | Cholesterol |
| 5 g | Dietary Fiber | | |

# Couscous with Feta, Olives, and Walnuts

*ALMOST INSTANT*

*Couscous is a favorite food in Morocco. Here it is combined with ingredients that are common throughout the Mediterranean.*

*Yield:* 6 side-dish servings

| | |
|---|---|
| Feta cheese, crumbled | 2 ounces (½ cup) |
| Calamata olives, chopped | ¼ cup |
| Green onions | 3, minced |
| Fresh basil leaves, minced | ¼ cup |
| Lemon zest | 2 teaspoons |
| Fresh-squeezed lemon juice | 3 tablespoons |
| Extra virgin olive oil | 3 tablespoons |
| Garlic | 2 cloves, minced |
| Salt | ¼ teaspoon |
| Black pepper | Several grinds |
| Dried couscous | 2 cups |
| Raw unsalted walnuts, chopped | ⅓ cup |

Combine the cheese, olives, onions, basil, and lemon peel in a medium bowl. Stir in the lemon juice and 2 tablespoons of the oil. Set aside.

Bring 3 cups of water to a boil in a medium saucepan. When the water boils, add the remaining tablespoon of oil, garlic, salt, and pepper, then stir in the couscous. Immediately cover the pan and remove it from the heat. Let stand 5 minutes without disturbing the lid.

Place the walnuts in a single layer in a dry heavy-bottomed skillet over medium-high heat. Shake the pan or stir frequently until the nuts are golden brown and emit a wonderful roasted aroma. Immediately remove them from the pan and set aside.

Fluff the cooked couscous with a fork and place it in a warmed serving dish. Add the cheese mixture and nuts and toss until well combined. Serve immediately.

---

Each serving provides:

| | | | |
|---|---|---|---|
| 378 | Calories | 51 g | Carbohydrate |
| 10 g | Protein | 391 mg | Sodium |
| 15 g | Fat | 8 mg | Cholesterol |
| 2 g | Dietary Fiber | | |

# Sweet and Hot Cauliflower
# with Couscous

*ALMOST INSTANT, VEGAN*

*A deliciously aromatic combination of spices makes this stew a mouth-watering favorite. It comes together quickly and makes a satisfying meal, perhaps followed by a flavorful leafy salad.*

*Yield:* 6 main-course servings

| | | |
|---|---|---|
| Whole pear tomatoes* | 1 | 28-ounce can |
| Olive oil | 1 | tablespoon plus 2 teaspoons |
| White onions | 2 | medium, chopped |
| Cauliflower, chopped | 6 | cups |
| Carrots | 2 | large, diced |
| Golden raisins | ½ | cup |
| Garlic | 2 | cloves, minced |
| Paprika | 1 | teaspoon |
| Ground cumin | 1 | teaspoon |
| Ground cinnamon | ½ | teaspoon |
| Ground cardamom | ½ | teaspoon |
| Salt | ½ | teaspoon |
| Cayenne | ⅛ | teaspoon |
| Fresh-squeezed lemon juice | 2 | tablespoons |
| Dried couscous | 1⅓ | cups |
| Fresh Italian parsley, minced | ¼ | cup |
| Fresh mint leaves, minced | ¼ | cup |

*You may substitute 3 pounds fresh pear tomatoes—blanched, peeled, and seeded—for the canned variety. See the directions on page 28.

Drain the juice from the can of tomatoes and reserve it for another use. Chop the tomatoes and set them aside in a bowl. Heat 1 tablespoon of the oil over medium heat in a high-walled skillet or Dutch oven that has a tight-fitting lid. Sauté the onions, cauliflower, and carrots in the oil for 5 minutes, stirring frequently, then add the tomatoes, raisins, garlic, paprika, cumin, cinnamon, cardamom, ¼ teaspoon of the salt, the cayenne, and 1 cup water. Cover the pan and reduce the heat to medium-low. Cook for 15 minutes, removing the lid to stir the mixture about midway through the cooking time. At the end of the cooking time, stir in the lemon juice, cover, and set aside briefly if the couscous is not yet done.

Meanwhile, bring 2 cups of water to a boil in a covered saucepan, along with the remaining ¼ teaspoon salt and the remaining 2 teaspoons oil. Stir the couscous into the water, immediately cover the pan, and remove it from the heat. Let stand at least 5 minutes without disturbing the lid. Just before serving, turn the couscous out onto a warmed serving platter, fluffing it up with a fork. Arrange the couscous in a ring around the edge of the platter. Spoon the hot cauliflower mixture inside the ring of hot couscous. Top evenly with parsley and mint and serve immediately.

---

Each serving provides:

| | | | |
|---|---|---|---|
| 312 | Calories | 60 g | Carbohydrate |
| 10 g | Protein | 425 mg | Sodium |
| 5 g | Fat | 0 mg | Cholesterol |
| 7 g | Dietary Fiber | | |

# Couscous with Black-Eyed Peas, Zucchini, and Tomatoes

*ALMOST INSTANT, VEGAN*

*If you keep frozen cooked beans in your freezer or canned ones in the pantry, this dish comes together quickly for an impressive feast in a flash. A leafy salad is a good accompaniment, as is chilled dark beer.*

*Yield:* 6 main-course servings

| | | |
|---|---|---|
| **Zucchini** | ¾ | **pound** |
| **Button mushrooms** | ½ | **pound** |
| **Whole pear tomatoes\*** | 1 | **28-ounce can** |
| **Olive oil** | 1 | **tablespoon plus 2 teaspoons** |
| **White onion** | 1 | **medium, diced** |
| **Garlic** | 2 | **cloves, minced** |
| **Freshly grated ginger** | 1 | **teaspoon** |
| **Whole coriander** | 1 | **teaspoon** |
| **Ground turmeric** | ½ | **teaspoon** |
| **Ground cinnamon** | ¼ | **teaspoon** |
| **Cayenne** | ¼ | **teaspoon** |
| **Cooked black-eyed peas, drained\*\*** | 2 | **cups** |
| **Bean cooking liquid or stock** | 1 | **cup** |
| **Salt** | ½ | **teaspoon** |
| **Fresh cilantro leaves, minced** | ¼ | **cup** |
| **Dried couscous** | 1⅓ | **cups** |

\*You may substitute 3 pounds fresh pear tomatoes—blanched, peeled, and seeded—for the canned variety. See the directions on page 28.

\*\*Cook 1 cup dried black-eyed peas according to the directions on page 29, or use canned black-eyed peas that do not include additives.

Trim the ends off the zucchini and cut them in half lengthwise, then cut each half crosswise into ½-inch slices. Set the zucchini aside. Brush or wipe any visible dirt from the mushrooms and quarter them. Set the mushrooms aside.

Drain the juice from the can of tomatoes and reserve it for another use. Chop the tomatoes and set them aside in a bowl. Heat 1 tablespoon of the oil over medium heat in a high-walled skillet or Dutch oven that has a tight-fitting lid. Sauté the onion for five minutes, stirring frequently, then add the tomatoes, garlic, ginger, coriander, tumeric, cinnamon, and cayenne. Sauté, stirring frequently, for 3 minutes. Stir in the black-eyed peas, bean cooking liquid or stock, zucchini, mushrooms, and ¼ teaspoon of the salt. Cover the pan and cook 15 minutes, removing the lid to stir the mixture midway through the cooking time. Stir in the cilantro, cover, and set aside if the couscous is not yet done.

Meanwhile, bring 2 cups of water to a boil in a covered saucepan, along with the remaining ¼ teaspoon salt and the remaining 2 teaspoons oil. Stir in the couscous, immediately cover the pan, and remove from the heat. Let stand at least 5 minutes without disturbing the lid. Just before serving, turn the couscous out onto a warmed serving platter, fluffing it up with a fork. Arrange the couscous in a ring around the edge of the platter. Spoon the stew inside the ring of hot couscous. Serve immediately.

---

Each serving provides:

| | | | |
|---|---|---|---|
| 309 | Calories | 55 g | Carbohydrate |
| 13 g | Protein | 404 mg | Sodium |
| 5 g | Fat | 0 mg | Cholesterol |
| 9 g | Dietary Fiber | | |

# Entrées
# from the Oven

This category of Mediterranean cooking encompasses a broad range of delicious main courses, from pizza and savory pastries to stuffed vegetables and elaborate casseroles.

In appearance, taste, aroma, and texture, these baked entrées are infinitely appetizing. The paper-thin filo pastries of the eastern Mediterranean practically melt on the tongue; herb-flecked custard filling is a delicious counterpoint to a flaky pastry crust; succulent vegetables are enhanced by a moist and flavorful rice or bread stuffing.

A number of these dishes come together rather quickly. Though the actual assembly time for moussaka or spanakopita is considerable, they can be made ahead and baked just before serving. These extra-special entrées are a labor of love that your lucky guests will appreciate.

Most of the dishes in this chapter keep well after baking, so they make wonderful leftovers. Reheat them briefly in the oven or microwave, or serve them at room temperature.

# Tips and Tools

- Purchase an oven thermometer and leave it in your oven. Adjust the temperature dial, if necessary, until the thermometer registers the proper temperature, then place the food in the oven.
- Filo dough (also spelled "phyllo"), paper-thin sheets of pastry dough, is sold frozen in many well-stocked supermarkets.
- A pastry brush is needed for preparing the filo sheets.
- A whisk and an egg beater (rotary or electric) are indispensable for soufflé preparation. A high-walled soufflé dish or gratin dish is required for baking soufflés.
- Stainless steel baking sheets, a selection of glass or ceramic pie plates and casserole dishes, and a soufflé dish are called for in this chapter.
- We provide recipes for pizza dough and pastry crust, but you may use commercially prepared versions purchased at the supermarket.

# Zucchini and Feta Casserole with Fresh Mint

*The mint gives this Greek-inspired casserole a delightfully fresh flavor. The texture is light and the taste is very satisfying. Sour and Sweet Herb Sauce on page 56 makes a great topping.*

*Yield:* 4 main-course servings

| | |
|---|---|
| **Zucchini** | 1 pound |
| **Eggs** | 3 large |
| **Yellow onion** | 1 medium, minced |
| **Fresh mint leaves, minced** | ¼ cup |
| **Fresh Italian parsley, minced** | ¼ cup |
| **Feta cheese, crumbled** | 3 ounces (¾ cup) |
| **Unbleached flour** | ¼ cup |
| **Salt** | ¼ teaspoon |
| **Cayenne** | ⅛ teaspoon |
| **Olive oil** | ¼ teaspoon |
| **Fine dry bread crumbs** | 3 tablespoons |

Preheat the oven to 350 degrees F. Trim off and discard the ends of the zucchini and coarsely grate them into a bowl. Beat the eggs briefly in a separate bowl, then add the zucchini, onion, mint, and parsley and stir to combine well. Add the cheese and stir it in. Stir in the flour, salt, and cayenne. Use the oil to rub down a 2-quart baking dish. Spoon the zucchini mixture evenly into the dish and top with the bread crumbs. Bake, covered, 35 minutes, until the casserole is set. Remove the lid and continue to bake for 5 minutes, until the top is lightly browned. Serve hot or at room temperature.

---

Each serving provides:

| | | | |
|---|---|---|---|
| 202 | Calories | 18 g | Carbohydrate |
| 11 g | Protein | 461 mg | Sodium |
| 10 g | Fat | 179 mg | Cholesterol |
| 3 g | Dietary Fiber | | |

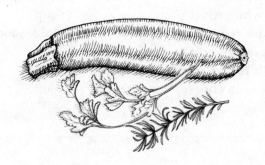

# Eggplant Parmigiana with Fresh Oregano

*There are many variations on this classic Italian dish. We have light-ened up the original by broiling the eggplant rather than breading and frying it. If your broiler pan is well tempered, no oil should be needed. The texture of this satisfying casserole is almost soufflé-like. Fresh oregano adds a bright flavor note, but 2 teaspoons of dried oregano may be substituted, added to the tomatoes along with the salt and pepper.*

*Yield:* 6 main-course servings

| | |
|---|---|
| **Eggplants** | 2 **pounds (2 medium)** |
| **Whole pear tomatoes°** | 1 **28-ounce can** |
| **Olive oil** | 1 **tablespoon plus ½ teaspoon** |
| **Garlic** | 4 **cloves, minced** |
| **Salt** | ¼ **teaspoon** |
| **Black pepper** | **Several grinds** |
| **Dry white wine** | ⅓ **cup** |
| **Fresh oregano leaves, minced** | 2 **tablespoons** |
| **Coarse dry bread crumbs** | 1 **cup** |
| **Fresh Italian parsley, minced** | ½ **cup** |
| **Parmesan cheese, finely grated** | 1 **cup** |

°You may substitute 3 pounds fresh pear tomatoes—blanched, peeled, and seeded—for the canned variety. See the directions on page 28.

Preheat the broiler. Wash and dry the eggplants and cut them crosswise into ¼-inch-thick slices. Place on the broiler pan and broil about 4 inches from the flame until the surface of the eggplant is well browned, about 5 minutes. Turn the slices over and broil 5 minutes. Eggplant slices should be fairly limp but not falling apart. (Alternatively, you may grill the eggplant slices until tender and nicely browned.)

Meanwhile, drain the tomatoes, reserving the juice for another use. Chop the tomatoes and set them aside in a bowl. Heat 1 tablespoon of the oil in a sauté pan or skillet over medium heat and sauté the garlic for about 30 seconds, then add the tomatoes, salt, and pepper and cook over medium heat, stirring frequently, until the tomatoes have cooked down to a thick sauce consistency, about 10 minutes. Stir in the wine and oregano and cook another 3 minutes.

Preheat the oven to 375 degrees F. Toss the bread crumbs with the parsley and set aside. Use the remaining ½ teaspoon oil to rub down a 2-quart casserole dish. Arrange half of the eggplant slices in an even layer on the bottom of the dish. Top evenly with half of the tomato sauce. Top the sauce evenly with half of the bread crumb mixture. Top with half of the Parmesan. Repeat the layers, ending with Parmesan. Bake uncovered for 30 minutes, until the top of the casserole is nicely browned.

---

Each serving provides:

| 228 | Calories | 29 g | Carbohydrate |
|---|---|---|---|
| 11 g | Protein | 729 mg | Sodium |
| 8 g | Fat | 12 mg | Cholesterol |
| 3 g | Dietary Fiber | | |

# Spiced Couscous Casserole

*This casserole combines couscous, the pasta popular in Moroccan cooking, with garbanzo beans, sweet red pepper, and bright green peas. It is pretty, flavorful, and satisfying.*

*Yield:* 6 main-course servings

| | | |
|---|---|---|
| Homemade Vegetable Stock* | 2½ | cups |
| Dried couscous | 1 | cup |
| Olive oil | 1 | tablespoon plus ¼ teaspoon |
| Red bell pepper | 1 | medium, diced |
| Green onions | 2, | minced |
| Cooked garbanzo beans, drained** | 1⅓ | cups |
| Shelled peas, fresh or frozen | 1 | cup |
| Dried tomatoes, minced | 2 | tablespoons |
| Ground cumin | 1 | teaspoon |
| Ground coriander | 1 | teaspoon |
| Ground turmeric | 1 | teaspoon |
| Ground cinnamon | ¼ | teaspoon |
| Salt | ¼ | teaspoon |
| Lowfat milk | ¾ | cup |
| Fresh cilantro leaves, minced | ¼ | cup |
| Lemon wedges | 1 | per serving |

*If you do not have Homemade Vegetable Stock on hand, make some according to the directions on page 32 or dissolve 1 large low-sodium vegetable broth cube in 2½ cups of hot water.

**Cook ⅔ cup of dried beans according to the directions on page 29, or use canned beans that do not contain additives.

Preheat the oven to 350 degrees F. Bring the stock to a boil in a saucepan that has a tight-fitting lid. Stir in the couscous, remove from the heat, cover, and let stand for 15 minutes.

Heat the 1 tablespoon of the oil in a sauté pan or skillet over medium heat. Add the bell pepper and onions and sauté for a minute or two, then stir in the garbanzo beans, peas, dried tomatoes, cumin, coriander, turmeric, cinnamon, and salt. Stir to combine. Pour in the milk. Heat through for about 2 minutes. Transfer the couscous to a large bowl and fluff it with a fork, then stir in the sautéed ingredients and cilantro. Use the remaining ¼ teaspoon oil to rub down a 2-quart casserole dish and add the couscous mixture. Cover and bake for 30 minutes. Serve with the lemon wedges, passing yogurt or sour cream, if desired.

---

Each serving provides:

| | | | |
|---|---|---|---|
| 257 | Calories | 44 g | Carbohydrate |
| 11 g | Protein | 229 mg | Sodium |
| 5 g | Fat | 2 mg | Cholesterol |
| 4 g | Dietary Fiber | | |

# Baked Noodles with Kidney Beans, Spiced Tomato Sauce, and Feta

*This simple casserole is classic comfort food, an example of Mediterranean cooking at its most humble and nourishing. It has a warming quality, so it is a winter favorite at our tables.*

*Yield:* 6 main-course servings

| | | |
|---|---|---|
| Whole pear tomatoes* | 1 | 28-ounce can |
| Button mushrooms | ½ | pound |
| Zucchini | ½ | pound |
| Dried egg noodles | 10 | ounces |
| Olive oil | 1 | tablespoon plus ½ teaspoon |
| White onion | 1 | medium, diced |
| Dried red chili flakes | ½ | teaspoon |
| Dry red or white wine | ½ | cup |
| Garlic | 3 | cloves, minced |
| Dried marjoram | 1 | teaspoon |
| Paprika | 1 | teaspoon |
| Dried thyme | ½ | teaspoon |
| Ground cinnamon | ¼ | teaspoon |
| Salt | ½ | teaspoon |
| Fresh lemon peel, minced | ½ | teaspoon |
| Cooked kidney beans, drained** | 1½ | cups |
| Plain nonfat yogurt | 1 | cup |

*You may substitute 3 pounds fresh pear tomatoes—blanched, peeled, and seeded—for the canned variety. See the directions on page 28.

**Cook ¾ cup dried kidney beans according to the directions on page 29, or used canned beans that do not contain additives.

| Feta cheese, crumbled | 4 | ounces (1 cup) |
|---|---|---|
| Black pepper | | Several grinds |
| Parmesan cheese, finely grated | 2 | tablespoons |

Put several quarts of water on to boil for the noodles. Drain the juice from the can of tomatoes and reserve it for another use. Chop the tomatoes and set them aside in a bowl. Wipe or brush any visible dirt from the mushrooms and quarter them. Set aside. Trim both ends from the zucchini, cut in half lengthwise, then cut each half crosswise into ½-inch slices. Set aside.

Cook the egg noodles in the boiling water until barely al dente, about 5 minutes. Immediately drain and set aside in a colander.

Meanwhile, use ½ teaspoon of the oil to rub down a 2-quart covered casserole dish. Set the dish aside. Preheat the oven to 375 degrees F. Heat the remaining 1 tablespoon oil in a heavy-bottomed sauté pan or skillet over medium heat. Sauté the onion, mushrooms, zucchini, and chili flakes for 5 minutes, stirring frequently, then add the tomatoes, wine, garlic, marjoram, paprika, thyme, cinnamon, salt, and lemon peel. Cook 5 minutes, stirring frequently. Add the drained noodles and kidney beans to the tomato sauce and stir to combine. Stir in the yogurt and feta and transfer the mixture to the oiled casserole dish. Grind on the black pepper and distribute the Parmesan evenly over the casserole. Bake, covered, 25 minutes, then remove the lid and bake 5 minutes longer. Serve very hot.

---

Each serving provides:

| | | | |
|---|---|---|---|
| 328 | Calories | 46 g | Carbohydrate |
| 16 g | Protein | 673 mg | Sodium |
| 9 g | Fat | 46 mg | Cholesterol |
| 5 g | Dietary Fiber | | |

# Spinach and Dill Filo Pie

*Filo—paper-thin pastry dough—is a common ingredient in Greek and Middle Eastern cuisine. It is widely available in the United States in the frozen foods section. Here we have created a somewhat traditional spanakopita pie, seasoning the spinach and feta with dill and nutmeg.*

*Yield:* 8 main-course servings

| | | |
|---|---|---|
| **Filo dough** | 8 | **ounces** |
| **Fresh spinach** | 1½ | **pounds** |
| | | **(2 bunches)** |
| **Green onions** | 4, | **minced** |
| **Part-skim ricotta cheese** | ½ | **cup** |
| **Lowfat milk** | ¼ | **cup** |
| **Eggs** | 2 | **large, beaten** |
| **Fresh dill, minced** | ¼ | **cup** |
| **Freshly grated nutmeg** | ½ | **teaspoon** |
| **Olive oil** | 2 | **tablespoons** |
| **Feta cheese, crumbled** | 6 | **ounces** |
| | | **(1½ cups)** |

The filo dough is quite delicate and must be at the optimum temperature for best results. Remove the filo dough from the freezer and thaw it in its original wrapping at room temperature for about 4 hours. Begin to prepare the filling about one hour before the dough is ready to use.

Wash the spinach and discard the stems. Place the wet spinach in a stockpot over medium-high heat, cover, and steam 5 minutes, until the spinach wilts. Drain the spinach in a colander and press it with the back of a wooden spoon to remove as much water as possible. Coarsely chop the spinach and place it in a large bowl. Add the green onions and stir to combine. In a separate bowl, beat the ricotta, milk, eggs, dill, and nutmeg together with a fork. Stir the spinach into this mixture.

When the dough has thawed for 4 hours, remove it from the package, unfold it, and cut half of the sheets in two. Refold the remaining dough, return it to its original wrapper, and reserve it in the refrigerator for another use. Cover the stack of dough you will be using with a barely damp tea towel to prevent it from drying out.

Preheat the oven to 350 degrees F. Lightly brush a 9 × 13 × 2-inch baking dish with some of the oil. Trim the stack of filo to fit the pan, if necessary. Lay down a single sheet of the filo pastry in the bottom of the dish. Sparingly brush the sheet with a bit of oil and cover with another sheet. Continue to oil and layer the sheets until you have used about half of them. Spread the spinach mixture evenly over this layer, then distribute the feta cheese evenly over the spinach. Cover with the remaining sheets, laying them down one at a time and continuing to brush each layer with a bit of oil, using the last bit of oil to brush the top of the last sheet. (At this point, you may refrigerate the dish for several hours, but let it stand at room temperature for about 30 minutes before baking.)

Bake for 35 to 40 minutes, until golden brown. Allow to cool slightly before cutting. Serve hot or at room temperature.

---

Each serving provides:

| 234 | Calories | 20 g | Carbohydrate |
|---|---|---|---|
| 11 g | Protein | 472 mg | Sodium |
| 13 g | Fat | 77 mg | Cholesterol |
| 3 g | Dietary Fiber | | |

# Filo Dough Filled with Zucchini and Parmesan Cheese

*Filled pastries—borekas as they are known in Israel and Turkey—are popular street vendor fare. Serve this delicious version as an appetizer, 2 per person, or as a supper entrée, 4 per person.*

*Yield:* 20 pastries

| | |
|---|---|
| **Filo dough** | 8 sheets |
| **Zucchini** | 1 pound |
| **Salt** | ½ teaspoon |
| **Olive oil** | ¼ cup |
| **White onion, minced** | ½ cup |
| **Cooking sherry** | ¼ cup |
| **Fresh basil leaves, minced** | ½ cup |
| **Garlic** | 3 cloves, minced |
| **Parmesan cheese, finely grated** | ¾ cup |
| **Egg** | 1 large, beaten |
| **Black pepper** | Several grinds |

The filo dough is quite delicate and must be at the optimum temperature for best results. Remove the filo dough from the freezer and thaw it in its original wrapping at room temperature for about 4 hours. Begin to prepare the filling about one hour before the dough is ready to use.

Cut off and discard the stem ends from the zucchini and coarsely grate them into a colander. Sprinkle with the salt and set aside in the sink to drain for 30 minutes. Rinse the zucchini well, then allow to drain for a few minutes before squeezing gently in a clean tea towel to remove as much water as possible.

Place 1 tablespoon of the oil in a skillet over medium-high heat and add the onion. Sauté, stirring frequently, for about 3 minutes, until the onion is translucent. Add the zucchini and sauté and stir for about 5 minutes, until the zucchini and onion are browning slightly. Stir in the sherry, basil, and garlic, then cover the pan and cook for 3 minutes. Remove the lid and continue to cook, stirring frequently, for another 2 to 3 minutes, until the liquid evaporates. Spoon the mixture into a large bowl. Set it aside to cool for 5 minutes or so, then stir in the Parmesan, egg, and pepper until well combined.

Preheat the oven to 400 degrees F. Lightly oil a large baking sheet and set it aside.

When the dough has thawed for 4 hours, carefully peel off 8 sheets. Refold the remaining dough, return it to its original wrapper, and reserve it in the refrigerator for another use. Place the 8 sheets on a flat work surface and cut them lengthwise into 3 equal strips measuring approximately 4 by 16 inches. Cover the stack of dough with a barely damp tea towel to prevent it from drying out. (You will have 4 extra strips in case one tears as you are preparing the pastries.)

Place one 4×16-inch strip of filo dough straight out in front of you and scantily brush it with some of the oil. Mound a tablespoon of the filling on the bottom right corner of the strip, about one inch up from the bottom, and in a bit from the side. Fold the bottom border up and over the filling, then fold the filled corner of the dough so the bottom edge meets the left side to form a triangle. Continue folding the triangle, as you would a flag, until you reach the end of the dough strip. Place the triangle seam side down on the baking sheet and brush the top with a bit of the oil.

Repeat with the remaining sheets of dough and filling, making sure that you brush the tops with oil as you place them on the baking sheet. (At this point, you may cover the baking sheet with plastic wrap and refrigerate for up to a day, but return the triangles to room temperature before baking.)

Bake the filo triangles for 12 to 15 minutes, until they are golden brown. Remove them from the baking sheet and allow them to cool for about 5 minutes before serving.

---

Each pastry provides:

| | | | |
|---|---|---|---|
| 83 | Calories | 7 g | Carbohydrate |
| 3 g | Protein | 162 mg | Sodium |
| 4 g | Fat | 13 mg | Cholesterol |
| 1 g | Dietary Fiber | | |

# Eggplant and Artichoke Moussaka

*This well-known Greek entrée (pronounced with the emphasis on the last syllable) typically includes a meat sauce. There are so many wonderful flavors in this meatless version, though, that even die-hard carnivores will love it. Making moussaka is a bit of a production, but the results are spectacular. Build a special dinner party around it and invite your worthiest friends.*

*Yield:* 6 main-course servings

| | | |
|---|---|---|
| **Eggplants** | 2 | **pounds (2 medium)** |
| **Water-packed artichoke hearts** | 2 | **14-ounce packages** |
| **Whole pear tomatoes**° | 2 | **28-ounce cans** |
| **Olive oil** | 1 | **tablespoon plus ½ teaspoon** |
| **Yellow onion** | 1 | **large, diced** |
| **Dry red wine** | ½ | **cup** |
| **Garlic** | 4 | **cloves, minced** |
| **Fresh lemon peel, minced** | ½ | **teaspoon** |
| **Ground cinnamon** | ½ | **teaspoon** |
| **Ground allspice** | ¼ | **teaspoon** |
| **Salt** | 1 | **teaspoon** |
| **Black pepper** | | **Several grinds** |
| **Whole bay leaf** | 1 | **large** |
| **Tomato paste** | ¼ | **cup** |
| **Unsalted butter** | 3 | **tablespoons** |
| **Unbleached white flour** | 3 | **tablespoons** |
| **Lowfat milk** | 2½ | **cups** |

°You may substitute 6 pounds fresh pear tomatoes—blanched, peeled, and seeded—for the canned variety. See the directions on page 28.

| Freshly ground nutmeg | ¼ | teaspoon |
| Egg yolks | 2 | large |
| Parmesan cheese, finely grated | ⅔ | cup |

Preheat the broiler. Wash and dry the eggplants and slice them crosswise into ½-inch slices. Place the slices on the broiler pan (no oil should be needed if the broiler pan is well-tempered). Broil about 4 inches from the flame until the surface of the eggplant is well-browned, about 5 minutes. Turn the slices over and broil an additional 8 to 10 minutes. The eggplant slices should be well-browned and tender. Transfer the eggplant to a plate and set aside. Rinse and drain the artichoke hearts and chop them coarsely. Set aside.

To make the tomato sauce, drain the juice from both cans of tomatoes and reserve it for another use, then coarsely chop the tomatoes and set them aside in a bowl. Heat 1 tablespoon of the oil in a heavy-bottomed saucepan over medium heat and sauté the onion for 5 minutes, stirring frequently. Add the tomatoes, wine, garlic, lemon peel, cinnamon, allspice, ½ teaspoon of the salt, the pepper, and the bay leaf. Bring to a simmer, reduce the heat to medium-low, cover, and cook 15 minutes, removing the lid to stir the sauce twice during the cooking time. Stir in the tomato paste and chopped artichoke hearts and set the sauce aside.

Preheat the oven to 375 degrees F. To make the white sauce, melt the butter in a heavy-bottomed saucepan over low heat, being careful not to let it brown. Add the flour and stir with a wooden spoon or wire whisk to incorporate it into the butter. It will thicken very quickly. Slowly whisk in the milk and bring to a simmer, whisking almost constantly to prevent the flour from sticking to the bottom of the pan. Simmer over low heat for 15 minutes, whisking frequently. Turn off the heat and whisk in the remaining ½ teaspoon salt and the nutmeg. Beat the egg yolks in a small bowl. Whisk about two tablespoons of the sauce into the yolks. Add another 2 tablespoons of sauce and whisk again. Now whisk the yolk mixture and ⅓ cup of the Parmesan into the sauce. (If the rest of the dish is not yet ready, transfer the sauce to a bowl and cover it with plastic wrap, allowing the plastic to lay directly on the surface of the sauce. Set the sauce aside at room temperature for up to 30 minutes while you finish the rest of the preparation, or refrigerate it for a day, but return it to room temperature before using. Remove and discard the plastic wrap and whisk the sauce again before adding it to the casserole.)

To assemble the casserole, use the remaining ½ teaspoon oil to rub down a large, high-walled baking pan or casserole dish. Make an even layer on the bottom of the dish using half the eggplant slices and top it evenly with half the tomato artichoke sauce. Sprinkle ⅓ cup of the Parmesan evenly over the tomato sauce. Add the remaining eggplant in an even layer and top with an even layer of the remaining tomato sauce. Finally, add the white sauce, ladling it evenly over the entire surface of the casserole.

Bake uncovered for 1 hour, until the top layer of white sauce is quite brown and almost crusty. Remove from the oven and allow the casserole to rest at room temperature for 10 minutes before serving.

---

Each serving provides:

| | | | |
|---|---|---|---|
| 360 | Calories | 42 g | Carbohydrate |
| 16 g | Protein | 1554 mg | Sodium |
| 18 g | Fat | 102 mg | Cholesterol |
| 5 g | Dietary Fiber | | |

# Basic Pizza Crust

*VEGAN*

*Use bread flour or unbleached white flour. The flour measure is given as a range because the exact amount will vary depending on the day's humidity and other weather conditions. The temperature of the water used to start the yeast is important—if it is too hot, it will kill the yeast; if it is too cold, the yeast will not be activated. We use an instant-read thermometer to make sure the water temperature is in the 105 to 115 degree F. range.*

*Yield:* 2 12-inch pizza crusts

| | |
|---|---|
| **Active dry yeast** | ¼ ounce (1 envelope) |
| **Lukewarm water** | 1½ cups |
| **Olive oil** | 2 tablespoons plus ½ teaspoon |
| **Salt** | ½ teaspoon |
| **Unbleached white flour** | 3½ cups |

Place the yeast in a large warm bowl and add the lukewarm water (105 to 115 degrees F.). Stir with a wooden spoon to dissolve the yeast, then set aside in a warm place until creamy in appearance, about 15 minutes. Stir in 2 tablespoons of oil and the salt, then add 2 cups of the flour. Stir to incorporate, using a large wooden spoon. The mixture will be very sticky at this point. Add 1 more cup of the flour and continue to stir until the dough begins to form a ball. Turn out onto a lightly floured work surface and knead the dough until it is soft and smooth, about 10 minutes, adding the remaining ½ cup flour as needed, a bit at a time, until the dough is no longer sticky. If necessary, add up to ½ cup more flour, a tablespoon at a time. Too much flour will result in a dry dough that can become a slightly tough crust, so don't add any more flour than necessary.

Lightly oil a large bowl with ½ teaspoon of oil. Place the dough ball in the oiled bowl, turn it to coat the entire surface with oil, and cover the bowl with a clean dish towel. Place the bowl in a warm, draft-free place for the dough to rise until doubled in volume, about 1½ hours. (An unlit oven or warm cupboard works well.) After it has risen, punch the dough down with your fist or fingertips to press out most of the air.

Place the dough on a lightly floured work surface and divide it into 2 balls of equal size. Working with 1 ball at a time, flatten it with your hands into a circle about 4 inches in diameter and 1 inch thick. Begin working from the center, pressing the dough outward with the heels of your hands. If the dough sticks to your hands, sprinkle lightly with flour. Push the dough into a 12-inch round that is slightly thicker at the edges. (You can also use a rolling pin to spread the dough into a 12-inch round.) If you are making only 1 pizza, the remaining dough ball may be wrapped tightly in plastic and frozen for up to 3 months. Thaw the dough at room temperature for a few hours before rolling out as directed. Proceed with the instructions of individual recipes.

---

Each crust provides:

| | | | |
|---|---|---|---|
| 235 | Calories | 42 g | Carbohydrate |
| 6 g | Protein | 136 mg | Sodium |
| 4 g | Fat | 0 mg | Cholesterol |
| 2 g | Dietary Fiber | | |

# Pizza with Zucchini, Artichokes, and Feta Cheese

*Picture yourself on a Greek island, eating this pizza straight from an outdoor wood-burning oven. It's simply delicious!*

*Yield:* 4 main-course servings

| | |
|---|---|
| **Pizza crust** | 1 **12-inch crust** |
| **Yellow cornmeal** | 2 **tablespoons** |
| **Water-packed artichoke hearts** | 1 **14-ounce can** |
| **Zucchini** | 1 **medium** |
| **Provolone cheese** | 2 **ounces, thinly sliced** |
| **Red onion, sliced paper-thin** | ¼ **cup** |
| **Fresh oregano leaves, minced** | 2 **tablespoons** |
| **Feta cheese, crumbled** | 2 **ounces (½ cup)** |
| **Black pepper** | **Several grinds** |

Prepare a pizza crust from the Pizza Dough recipe on page 204 or use a commercial crust for an Almost Instant pizza. Place the uncooked crust on a round pizza pan or a baker's peel that has been sprinkled with the cornmeal. Preheat a coal or gas grill to high, about 500 degrees F., or preheat the oven to 450 degrees F.

Drain the artichoke hearts and coarsely chop them. Remove the ends of the zucchini and cut it into very thin oblong slices. Distribute the provolone slices so that they cover most of the pizza crust, leaving about a 1-inch border. Arrange the onion slices over the provolone, then place the zucchini slices and the artichoke hearts on top of the onion. Distribute the oregano and the feta cheese over the top and grind on pepper to taste.

Transfer the pizza to the hot grill and cover the grill, or place the pizza in the hot oven. Bake for 15 to 20 minutes, until the crust is crisp and the provolone has melted. Serve immediately.

---

Each serving provides:

| | | | |
|---|---|---|---|
| 365 | Calories | 53 g | Carbohydrate |
| 15 g | Protein | 719 mg | Sodium |
| 11 g | Fat | 23 mg | Cholesterol |
| 3 g | Dietary Fiber | | |

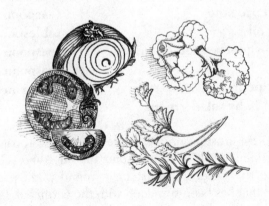

# Pizza with Garlic Tomato Sauce, Ricotta, and Fresh Greens

*ALMOST INSTANT*

*This unique pizza makes a wonderful first course at an Italian-inspired dinner party or a delightful weekend lunch. Needless to say, you do not need a salad to complete the meal.*

*Yield:* 4 main-course servings

| | | |
|---|---|---|
| Pizza crust | 1 | 12-inch crust |
| Yellow cornmeal | 2 | tablespoons |
| Fresh pear tomatoes | ½ | pound |
| Tomato paste | 2 | tablespoons |
| Garlic | 2 | cloves, minced |
| Parmesan cheese, finely grated | 2 | tablespoons |
| Calamata olives, chopped | ¼ | cup |
| Part-skim ricotta cheese | ½ | cup |
| Lowfat sour cream | 2 | tablespoons |
| Dried oregano | 1 | teaspoon |
| Olive oil | 1 | tablespoon |
| Fresh-squeezed lemon juice | 1 | teaspoon |
| Salt | ⅛ | teaspoon |
| Black pepper | Several grinds | |
| Mixed baby salad greens | 1½ cups | |

Prepare a pizza crust according to the directions on page 204, or use a commercially prepared one for an Almost Instant pizza. Place the uncooked crust on a round pizza pan or a baker's peel that has been sprinkled with the cornmeal. Preheat a coal or gas grill to high, about 500 degrees F., or preheat the oven to 450 degrees F.

Without peeling them, cut the tomatoes into quarters and place them in a blender. Add the tomato paste and garlic, then puree until smooth and set aside. Sprinkle the Parmesan cheese evenly over the crust, then evenly top with the pureed tomatoes, leaving a 1-inch border free of sauce. Distribute the olives on top of the sauce.

In a bowl, combine the ricotta cheese, sour cream, and ½ teaspoon of the oregano, then place 6 heaping tablespoons of the mixture on the pizza, within the ring of sauce but toward its outer edge. Crumble the remaining ½ teaspoon oregano over the pizza.

Transfer the pizza to the hot grill and cover the grill, or place the pizza in the hot oven. Bake for 15 to 20 minutes, until the crust is crisp and the cheese has softened and browned a bit.

Meanwhile, whisk together the oil, lemon juice, salt, and pepper. Place the greens in a small bowl and drizzle with the dressing. Remove the pizza from the grill and cut into six wedges. Mound the greens in the center of the pizza and serve immediately.

------------

Each serving provides:

| | | | |
|---|---|---|---|
| 399 | Calories | 54 g | Carbohydrate |
| 13 g | Protein | 641 mg | Sodium |
| 15 g | Fat | 15 mg | Cholesterol |
| 3 g | Dietary Fiber | | |

# Green Peppers Stuffed with Dill Minted Rice

*These peppers are stuffed with deliciously seasoned rice. You may serve them as a side dish for 8 people or as an entrée as suggested below.*

*Yield:* 4 main-course servings

| | |
|---|---|
| Olive oil | 2 tablespoons |
| Dry sherry | 2 tablespoons |
| Yellow onion | 1 medium, chopped |
| Uncooked long-grain white rice | 1 cup |
| Fresh pear tomatoes | ½ pound, diced |
| Dried currants | ¼ cup |
| Fresh dill, minced | ¼ cup |
| Fresh mint leaves, minced | ¼ cup |
| Salt | 1 teaspoon |
| Ground allspice | ½ teaspoon |
| Green bell peppers | 4 large |
| Whole wheat pita bread | 4 rounds |
| Pine nuts | 2 tablespoons |
| Plain nonfat yogurt | 1 cup |

Place the oil and sherry in a large sauté pan or skillet over medium heat. Add the onion and sauté until translucent, about 3 minutes. Add 2 cups of water, the rice, tomatoes, currants, dill, mint, salt, and allspice. Cover the pan, increase the heat to high, and bring to a boil. Reduce the heat to very low and simmer for 20 minutes. Turn off the heat and set aside without disturbing the lid for 5 minutes.

Meanwhile, preheat the oven to 350 degrees F. Cut the peppers in half lengthwise. Remove and discard the stems, seeds, and white membranes, then place the pepper halves in a large shallow baking dish, hollow side up. When the rice is cooked, remove it from the heat and spoon equal amounts into the pepper halves. Reserve any rice that doesn't fit into the peppers. Add hot water to the dish to measure about ½ inch up the sides of the peppers. Cover the dish and bake for 40 to 45 minutes, until the peppers are tender. Wrap the pita bread in foil and place it in the oven 10 minutes before serving.

While the peppers are baking, place the pine nuts in a dry, heavy-bottomed skillet and toast over medium-high heat for several minutes. Stir or shake the pan frequently until the nuts are lightly browned and emit a wonderful roasted aroma. Immediately remove them from the pan and set aside.

Remove the peppers from the oven and place 2 halves on each plate, along with a portion of the reserved rice, if any. Garnish with the pine nuts and serve, passing the yogurt and pita bread.

---

Each serving provides:

| 509 | Calories | 85 g | Carbohydrate |
|---|---|---|---|
| 16 g | Protein | 852 mg | Sodium |
| 12 g | Fat | 1 mg | Cholesterol |
| 7 g | Dietary Fiber | | |

# Red Peppers Stuffed with Bread, Walnuts, and Fresh Herbs

*Many vegetables that thrive in the Mediterranean climate are perfect for stuffing. These scrumptious peppers make a wonderful light main course to serve with a leafy salad and a distinctive vegetable side dish such as the Green Beans and Carrots Braised in Wine (page 236). Be sure to use slightly stale, but not dry, cubes of coarse country bread for the stuffing. Select peppers that are fairly even on the bottom so they will stand upright in the baking dish.*

*Yield:* 4 main-course servings

| | |
|---|---|
| **Red bell peppers** | **4 large** |
| **Onion** | **½ medium, finely diced** |
| **Celery** | **1 small rib, finely diced** |
| **Salt** | **½ teaspoon** |
| **Fresh Italian parsley, minced** | **¼ cup** |
| **Fresh thyme leaves** | **1 teaspoon** |
| **Fresh rosemary, minced** | **½ teaspoon** |
| **Garlic** | **1 clove, minced** |
| **Black pepper** | **Several grinds** |
| **Thick-crusted unsliced bread, cut into ¾-inch cubes** | **2 cups** |
| **Dry white wine** | **½ cup** |
| **Fresh lemon peel, minced** | **½ teaspoon** |
| **Raw, unsalted walnuts, coarsely chopped** | **⅓ cup** |
| **Fontina or cheddar cheese, shredded** | **½ cup** |
| **Egg** | **1 large, beaten** |
| **Olive oil** | **½ teaspoon** |

Preheat the oven to 375 degrees F. Slice the stem ends off the peppers and reach inside to remove and discard the seeds and thick white membranes. Cut off any pepper flesh connected to the stems and finely chop it, discarding the stems themselves. Set the whole peppers aside.

Place the chopped red bell pepper, onion, celery, and salt in a skillet over medium heat, along with ½ cup water. Bring to a simmer and cook 3 minutes, stirring frequently. Stir in the parsley, thyme, rosemary, garlic, and black pepper. Stir and cook for 2 minutes, or until most of the moisture is gone, then scrape the mixture into a large mixing bowl. Add the bread cubes, wine, and lemon peel and toss to combine well. Add a few tablespoons of additional wine or water, if necessary, to create a moist but not mushy filling. Stir in the walnuts, cheese, and egg until well combined. Spoon equal amounts of the filling into the peppers, packing it in firmly with a wooden spoon.

Use the oil to rub down a baking dish just big enough to hold the peppers. Place the peppers in the dish, touching each other for support, and pour in hot water to a depth of 1 inch. Cover the dish and bake for 40 minutes, until the peppers are tender. Carefully remove them from the dish and set aside on a platter. Serve whole, or cut each pepper in half before serving.

---

Each serving provides:

| 235 | Calories | 20 g | Carbohydrate |
|---|---|---|---|
| 9 g | Protein | 520 mg | Sodium |
| 13 g | Fat | 70 mg | Cholesterol |
| 3 g | Dietary Fiber | | |

# Stuffed Zucchini with Walnuts, Olives, and Madeira

*Inspired by the sunny flavors of Greece, these zucchini boats are a Mediterranean delight. Not counting the baking time, they come together quickly. For this dish, select zucchini at the market that are a bit longer and thicker than average. They should weigh about a half pound each.*

*Yield:* 4 main-course servings

| | | |
|---|---|---|
| **Zucchini** | 4 | **large** |
| **Lemon** | ½ | **medium** |
| **Olive oil** | 1 | **tablespoon** |
| **Red bell pepper, finely chopped** | ½ | **cup** |
| **Garlic** | 3 | **cloves, minced** |
| **Dried basil** | 1 | **tablespoon** |
| **Dried red chili flakes** | ¼ | **teaspoon** |
| **Salt** | ½ | **teaspoon** |
| **Coarse dry bread crumbs** | 1½ | **cups** |
| **Raw, unsalted walnuts, chopped** | ⅓ | **cup** |
| **Calamata olives, slivered** | ¼ | **cup** |
| **Madeira** | ½ | **cup** |
| **Egg** | 1 | **large** |

Preheat the oven to 350 degrees F. Wash and dry the zucchini and cut them in half lengthwise. Using a spoon or melon baller, carefully scrape out and reserve the zucchini pulp, leaving a ¼-inch shell. Rub the inside of these shells with the cut lemon and set them aside. Mince the zucchini pulp and set aside.

Heat the oil in a heavy-bottomed sauté pan or skillet over medium heat and sauté the minced zucchini, red bell pepper, garlic, basil, chili flakes, and salt for 15 minutes, stirring frequently.

Combine the bread crumbs, walnuts, and olives in a mixing bowl. Stir in the zucchini mixture until well combined. Whisk the Madeira with the egg briefly and stir this into the stuffing until well combined. Stuff the zucchini shells with the filling and arrange them in a row in a 9×13-inch baking dish. Add hot water to the dish to a depth of about ¼ inch and cover the dish tightly. Bake for 30 minutes. Remove the lid and bake 5 minutes longer. Serve hot.

---

Each serving provides:

| 352 | Calories | 39 g | Carbohydrate |
|-----|----------|------|--------------|
| 11 g | Protein | 799 mg | Sodium |
| 17 g | Fat | 57 mg | Cholesterol |
| 4 g | Dietary Fiber | | |

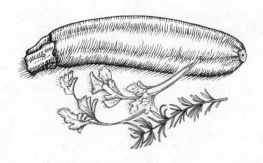

# Eggplants Stuffed with Rice, Tomatoes, Herbs, and Pine Nuts

*There are many Mediterranean variations on the stuffed eggplant theme. This one brings together many of the favorite foods of Italy to create an exemplary main course. The Baked Winter Squash with Garlic and Sage (page 260) can share the oven with the eggplants and makes a colorful side dish. A fresh tomato salad would finish the meal nicely. For a vegan variation, simply omit the Parmesan; the results will be delicious, if not quite authentic.*

*Yield:* 4 main-course servings

| Eggplants | 2 | pounds (2 medium) |
|---|---|---|
| Canned diced tomatoes | 1 | 14½-ounce can |
| Cooked white or brown rice | 1½ | cups |
| Pine nuts | ¼ | cup |
| Green onions | 4, | minced |
| Garlic | 2 | cloves, minced |
| Dried oregano | 1 | teaspoon |
| Dried marjoram | 1 | teaspoon |
| Dried basil | 1 | teaspoon |
| Dried rosemary | 1 | teaspoon |
| Salt | ½ | teaspoon |
| Black pepper | Several grinds | |
| Parmesan cheese, finely grated | ¼ | cup |

Preheat the broiler. Wash and dry the eggplants and cut them in half lengthwise. Place the eggplants cut side up 4 inches under the broiler for 10 minutes. They will char a bit on top. Remove them from the oven and set aside to cool for a few minutes. Turn off the broiler and preheat the oven to 375 degrees F.

Drain the tomatoes, reserving the juice for another use. In a large bowl, combine the rice with the tomatoes, pine nuts, green onions, garlic, oregano, marjoram, basil, rosemary, salt, and pepper. When the eggplants are cool enough to handle, use a sharp knife to cut out the eggplant pulp, leaving about a ½-inch shell. Finely chop the eggplant pulp and add it to the rice mixture, stirring to combine well. Mound the filling into the eggplant shells and sprinkle each one evenly with 1 tablespoon of the Parmesan. Place the stuffed eggplants on a baking sheet.

Bake for 35 to 40 minutes, until the eggplant shells are fork-tender in their thickest part and the Parmesan is lightly browned. Serve very hot.

---

Each serving provides:

| 240 | Calories | 43 g | Carbohydrate |
|------|----------|------|--------------|
| 9 g | Protein | 537 mg | Sodium |
| 5 g | Fat | 4 mg | Cholesterol |
| 4 g | Dietary Fiber | | |

# Cabbage Stuffed with Rice and Gorgonzola

*Rice and gorgonzola cheese make a tasty filling for cabbage leaves in this Mediterranean flight of fancy. For a memorable meal, serve them with a distinctive vegetable side dish such as Mustard Glazed Carrots (page 244).*

*Yield:* 6 main-course servings

| | |
|---|---|
| Green cabbage | 12 large leaves |
| Whole pear tomatoes* | 1 28-ounce can |
| Uncooked long-grain white rice | ½ cup |
| Dried marjoram | 1 teaspoon |
| Salt | ¼ teaspoon |
| Black pepper | Several grinds |
| Olive oil | 1 tablespoon |
| Yellow onion | 1 medium, chopped |
| Garlic | 3 cloves, minced |
| Gorgonzola cheese, crumbled | 4 ounces (1 cup) |

Use a sharp knife to cut the core out of the cabbage. Carefully remove 12 of the large outer leaves, peeling them off from the bottom up. Drain the tomatoes, reserving their juice for another use. Chop the tomatoes and set them aside in a bowl.

Bring 1 cup of water to a boil over high heat in a small saucepan that has a tight-fitting lid. Add the rice, marjoram, ⅛ teaspoon of the salt, and a few grinds of pepper. Cover, reduce the heat to very low, and cook 20 minutes. Turn off the heat and leave the lid in place for at least 5 minutes.

---

*You may substitute 3 pounds fresh pear tomatoes—blanched, peeled, and seeded—for the canned variety. See the directions on page 28.

*Entrées from the Oven*

While the rice is cooking place the oil in a sauté pan or skillet over medium heat. Add the onion and garlic and sauté for 3 to 4 minutes, until the onion is translucent. Add the tomatoes and the remaining ⅛ teaspoon salt and a few grinds of pepper and cook for 20 to 25 minutes, stirring frequently, until the sauce becomes quite thick and has reduced by about half. Remove from the heat and set aside.

Meanwhile, arrange the whole cabbage leaves on a steamer rack inside a large pot and place about 2 inches of water into the pot. Cover and steam over medium-high heat for 15 to 20 minutes, until the leaves are tender enough to be flexible but still have a lot of body. Immediately submerge them in cold water to stop the cooking, then drain them well in a colander and set them aside.

Preheat the oven to 350 degrees F. When the rice is cooked, transfer it to a bowl and stir in the cheese. Spoon one-twelfth of the filling (about 2 tablespoons) onto the lower portion of each cabbage leaf. Fold the bottom one-third of the thick stem end of the leaf over the filling. Fold in the sides, then roll the leaf up. Repeat with the remaining leaves.

Spoon half of the sauce evenly into a 9×11-inch baking dish. Arrange the cabbage rolls on top, then top the rolls with the remaining sauce. Cover the dish and bake for 20 minutes. Serve immediately.

---

Each serving provides:

| | | | |
|---|---|---|---|
| 186 | Calories | 22 g | Carbohydrate |
| 7 g | Protein | 573 mg | Sodium |
| 8 g | Fat | 14 mg | Cholesterol |
| 2 g | Dietary Fiber | | |

# Pastry Crust

*This versatile pastry crust can be used for either savory or sweet pies. A few tries will convince you that there is nothing difficult about making pie crust from scratch, and then you're on your way to becoming a master pastry maker.*

*Yield:* 2 9-inch or 10-inch crusts

| | | |
|---|---|---|
| **Unbleached white flour** | **1½** | **cups** |
| **Whole wheat pastry flour** | **½** | **cup** |
| **Salt** | **½** | **teaspoon** |
| **Unsalted butter (cold)** | **½** | **cup (1 stick)** |
| **Ice water** | **3 to 4 tablespoons** | |

Sift the flours and salt together in a bowl. Cut the butter into small cubes and add the pieces to the flour. Use a pastry cutter or 2 knives to cut the butter into the flour until the mixture has the texture of coarse crumbs. (You may also do this with your hands, rubbing the butter into the flour.) Add 3 tablespoons of the water, using your fingers to incorporate it. Gather the mixture into a ball, sprinkling on additional water about a teaspoon at a time, if necessary, to make all the dry ingredients adhere. You do not want a sticky dough, so add no more water than is necessary.

Cover one of the dough balls with waxed paper, flatten it with your palm into a thick circle, and let it rest 30 minutes in the refrigerator before rolling it out. If you are making only one pie at present, wrap the extra dough ball in plastic wrap and freeze it for future use. (Defrost frozen dough in the refrigerator for several hours before rolling it out.)

Remove the dough from the refrigerator and allow it to rest at room temperature for 20 minutes before rolling it out with a rolling pin. Roll it out with firm strokes, applying even pressure, to a circle about ⅛ inch thick. Fold the circle into quarters and lay the dough into the pie or quiche pan with the corner in the approximate center of the pan. Unfold the dough to cover the pan, then gently press it into place, conforming to the shape of the pan, and allowing an overhang of about 1 inch. Fold the overhanging dough under and crimp the edge, then proceed as directed in individual recipes.

---

Each crust provides:

| | | | |
|---|---|---|---|
| 146 | Calories | 16 g | Carbohydrate |
| 2 g | Protein | 91 mg | Sodium |
| 8 g | Fat | 22 mg | Cholesterol |
| 1 g | Dietary Fiber | | |

# Asparagus and Pimiento Pie
## with Goat Cheese and Mustard

*Savory pies are served frequently in many parts of the Mediterranean region. Fillings are created from whatever is on hand or from ingredients purchased at the morning market. This delicious version is a salute to Spring.*

*Yield:* 6 main-course servings

| | |
|---|---|
| Pastry crust | 1 9-inch or 10-inch crust |
| Fresh asparagus | 1 pound |
| Dry white wine | ⅓ cup plus 1 tablespoon |
| Pimiento, diced | 1 2-ounce jar, drained |
| Garlic | 1 clove, minced |
| Soft goat cheese (chèvre) | 3 ounces |
| Dijon mustard | 1 tablespoon |
| Eggs | 3 large, lightly beaten |
| Freshly grated nutmeg | ¼ teaspoon |
| Salt | ¼ teaspoon |
| Black pepper | Several grinds |

Preheat the oven to 375 degrees F. Prepare a pastry crust according to the directions on page 216, using a 9-inch, high-walled pie or quiche pan. (You may substitute a commercially prepared ready-to-bake crust, if you wish.) Gently line the pan with the crust, allowing an overhang of about 1 inch. Fold the overhanging dough under and crimp the edge.

Pierce the bottom of the crust with a fork in several places. Lay a sheet of foil inside the crust and conform its shape to that of the dish. The foil should cover the crimped edge of the crust. Place about 1 cup of dried beans (or commercial baking weights) in the dish to prevent the bottom of the crust from ballooning. Bake for 10 minutes, then allow to cool slightly before removing the foil and beans, which can be saved for your next pastry crust. Set the crust aside.

Rinse the asparagus to remove any grit caught in the tips, and pat it dry. Snap off and discard the tough ends, then cut the spears diagonally into 1-inch-long pieces. Place them in a sauté pan or skillet with ⅓ cup of the wine, the pimiento, and garlic and bring to a simmer over high heat. Simmer 5 minutes, stirring frequently. The pan should be nearly dry. Remove from the heat.

In a medium bowl, mash together the goat cheese and mustard. Whisk in the eggs, nutmeg, salt, pepper, and remaining 1 tablespoon wine until smooth and well combined. Stir the asparagus mixture into the cheese mixture and transfer it to the prebaked crust. Bake for 30 to 35 minutes, until the crust is golden and the filling is set. Set aside to cool for 10 to 15 minutes before slicing into wedges. Serve warm or at room temperature.

---

Each serving provides:

| | | | |
|---|---|---|---|
| 243 | Calories | 19 g | Carbohydrate |
| 10 g | Protein | 339 mg | Sodium |
| 15 g | Fat | 135 mg | Cholesterol |
| 1 g | Dietary Fiber | | |

# Caramelized Onion Quiche

*Pissaladière is a traditional Provençal onion pizza. In this twist on the standard theme, we have caramelized the onions to develop their sweetness and combined them with eggs to create a quiche. Serve this with a glass of merlot and picture yourself dining in the south of France.*

*Yield:* 6 main-course servings

| | |
|---|---|
| **Pastry crust** | 1  **9-inch or 10-inch crust** |
| **Yellow onions** | 3  **pounds** |
| **Olive oil** | 2  **tablespoons** |
| **Brandy** | 2  **tablespoons** |
| **Dried thyme** | 1  **teaspoon** |
| **Salt** | ¼ **teaspoon** |
| **Eggs** | 4  **large** |
| **Lowfat milk** | 1  **cup** |

Preheat the oven to 400 degrees F. Prepare a pastry crust according to the directions on page 216, using a 9-inch, high-walled pie or quiche pan. (You may substitute a commercially prepared ready-to-bake crust, if you wish.) Gently line the pan with the crust, allowing an overhang of about 1 inch. Fold the overhanging dough under and crimp the edge.

Pierce the bottom of the crust with a fork in several places. Lay a sheet of foil inside the crust and conform its shape to that of the dish. The foil should cover the crimped edge of the crust. Place about 1 cup of dried beans (or commercial baking weights) in the dish to prevent the bottom of the crust from ballooning. Bake for 10 minutes, then allow to cool slightly before removing the foil and beans, which can be saved for your next pastry crust. Set the crust aside and reduce the oven temperature to 375 degrees F.

Meanwhile, peel the onions and thinly slice them. Heat the oil in a very large skillet over medium heat. Add the onions, reduce the heat to medium-low, and sauté, stirring frequently, for 35 to 40 minutes, until the onions are very soft and nicely browned. Add the brandy, thyme, and salt and cook for 5 additional minutes, stirring frequently.

Place the eggs in a medium bowl and whisk them until they are light. Whisk in the milk, then stir in the onions. Pour this evenly into the partially baked crust and bake for 40 minutes. Remove from the oven and allow to cool at least 10 minutes before serving. Serve warm or at room temperature.

---

Each serving provides:

| | | | |
|---|---|---|---|
| 358 | Calories | 38 g | Carbohydrate |
| 11 g | Protein | 297 mg | Sodium |
| 18 g | Fat | 169 mg | Cholesterol |
| 4 g | Dietary Fiber | | |

# Poached Eggs with
# Dill Yogurt Sauce

*Eggs play an important role in the cuisines of many countries. In the Turkish diet they are often enjoyed for lunch or as an appetizer before dinner. We also enjoy this delicious preparation as a brunch entrée.*

*Yield:* 4 main-course servings

| | |
|---|---|
| **Plain nonfat yogurt** | 1 **cup** |
| **Garlic** | 1 **clove, minced** |
| **Whole wheat pita bread** | 4 **rounds** |
| **White vinegar** | 1 **tablespoon** |
| **Eggs** | 4 **large** |
| **Unsalted butter** | 1 **tablespoon** |
| **Fresh dill, minced** | 1 **tablespoon** |
| **Paprika** | ½ **teaspoon** |

Preheat the oven to 300 degrees F. In a small bowl, stir together the yogurt and garlic. Spoon equal amounts into four 3-inch ramekins and place them in the oven to warm while you poach the eggs. Wrap the pita bread in foil and place it in the oven to warm.

Place several inches of water in a nonreactive sauté pan or skillet (such as stainless steel) and bring it to a boil over high heat. Reduce the heat to medium-high and add the vinegar. Crack the eggs one at a time and gently slide them into the simmering water. Poach the eggs for 3 to 4 minutes, spooning hot water over the tops, until the yolks are barely set. Carefully remove the eggs from the water with a slotted spoon and drain carefully.

Place a poached egg atop the yogurt in each ramekin and return the ramekins to the oven, turning off the heat. Melt the butter in a small pan and add the dill and paprika. Cook for about a minute then evenly distribute over the eggs. Serve immediately, accompanied with the warmed pita bread.

---

Each serving provides:

| | | | |
|---|---|---|---|
| 276 | Calories | 29 g | Carbohydrate |
| 16 g | Protein | 372 mg | Sodium |
| 10 g | Fat | 222 mg | Cholesterol |
| 3 g | Dietary Fiber | | |

# Mushroom and Corn Soufflé with Tomato Coulis

*A soufflé always makes a magnificent presentation, and this one looks particularly pretty served atop the deep red tomato sauce. It will start a dinner party for six with panache, or you may serve it as a main course for four, with the addition of a substantial vegetable dish, bread, and a salad.*

*Yield:* 6 first-course servings

### The soufflé

| | | |
|---|---|---|
| Whole eggs | 5 | large |
| Unsalted butter | 2 | tablespoons plus ½ teaspoon |
| Button mushrooms | ½ | pound |
| Shallot | 1 | medium |
| Salt | ½ | teaspoon |
| Dry white wine | ⅓ | cup |
| Fresh or frozen corn kernels* | 1 | cup |
| Dried tarragon | 1 | teaspoon |
| Dried thyme | ¼ | teaspoon |
| Unbleached white flour | 3 | tablespoons |
| Lowfat milk | 1½ | cups |
| Parmesan cheese, finely grated | ¼ | cup |

*If using fresh corn, you will need about 2 medium ears to yield 1 cup corn kernels.

### The sauce

| | | |
|---|---|---|
| Whole pear tomatoes** | 1 | 28-ounce can |
| Shallots | 2 | medium |
| Dry white wine | ⅓ | cup |
| Salt | ¼ | teaspoon |
| Black pepper | Several grinds | |
| Capers, drained and minced | 2 | teaspoons |
| Dried tarragon | 1 | teaspoon |

A few hours ahead of time, carefully separate the eggs, reserving 3 of the yolks for another use. (They will stay fresh for a day or two in a tightly covered container in the refrigerator.) Hold the 2 egg yolks you will need for the soufflé in a small covered dish in the refrigerator, and leave the whites out in a covered bowl to come to room temperature. Make sure no egg yolk has dripped into the egg whites; even a drop will prevent the whites from whipping properly.

An hour before dinnertime, preheat the oven to 375 degrees F. Use ½ teaspoon of the butter to rub down a 2-quart soufflé or gratin dish and set it aside. Wipe or brush the mushrooms clean and coarsely chop them. Peel and mince the shallot. Place the mushrooms and shallot in a sauté pan or skillet with the salt and the wine and bring to a simmer over medium heat. Stir and cook 3 minutes, then add the corn, tarragon, and thyme and cook about 5 minutes, until the vegetables are tender and most of the liquid has evaporated. Set this mixture aside in a large bowl.

In a large, heavy-bottomed saucepan, melt the remaining 2 tablespoons butter over medium-low heat until it foams, then

---

**You may substitute 3 pounds fresh pear tomatoes—blanched, peeled, and seeded—for the canned variety. See the directions on page 28.

stir in the flour. Cook for 1 minute to slightly brown the flour, then slowly whisk in the milk. Cook for about 7 minutes, stirring frequently with a wooden spoon, until the sauce is well thickened. Stir in the Parmesan, then remove the saucepan from the heat and beat in the egg yolks one at a time. Add the white sauce to the mushroom mixture in the bowl and stir to combine well.

In a large bowl, beat the egg whites with a wire whisk until soft peaks form, then stir briskly with a wooden spoon for a few strokes to set the whites. Do not overbeat; you do not want the whites to dry out. Gently fold half the egg whites into the mushroom mixture. When incorporated, fold in the remaining egg whites. Carefully transfer the mixture to the buttered dish and bake for 30 to 35 minutes, until it rises and is medium brown on the top.

Meanwhile, make the sauce. Drain the juice from the canned tomatoes, reserving it for another use. Finely chop the tomatoes and place them in a medium saucepan. Peel and thinly slice the shallots. Add the shallots, wine, salt, and pepper to the tomatoes. Bring to a simmer over medium heat and cook 10 minutes, stirring frequently. Add the capers and tarragon, reduce the heat to low, and cook 5 to 10 minutes, until the tomatoes cook down to a medium-thick sauce consistency.

Place the hot sauce in a warmed sauce boat or bowl with ladle and take it to the table. Transfer the soufflé to the table after your guests are seated, setting it down carefully so it does not collapse. Place a portion of the sauce on the bottom of each warmed plate and serve a portion of the soufflé on top of the sauce.

---

Each serving provides:

| 195 | Calories | 19 g | Carbohydrate |
| 11 g | Protein | 647 mg | Sodium |
| 9 g | Fat | 89 mg | Cholesterol |
| 2 g | Dietary Fiber | | |

*Entrées from the Oven*

# Hot Vegetable Dishes

Outdoor markets are a trademark of the Mediterranean, from the largest city to the smallest village, and the vegetables from these markets are an important part of the diet. Many cooks shop on an almost daily basis and build meals around the most succulent and inviting seasonal ingredients available at market stalls.

Fresh and dried herbs, fruity olive oil, aged cheeses, garlic and its relatives—these are some of the pantry staples that are used by Mediterranean cooks to create an infinite variety of delicious hot vegetable dishes. A drizzle of the best olive oil, a squeeze of fresh lemon, and a pinch of salt and pepper will turn plain cooked vegetables into something extraordinary.

Beyond this most simple approach is a wide variety of techniques and seasonings employed in the Mediterranean to make delicious use of the region's abundant produce. This chapter provides a sampling of our favorites.

## Tips and Tools

- Most vegetables taste best when cooked to the al dente stage, retaining some firmness but easily pierced with a fork. Overcooking renders them unappetizing, so test frequently and serve vegetables when they are barely tender for best results.

- A collapsible steaming tray, made of perforated stainless steel, is a valuable aid in vegetable cooking. You will also need a large saucepan with a tight-fitting lid for vegetable steaming.

- Sauté pans or skillets in a variety of sizes are frequently used in vegetable cookery. For braising, one with a tight-fitting lid is required.

# Garlic Sautéed Arugula

*ALMOST INSTANT, VEGAN*

*The peppery flavor of arugula makes it delicious in cold salad preparations as well as sautéed, as described here. It makes a wonderful side dish for a pasta or risotto or with the Cannellini Beans with Grilled Portobello Mushrooms (page 292).*

*Yield:* 4 side-dish servings

| | |
|---|---|
| **Fresh arugula** | **1 pound** |
| **Olive oil** | **1 tablespoon** |
| **Garlic** | **2 cloves, minced** |

Carefully wash the arugula, discarding the thickest part of the stems. Spin or pat the arugula dry and coarsely chop it. Heat the oil over medium heat in a sauté pan or skillet and add the garlic. Cook for about 30 seconds, then stir in the arugula and 2 tablespoons of water. Cover the pan and cook for 6 to 8 minutes, until the arugula wilts. Serve hot.

---

Each serving provides:

| 54 | Calories | 5 g | Carbohydrate |
|---|---|---|---|
| 3 g | Protein | 35 mg | Sodium |
| 4 g | Fat | 0 mg | Cholesterol |
| 3 g | Dietary Fiber | | |

# Artichokes Braised
# with Parsley and Lemon

*VEGAN*

*This mouth-watering recipe works best with medium-size artichokes. The preparation might seem wasteful, as the outer leaves of the artichokes are removed before cooking and only the tender inner leaves and bottoms are used in the recipe. However, the outer leaves may be steamed separately and eaten in the conventional way with mayonnaise.*

*Yield:* 8 side-dish servings

| | |
|---|---|
| **Lemon juice or vinegar** | **6 tablespoons** |
| **Artichokes** | **2 pounds** |
| | **(4 medium)** |
| **Olive oil** | **3 tablespoons** |
| **Fresh-squeezed lemon juice** | **⅓ cup** |
| **Garlic** | **5 cloves, minced** |
| **Dried red chili flakes** | **¼ teaspoon** |
| **Salt** | **¼ teaspoon** |
| **Black pepper** | **Several grinds** |
| **Fresh Italian parsley, minced** | **½ cup** |

Prepare acidulated water in a large bowl by combining 2 quarts of cold water with 6 tablespoons of lemon juice or vinegar. Set aside near your work surface.

Trim the artichokes, working with 1 artichoke at a time. Use your hands to snap off all the tough outer leaves until you get down to the pale leaves at the center. Set the leaves you have removed aside for another use, or discard them.

Use a sharp knife to cut off the leaf tips, leaving only the base of the yellowish green leaves attached to the artichoke bottom. Cut off ¼ inch of the stem end, then peel the stem and the bottom of each artichoke. Drop the artichoke into the acidulated water when you are finished trimming it. Proceed until you have trimmed all the artichokes in this manner, and they are all in the water.

Remove the artichoke hearts from the water one at a time and quarter them from stem to top. Use a paring knife or melon baller to scrape out the fuzzy "choke" portion. Finally, slice each quarter lengthwise into thirds or fourths, depending on their size. You want wedges about ¼-inch thick. As you go, drop the artichoke pieces back into the acidulated water.

Heat the oil over medium heat in a large sauté pan or skillet that has a tight-fitting lid. Add ½ cup of fresh water, the lemon juice, garlic, chili flakes, salt, and pepper. Remove the artichoke pieces from the acidulated water and drain them briefly on a clean tea towel. Add them to the pan, toss to coat, cover, and cook 15 to 20 minutes, until barely fork-tender, stirring once at the halfway point. Remove the lid to check the artichokes frequently toward the end of the cooking time, as the liquid will almost be cooked away. If the liquid evaporates before the artichokes are done, add a tablespoon of water as needed and continue to cook. When the artichokes are fork-tender, remove from the heat, toss with the parsley, and transfer to a serving dish. Serve hot or at room temperature.

---

Each serving provides:

| | | | |
|---|---|---|---|
| 109 | Calories | 15 g | Carbohydrate |
| 4 g | Protein | 177 mg | Sodium |
| 5 g | Fat | 0 mg | Cholesterol |
| 6 g | Dietary Fiber | | |

# Braised Green Tomatoes with Basil Sauce

*ALMOST INSTANT, VEGAN*

*The peppery taste of the basil, along with the tang of the vinegar, turns the simple green tomato into a delicious side dish.*

*Yield:* 6 side-dish servings

| | |
|---|---|
| **Green tomatoes** | 1  **pound** |
| **Dry sherry** | 2  **tablespoons** |
| **Extra virgin olive oil** | 2  **tablespoons** |
| **White wine vinegar** | 1  **tablespoon** |
| **Fresh basil leaves, chiffonade**° | ½ **cup** |
| **Garlic** | 2  **cloves, minced** |
| **Salt** | ⅛ **teaspoon** |
| **Black pepper** | **Several grinds** |

Cut out and discard the stem ends of the tomatoes and cut them crosswise into ¼-inch slices. Place ¼ cup of water and the sherry in a sauté pan or skillet that has a tight-fitting lid. Add the tomato slices, cover the pan, and cook over medium heat 10 to 12 minutes, until the tomatoes are tender and most of the water has evaporated.

°Chiffonade is the French term for a particular method of preparing fresh herbs. Stack the herb leaves on top of each other and roll slightly so you can hold them tightly in place, then use a sharp knife to slice the stack crosswise into paper-thin shreds.

Meanwhile, place the oil, vinegar, basil, garlic, salt, and pepper in a small skillet. Cook over medium heat for 2 to 3 minutes, until the basil wilts. Place the tomatoes in a serving dish and top with the basil sauce. Serve immediately.

---

Each serving provides:

| | | | |
|---|---|---|---|
| 62 | Calories | 5 g | Carbohydrate |
| 1 g | Protein | 54 mg | Sodium |
| 5 g | Fat | 0 mg | Cholesterol |
| 1 g | Dietary Fiber | | |

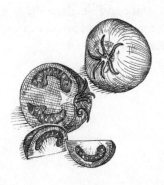

# Spicy Braised Broccoli

*ALMOST INSTANT, VEGAN*

*There are so many ways to enjoy broccoli, and this simple preparation is sure to please.*

*Yield:* 6 side-dish servings

| | | |
|---|---|---|
| **Broccoli** | 1¼ | **pounds** |
| **Fresh tomatoes** | ½ | **pound** |
| | | **(1 medium)** |
| **Olive oil** | 1 | **tablespoon** |
| **Garlic** | 2 | **cloves, minced** |
| **Dried red chili flakes** | ¼ | **teaspoon** |
| **Madeira** | ¼ | **cup** |
| **Salt** | ¼ | **teaspoon** |
| **Lemon zest** | 2 | **teaspoons** |

Trim off and discard the tough stem ends of the broccoli. Peel the remaining stalks if they are particularly thick-skinned. Coarsely chop the stalk and heads. Set aside. Remove and discard the stems from the tomatoes and coarsely chop them, retaining their juice. Set aside.

Put the oil in a heavy-bottomed sauté pan or skillet over medium heat and add the garlic and chili flakes. Sauté for about 1 minute, then add the Madeira, salt, and ¼ cup water. Stir in the broccoli and tomatoes, then cover the pan. Cook for 12 to 14 minutes, until the broccoli is fork-tender. Transfer to a bowl and garnish with the lemon zest. Serve immediately, passing Parmesan cheese, if desired.

---

Each serving provides:

| | | | |
|---|---|---|---|
| 55 | Calories | 7 g | Carbohydrate |
| 3 g | Protein | 115 mg | Sodium |
| 3 g | Fat | 0 mg | Cholesterol |
| 3 g | Dietary Fiber | | |

# Green Beans and Carrots Braised in Wine

*ALMOST INSTANT, VEGAN*

*This simple vegetable side dish is a classic. Once you have mastered the braising technique described here, you can cook any of your favorite vegetables this way.*

*Yield:* 6 side-dish servings

| | |
|---|---|
| **Fresh green beans** | **¾ pound** |
| **Carrots** | **½ pound** |
| **White onion** | **½ medium** |
| **Olive oil** | **1 tablespoon** |
| **Salt** | **¼ teaspoon** |
| **Black pepper** | **Several grinds** |
| **Dry white wine** | **⅔ cup** |
| **Fresh Italian parsley, minced** | **2 tablespoons** |

Pinch off and discard the stems ends of the beans and string them, if necessary. Peel the carrots and cut them into ¼-inch sticks approximately the same length as the beans. Cut the onion half into ¼-inch slices.

Heat the oil over medium heat in a heavy-bottomed sauté pan or skillet that has a tight-fitting lid. Add the beans, carrots, onion, salt, and pepper and stir and sauté about 7 minutes, until the vegetables are browning just a bit.

Holding the lid of the pan in one hand, pour in the wine and immediately cover the pan. Cook 5 minutes, then remove the lid and stir. Replace the lid and cook 5 minutes longer, then remove the lid. Leave the pan uncovered and continue to cook, stirring frequently, until almost all the liquid has evaporated, leaving only a few tablespoons of thick sauce on the vegetables. Transfer to a pretty serving dish and sprinkle with the parsley. Serve hot.

---

Each serving provides:

| | | | |
|---|---|---|---|
| 82 | Calories | 1 g | Carbohydrate |
| 3 g | Protein | 107 mg | Sodium |
| 3 g | Fat | 0 mg | Cholesterol |
| 3 g | Dietary Fiber | | |

# Fresh Peas and Shallots
# with Provençal Herbs

*ALMOST INSTANT*

*There is nothing quite like freshly harvested garden peas, especially when cooked with butter, shallots, and herbs. You will need to buy about 2 pounds of plump pea pods to yield 2½ cups shelled peas. This dish is a sure-fire way to evoke the mood of southern France.*

*Yield:* 4 side-dish servings

| | | |
|---|---|---|
| **Shallots** | 3 | **medium** |
| **Unsalted butter** | 1 | **tablespoon** |
| **Fresh shelled peas** | 2½ | **cups** |
| **Herbes de Provence (page 38)** | 1 | **teaspoon** |
| **Salt** | ¼ | **teaspoon** |
| **Black pepper** | **Several grinds** | |
| **Dry white wine** | ½ | **cup** |
| **Heavy cream** | 2 | **tablespoons** |
| **Freshly grated nutmeg** | ¼ | **teaspoon** |

Peel and thinly slice the shallots. In a heavy-bottomed skillet or sauté pan with a tight-fitting lid, melt the butter over medium heat and sauté the shallots 3 to 4 minutes, until they are beginning to brown slightly. Add the peas, herbes de Provence, salt, and pepper and stir.

Holding the lid to the pan in one hand, pour in the wine and immediately cover the pan. Reduce the heat to low and cook the peas for 6 minutes. Stir the peas, then replace the lid and cook an additional 6 minutes. Remove the lid and add the cream to the skillet. Stir and cook, uncovered, 4 to 6 minutes longer, until the liquid has reduced to a thick sauce and the peas are tender, but not at all mushy. You may add another tablespoon or two of wine, if necessary, to prevent the pan from going dry. Transfer the peas to a warmed serving dish, top with nutmeg, and serve very hot.

---

Each serving provides:

| | | | |
|---|---|---|---|
| 155 | Calories | 19 g | Carbohydrate |
| 6 g | Protein | 141 mg | Sodium |
| 6 g | Fat | 19 mg | Cholesterol |
| 3 g | Dietary Fiber | | |

# Potatoes with Parsley Paprika Sauce

*ALMOST INSTANT, VEGAN*

*Potatoes are loved the world over. They were introduced to Spain from South America in the sixteenth century and became a staple of the Spanish diet. In the Castilian region of Spain they are often enjoyed this way.*

*Yield:* 4 side-dish servings

| | | |
|---|---|---|
| **Russet potatoes** | **1½** | **pounds (3 large)** |
| **Olive oil** | **2** | **tablespoons** |
| **White onion, minced** | **½** | **cup** |
| **Garlic** | **3** | **cloves, minced** |
| **Unbleached white flour** | **1** | **tablespoon** |
| **Paprika** | **1** | **teaspoon** |
| **Salt** | **1** | **teaspoon** |
| **Fresh Italian parsley, minced** | **¼** | **cup** |
| **Whole bay leaf** | **1** | **large** |

Scrub the potatoes and, without peeling them, cut them into ½-inch cubes. Set them aside.

Place the oil in a heavy-bottomed sauté pan or skillet over medium heat. Add the onion and garlic and sauté for a minute or two, then stir in the potatoes. Sprinkle the flour, paprika, and salt evenly over the potatoes and stir to coat. Add the parsley, bay leaf, and enough hot water to barely submerge the potatoes. Cover the pan and cook until the potatoes are tender, about 20 minutes. Remove the lid to check the potatoes frequently during the last few minutes of cooking, as most of the liquid will be absorbed and you do not want to burn the potatoes. If too much liquid remains when the potatoes are tender, remove the lid, increase the heat to medium-high and continue to cook for a few minutes, stirring occasionally, to reduce the liquid to a thick sauce consistency. Serve immediately.

---

Each serving provides:

| | | | |
|---|---|---|---|
| 265 | Calories | 48 g | Carbohydrate |
| 5 g | Protein | 548 mg | Sodium |
| 7 g | Fat | 0 mg | Cholesterol |
| 3 g | Dietary Fiber | | |

# Steamed Cauliflower
# with Garlic Paprika Sauce

*ALMOST INSTANT, VEGAN*

*This simple sauce is the perfect complement to the strong flavor of cauliflower, and its bright red color is brilliant on the snowy white vegetable.*

*Yield:* 4 side-dish servings

| | | |
|---|---|---|
| **Cauliflower** | 1½ | **pounds** |
| **Garlic** | 3 | **cloves, minced** |
| **Fresh Italian parsley, minced** | 3 | **tablespoons** |
| **Salt** | ½ | **teaspoon** |
| **Olive oil** | 2 | **tablespoons** |
| **Red wine vinegar** | 1 | **tablespoon** |
| **Paprika** | 2 | **teaspoons** |

Trim the outer leaves and core from the cauliflower, then separate it into florets. Place the cauliflower on a steamer rack in a saucepan with a tight-fitting lid. Add about an inch of water, cover, and cook over medium-high heat 10 to 12 minutes, until the cauliflower is fork-tender.

Meanwhile, combine the garlic, parsley, and salt in a blender and puree. With the motor running, add the oil in a slow, steady stream. Add the vinegar and paprika along with

2 tablespoons of water and puree once again. Transfer the sauce to a small pan and simmer over low heat for about 2 minutes. Place the hot cauliflower in a warm serving dish and pour the sauce evenly over it. Serve immediately.

---

Each serving provides:

| | | | |
|---|---|---|---|
| 102 | Calories | 9 g | Carbohydrate |
| 3 g | Protein | 289 mg | Sodium |
| 7 g | Fat | 0 mg | Cholesterol |
| 4 g | Dietary Fiber | | |

# Mustard Glazed Carrots

*ALMOST INSTANT*

*Any carrots will do for this side dish, but garden-fresh "baby" carrots, purchased with their tops still attached, lend themselves best to this preparation. If you will be waiting a couple of days before cooking the carrots, remove their greens before wrapping them in plastic and storing them in the refrigerator. If left attached, the greens will continue to draw nutrients and sweetness from the carrots.*

*Yield:* 4 side-dish servings

| | |
|---|---|
| **Small carrots** | **1 pound** |
| **Dijon mustard** | **2 tablespoons** |
| **Honey** | **1 tablespoon** |
| **Unsalted butter** | **1 tablespoon** |
| **Fresh-squeezed lemon juice** | **3 tablespoons** |
| **Dried sage, crumbled** | **1 teaspoon** |
| **Salt** | **⅛ teaspoon** |

Clip the tops from the carrots, leaving about ½-inch of the green stems attached for added color. Scrub the carrots, but do not peel them.

Combine the mustard, honey, butter, lemon juice, sage, and salt in a small saucepan. Cook over very low heat about 12 minutes, stirring frequently. When a thick sauce develops, remove it from the heat, and set it aside in a warm place.

Meanwhile, place the whole carrots on a steamer rack in a saucepan that has a tight-fitting lid and add an inch or two of cold water to the pan. Cover and cook over medium-high heat for 6 to 12 minutes, depending on the size of the carrots, until they are just fork-tender. Be careful not to overcook them.

Remove the carrots from the steamer rack and transfer them to a warmed serving dish. Add the hot sauce and gently turn the carrots to coat them well, reheating over low heat if necessary.

---

Each serving provides:

| 77 | Calories | 11 g | Carbohydrate |
|---|---|---|---|
| 1 g | Protein | 187 mg | Sodium |
| 4 g | Fat | 8 mg | Cholesterol |
| 2 g | Dietary Fiber | | |

# Asparagus with Watercress and Green Onion Sauce

*ALMOST INSTANT*

*Asparagus and watercress both appear in the spring. This dish combines them beautifully. We enjoy fresh asparagus as often as we can during its short season.*

*Yield:* 8 side-dish servings

| | |
|---|---|
| **Egg** | **1 medium** |
| **Fresh asparagus** | **2 pounds** |
| **Watercress leaves** | **½ cup** |
| **Fresh-squeezed lemon juice** | **2 tablespoons** |
| **Salt** | **⅛ teaspoon** |
| **Black pepper** | **Several grinds** |
| **Green onions** | **2, chopped** |
| **Olive oil** | **3 tablespoons** |

Put the eggs into a pan and cover with cold water. Bring to a boil over medium-high heat, then reduce the heat to medium and boil 10 minutes. Immediately transfer the eggs to a bowl of ice water to cool for 10 minutes. Peel, finely chop, and set aside.

Meanwhile, wash the asparagus carefully to remove any traces of soil. Snap off the tough ends. Place on a steamer rack in a pan with a tight-fitting lid. Add 2 inches of water to the pan and cook over medium-high heat until just fork-tender, about 6 minutes, depending on the thickness of the stems. Be careful not to overcook—when in doubt, it is better to err on the undercooked side.

Combine the oil, lemon juice, salt, and pepper in a small bowl. Place the watercress and onions in a blender. Switch on the low setting and add the oil and lemon juice mixture in a slow, steady stream. The resulting sauce will be a bright springtime green. Arrange the cooked asparagus on a serving platter and top with the sauce. Sprinkle on the chopped egg and serve hot or at room temperature.

---

Each serving provides:

| 75 | Calories | 4 g | Carbohydrate |
|----|----------|-----|--------------|
| 3 g | Protein | 52 mg | Sodium |
| 6 g | Fat | 28 mg | Cholesterol |
| 1 g | Dietary Fiber | | |

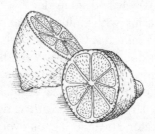

# Chard with Raisins and Pine Nuts

*ALMOST INSTANT, VEGAN*

*This Catalan-inspired dish can also be made with spring's first collard greens, with equally delicious results.*

*Yield:* 4 side-dish servings

| | |
|---|---|
| **Pine nuts** | 2 **tablespoons** |
| **Golden raisins** | 2 **tablespoons** |
| **Swiss chard** | 1½ **pounds** |
| **Olive oil** | 1 **tablespoon** |
| **Garlic** | 2 **cloves, minced** |
| **White onion, minced** | 2 **tablespoons** |
| **Salt** | ¼ **teaspoon** |
| **Black pepper** | **Several grinds** |

Place the pine nuts in a dry, heavy-bottomed skillet in a single layer over medium heat. Stir or shake the pan frequently until the nuts are lightly browned. Immediately remove them from the pan and set aside. When they have cooled for a few minutes, chop them coarsely and set aside.

Cover the raisins with boiling water and allow them to plump for at least 5 minutes. Carefully wash the chard, separating the stalks from the leaves. Discard the thick, tough ends of the stalks and thinly slice the remaining stalks crosswise. Set aside. Coarsely chop the green leaves. Place the stalks on a steamer rack in a large stockpot with a tight-fitting lid. Add about an inch of water, cover, and cook over medium-high heat 5 minutes. Add the chopped leaves to the steamer tray and continue to cook for about 3 minutes, until the leaves just wilt. Drain the chard thoroughly and set aside. Drain the raisins.

Heat the oil over medium heat in a sauté pan or skillet. Add the garlic and onion and sauté for about 3 minutes, until the onion is barely translucent. Add the chard and raisins to the skillet, along with the salt and pepper. Cook for 2 to 3 minutes, then transfer to a warmed serving dish. Top evenly with the pine nuts and serve very hot.

---

Each serving provides:

| 96 | Calories | 11 g | Carbohydrate |
|---|---|---|---|
| 4 g | Protein | 438 mg | Sodium |
| 6 g | Fat | 0 mg | Cholesterol |
| 2 g | Dietary Fiber | | |

# Okra with Olives, Tomatoes, Herbs, and Lemon

*VEGAN*

*Okra is unappreciated in much of the world. In Greece, however, it is in favor and cooks have many ways of preparing it. We invented this succulent stewed okra dish in the spirit of Greek cooking. As befits a rustic dish, the olives are added whole. To avoid any unpleasant surprises, let your diners know that the pits are there. You may also serve it as a main course for four, along with a favorite grain side dish such as the Toasted Vermicelli and Rice Pilaf (page 266), crusty bread, and a tart, leafy salad.*

*Yield:* 6 side-dish servings

| | |
|---|---|
| **Whole pear tomatoes*** | 1  28-ounce can |
| **Fresh okra** | 1  pound |
| **Olive oil** | 1  tablespoon |
| **White onion** | 1  medium, diced |
| **Dried red chili flakes** | ½ teaspoon |
| **Garlic** | 4  cloves, minced |
| **Dried oregano** | 1  teaspoon |
| **Dried thyme** | ½ teaspoon |
| **Dried rosemary** | ½ teaspoon |
| **Salt** | ¼ teaspoon |
| **Oil-cured black olives, unpitted** | 1  cup |
| **Fresh lemon peel, minced** | ½ teaspoon |

*You may substitute 3 pounds fresh pear tomatoes—blanched, peeled, and seeded—for the canned variety. See the directions on page 28.

Drain the juice from the can of tomatoes and reserve it for another use. Coarsely chop the tomatoes and set them aside in a bowl. Rinse the okra pods and pat them dry with a tea towel. Use a paring knife to slice off most of the stem portion, leaving the base of the pods intact. Cut the okra pods in half crosswise at a slant and set them aside in a bowl or colander.

Heat the oil in a heavy-bottomed skillet over medium heat and sauté the onion and chili flakes for 5 minutes, stirring frequently. Add the tomatoes, garlic, oregano, thyme, rosemary, and salt, then stir in the okra. Bring to a simmer, reduce the heat to medium-low, cover, and cook 20 minutes. Remove the lid and stir in the whole olives and the lemon peel. Replace the lid and cook an additional 5 to 10 minutes, until the okra is very tender but not at all mushy. Serve hot.

---

Each serving provides:

| 162 | Calories | 17 g | Carbohydrate |
|---|---|---|---|
| 4 g | Protein | 1046 mg | Sodium |
| 11 g | Fat | 0 mg | Cholesterol |
| 2 g | Dietary Fiber | | |

# Potato and Cauliflower Puree with Goat Cheese and Fresh Oregano

*ALMOST INSTANT*

*This puree makes an elegant and delicious side dish, lighter in texture and more distinctive than simple mashed potatoes. For a formal dinner, you may pour the puree into individual buttered ramekins and broil them briefly to brown the tops; however, we usually simply mound it onto the dinner plate alongside any hearty vegetable and herb stir-fry.*

*Yield:* 6 side-dish servings

| | |
|---|---|
| **Cauliflower** | 1 **pound (1 small)** |
| **Garlic** | 6 **cloves** |
| **Russet potatoes** | 1½ **pounds (3 large)** |
| **Soft goat cheese (chèvre)** | 2 **ounces, cubed** |
| **Half-and-half** | 2 **tablespoons** |
| **Fresh oregano leaves, minced** | 2 **teaspoons** |
| **Freshly grated nutmeg** | ½ **teaspoon** |
| **Salt** | ½ **teaspoon** |
| **Black pepper** | **Several grinds** |

Bring a large pot of water to a boil for the vegetables. Trim off and discard the cauliflower leaves and the toughest part of the core and coarsely chop the head. Peel the garlic cloves but leave them whole. Peel the potatoes and dice them. (If the water is not yet boiling, place the diced potatoes in a bowl of cold water so they do not start to discolor.)

When the water is boiling, add the cauliflower, potatoes, and whole garlic cloves. Return to a boil and cook 15 to 20 minutes, until the cauliflower and potatoes are very tender but not falling apart. Reserve ⅓ cup of the cooking water, then drain the vegetables and place them in a food processor, along with the chèvre, half-and-half, oregano, nutmeg, salt, and pepper. Puree thoroughly, adding some or all of the reserved cooking water, as necessary, to achieve a perfectly smooth texture. Serve very hot.

---

Each serving provides:

| 150 | Calories | 27 g | Carbohydrate |
|---|---|---|---|
| 5 g | Protein | 230 mg | Sodium |
| 3 g | Fat | 6 mg | Cholesterol |
| 3 g | Dietary Fiber | | |

# Tarragon Creamed Mushrooms Au Gratin

*Mushrooms are widely enjoyed throughout Italy and in the south of France and are often picked wild. This recipe calls for easy-to-obtain button mushrooms and dried porcini mushrooms. You may prepare it several hours ahead of time and hold it in the refrigerator, but bring it to room temperature before baking it. We give instructions for using individual au gratin dishes, but you can also use one larger au gratin or casserole dish.*

*Yield:* 4 side-dish servings

| | |
|---|---|
| **Dried porcini mushrooms** | ½ ounce |
| **Unsalted butter** | 2 tablespoons plus 1 teaspoon |
| **Button mushrooms** | 1 pound |
| **Unbleached white flour** | 1 tablespoon |
| **Dried tarragon** | ½ teaspoon |
| **Heavy cream** | 2 tablespoons |
| **Salt** | ⅛ teaspoon |
| **Black pepper** | Several grinds |
| **Fresh-squeezed lemon juice** | 1 tablespoon |
| **Fine dry bread crumbs** | ¼ cup |

Place the porcini mushrooms in a bowl or saucepan and pour 1 cup of boiling water over them. Cover the bowl and set aside for 30 minutes.

Meanwhile, lightly rub four individual au gratin dishes or one larger dish with 1 teaspoon of the butter and set aside. Brush or wipe any visible dirt from the button mushrooms and quarter them to create wedges. Set aside.

Preheat the oven to 375 degrees F. Lift the porcini mushrooms out of their soaking liquid, reserving the liquid. Squeeze the mushrooms gently so their juice drips back into the soaking liquid. Finely dice the mushrooms and set them aside. Strain the soaking liquid through a paper coffee filter and set it aside.

Melt 1 tablespoon of the remaining butter over medium heat in a skillet. Before it browns, add the button and porcini mushrooms and stir to coat with butter. Sauté about 5 minutes, stirring occasionally, until the mushrooms begin to brown and release a little of their juice. Use a slotted spoon to transfer the mushrooms to the buttered dish(es).

Place the remaining 1 tablespoon butter in the skillet and melt over low heat. Add the flour and tarragon and stir with a wooden spoon or wire whisk to incorporate it into the butter. Cook about 30 seconds, stirring constantly, to brown the flour a little. Add about half the mushroom soaking liquid and whisk continuously until the sauce has begun to thicken, then whisk in the remaining liquid and the cream, salt, and pepper. Cook over medium heat, whisking frequently, until the sauce is thick, about 7 minutes. Remove from the heat and stir in the lemon juice.

Pour the sauce evenly over the mushrooms. Top evenly with the bread crumbs. Bake about 20 minutes, until the bread crumbs are lightly browned. Serve hot.

---

Each serving provides:

| | | | |
|---|---|---|---|
| 161 | Calories | 15 g | Carbohydrate |
| 4 g | Protein | 119 mg | Sodium |
| 11 g | Fat | 30 mg | Cholesterol |
| 2 g | Dietary Fiber | | |

# Sage Roasted Winter Vegetables

*VEGAN*

*Winter root vegetables are often overlooked, yet they offer unique flavors and are powerhouses of nutrition. This is an earthy and satisfying side dish.*

*Yield:* 6 side-dish servings

| | |
|---|---|
| **Red-skinned yam** | ¾ **pound** |
| **Parsnip** | ¾ **pound** |
| **Turnips** | ¾ **pound** |
| **Rutabagas** | ¾ **pound** |
| **Fennel bulb** | ¾ **pound** |
| **Olive oil** | ¼ **cup** |
| **Rubbed sage** | 2 **teaspoons, crushed** |
| **Salt** | 1 **teaspoon** |
| **Black pepper** | **Several grinds** |

Preheat the oven to 450 degrees F. Scrub the yam and cut it in half lengthwise, then crosswise into ¼-inch slices. Place in a large bowl. Peel the parsnip, turnips, and rutabagas. Cut the parsnip crosswise into ¼-inch slices. Add to the yam. Quarter the turnips and rutabagas, then cut them into ¼-inch slices. Add to the yam. Trim off the stalks of the fennel and slice the bulb in half. Cut the bulb into ¼-inch slices, retaining the stalks for another use, such as soup stock. Add the fennel to the other vegetables in the bowl.

In a small bowl, whisk together the oil and sage. Drizzle over the vegetables and toss well to coat. Place them in a single layer on a large, dry baking sheet and sprinkle evenly with the salt and pepper.

Place them in the oven and roast for 10 minutes. Stir the vegetables around on the sheet, turning the pieces over, and continue to cook for 20 minutes, stirring them again about halfway through the cooking time. When the vegetables are fork-tender and slightly browned, serve them immediately.

---

Each serving provides:

| | | | |
|---|---|---|---|
| 249 | Calories | 40 g | Carbohydrate |
| 4 g | Protein | 446 mg | Sodium |
| 10 g | Fat | 0 mg | Cholesterol |
| 6 g | Dietary Fiber | | |

# Asparagus with Cumin Scrambled Eggs

*ALMOST INSTANT*

*In Spain, vegetables are frequently combined with eggs and served as a side dish or light supper. Enjoy this dish anytime fresh tender asparagus is available.*

*Yield:* 4 side-dish servings

| | |
|---|---|
| **Fresh asparagus** | 1 pound |
| **Eggs** | 4 large |
| **Ground cumin** | ½ teaspoon |
| **Salt** | ¼ teaspoon |
| **Black pepper** | Several grinds |
| **Unsalted butter** | 1 tablespoon |
| **Paprika** | ¼ teaspoon |
| **Lemon wedges** | 1 per serving |

Rinse the asparagus spears and snap off the tough stem ends. Cut them at a slant into 1-inch pieces and place on a steamer rack in a saucepan that has a tight-fitting lid. Add about an inch of cold water, cover, and cook over medium-high heat 6 to 8 minutes, until the asparagus is barely fork-tender. Remove from the pan immediately and rinse with cold water to stop the cooking. Set aside.

Meanwhile, break the eggs into a bowl and stir in the cumin, salt, and pepper to just combine. Melt the butter in a large heavy-bottomed skillet over medium heat. Add the eggs and stir them with a wooden spoon. Cook 2 to 3 minutes until they are almost set, then add the asparagus and continue to cook for 1 to 2 minutes until the eggs are set and the asparagus is heated through. Transfer to a warmed serving bowl and sprinkle with the paprika. Serve immediately, with the lemon wedges on the side.

---

Each serving provides:

| | | | |
|---|---|---|---|
| 123 | Calories | 5 g | Carbohydrate |
| 8 g | Protein | 206 mg | Sodium |
| 8 g | Fat | 221 mg | Cholesterol |
| 1 g | Dietary Fiber | | |

# Baked Winter Squash
# with Garlic and Sage

*VEGAN*

*This savory and succulent vegetable side dish is a wonderful autumn
treat. It looks beautiful on the plate alongside any pasta or risotto.
Leftovers are delicious, reheated in the microwave or briefly sautéed.
Any variety of squash, such as butternut or acorn, may be used.*

*Yield:* 6 side-dish servings

| | |
|---|---|
| **Winter squash** | **3 pounds** |
| **Olive oil** | **2 tablespoons** |
| **Garlic** | **3 cloves, minced** |
| **Ground sage** | **1 teaspoon** |
| **Salt** | **½ teaspoon** |
| **Black pepper** | **Several grinds** |
| **Dry white wine** | **¼ cup** |

Preheat the oven to 375 degrees F. Cut the squash(es) open and
scrape out and discard the seeds and stringy pulp. Cut the
squash(es) into several pieces, then slice off and discard the peel
from each piece. Dice the squash and toss it with the oil in a
casserole dish. Add the garlic, sage, salt, and pepper and toss
again until well combined. Pour the wine into the dish, cover, and
bake 35 to 40 minutes, until the squash is perfectly tender. Serve
very hot.

---

Each serving provides:

| | | | |
|---|---|---|---|
| 112 | Calories | 16 g | Carbohydrate |
| 3 g | Protein | 184 mg | Sodium |
| 5 g | Fat | 0 mg | Cholesterol |
| 3 g | Dietary Fiber | | |

# Grain and Bean Dishes

Grains and dried beans play a major role in the traditional cuisines of the Mediterranean basin. These ancient crops grow well throughout the region, and once dried they can be stored almost indefinitely. Humble and nutritious, these foods appear frequently on the Mediterranean table in a mouthwatering variety of dishes.

Rice is perhaps the most popular Mediterranean grain, enjoyed as pilaf, risotto, or paella. Other grains, such as cornmeal (Italian polenta) and cracked wheat (Middle Eastern bulgur), are also important traditional foods.

Dried legumes—prominently garbanzos, lentils, and fava beans—are regional favorites. We feature them in this chapter; however, they also appear frequently elsewhere in the book.

Here we include a few grain and bean main courses and quite a number of outstanding side dishes. For us, they have become beloved staples.

## Tips and Tools

- Supermarkets carry a few kinds of dried grains and beans. For best selection and economy, however, you may wish to seek out a natural food store that sells dried foods in bulk or an ethnic market.

- Store dried grains and beans in airtight containers in a cool, dry place out of direct sunlight. Under these conditions, they will last indefinitely.

- For steaming grains, you will need a saucepan with a tight-fitting lid.

- A large saucepan or stockpot is necessary for soaking and cooking beans.

- For detailed bean-cooking instructions, see page 29. If you purchase canned beans rather than cooking them at home, look for brands that do not contain additives.

# Brown Rice and Lentil Pilaf

*VEGAN*

*Simple and nutritious, this delicious side dish goes well with any Mediterranean-inspired vegetable stew or stir-fry. Any leftovers will keep well in the refrigerator, to be used over the course of a day or two.*

*Yield:* 8 side-dish servings

| | | |
|---|---|---|
| **Olive oil** | **2** | **tablespoons** |
| **Onion** | **1** | **medium, diced** |
| **Dried red chili flakes** | **½** | **teaspoon** |
| **Uncooked long-grain brown rice** | **1½** | **cups** |
| **Dried brown lentils** | **⅓** | **cup** |
| **Salt** | **½** | **teaspoon** |
| **Whole bay leaf** | **1** | **large** |

Heat the oil over medium heat in a heavy-bottomed saucepan that has a tight-fitting lid and sauté the onion and chili flakes, stirring frequently, for 5 minutes. Add the rice and lentils and stir and cook 5 minutes to toast the rice a little. (This toasted flavor adds a lot to the finished dish, so don't skimp on this step.) Add 3¼ cups water, the salt, and the bay leaf and bring to a boil over medium-high heat. Reduce the heat to very low, cover, and cook 45 to 50 minutes, until all the liquid is absorbed and the rice is tender. Remove from the heat and set the pilaf aside, without disturbing the lid, for at least 5 minutes before transferring it to a warmed serving dish. Serve very hot.

---

Each serving provides:

| | | | |
|---|---|---|---|
| 194 | Calories | 33 g | Carbohydrate |
| 5 g | Protein | 136 mg | Sodium |
| 5 g | Fat | 0 mg | Cholesterol |
| 2 g | Dietary Fiber | | |

# Rice Pilaf with Dried Fruit and Preserved Lemons

*This exotic flavor combination hails from North Africa. The blend of salty, sweet, and nutty flavors is scrumptious.*

*Yield:* 4 side-dish servings

| | | |
|---|---|---|
| **Unsalted butter** | 2 | **tablespoons** |
| **Uncooked long-grain white rice** | 1 | **cup** |
| **Saffron threads** | ¼ | **teaspoon** |
| **Homemade Vegetable Stock\*** | 2 | **cups** |
| **Salt** | ¼ | **teaspoon** |
| **Pine nuts** | 3 | **tablespoons** |
| **Walnuts, chopped** | ¼ | **cup** |
| **Preserved Lemon (page 36)** | 1 | **lemon** |
| **Dried apricot halves** | 12 | **halves, sliced** |
| **Golden raisins** | ¼ | **cup** |

Melt 1 tablespoon of the butter over medium heat in a saucepan that has a tight-fitting lid. Add the rice and saffron and stir for about 1 minute, then add the stock and salt, increase the heat to high, and bring to a boil. Cover the pan, reduce the heat to very low, and cook 20 minutes. Remove from the heat and set aside, without disturbing the lid, for 10 minutes.

Place the pine nuts in a dry, heavy-bottomed skillet in a single layer over medium heat. Stir or shake the pan frequently until the nuts are lightly browned. Immediately

---

\*If you do not have Homemade Vegetable Stock on hand, make some according to the directions on page 32 or dissolve 1 large low-sodium vegetable broth cube in 2 cups of hot water.

remove them from the pan and set aside. Repeat this process with the walnuts and set aside. Separate the preserved lemon into quarters, discarding the pulp. Thinly slice the peel lengthwise and set it aside.

Melt the remaining 1 tablespoon butter in a small skillet over medium-high heat and add the apricots, raisins, and toasted nuts. Cook for about a minute, then stir this mixture into the cooked rice. Transfer to a warm serving dish and garnish with the lemon peel. Serve immediately.

---

Each serving provides:

| 390 | Calories | 61 g | Carbohydrate |
|---|---|---|---|
| 8 g | Protein | 488 mg | Sodium |
| 15 g | Fat | 17 mg | Cholesterol |
| 3 g | Dietary Fiber | | |

# Toasted Vermicelli and Rice Pilaf

*This unusual pilaf has roots in the eastern Mediterranean. It is quite versatile. We like to serve it with a stewed vegetable such as the Okra with Olives, Tomatoes, Herbs, and Lemon (page 250). Simply substitute olive oil for the butter if you want to make a vegan version.*

*Yield:* 6 side-dish servings

| | | |
|---|---|---|
| **Dried vermicelli** | 4 | **ounces** |
| **Unsalted butter** | 1 | **tablespoon** |
| **Uncooked long-grain white rice** | 1½ | **cups** |
| **Garlic** | 1 | **clove, minced** |
| **Salt** | ¼ | **teaspoon** |
| **Black pepper** | **Several grinds** | |
| **Fresh Italian parsley, minced** | ½ | **cup** |
| **Homemade Vegetable Stock\*** | 4½ | **cups** |

Preheat a toaster oven or conventional oven to 400 degrees F. With your hands, break the vermicelli into pieces about 1 to 2 inches in length. Place the broken vermicelli on a baking sheet and toast for 5 to 8 minutes, stirring or shaking the pan occasionally, until the vermicelli is lightly and evenly browned. Immediately remove it from the baking sheet and set it aside.

Melt the butter in a heavy-bottomed saucepan over medium heat and sauté the rice and garlic for 3 minutes, stirring frequently. Add the toasted vermicelli, salt, pepper, parsley,

*If you do not have Homemade Vegetable Stock on hand, make some according to the directions on page 32 or dissolve 2 large low-sodium vegetable broth cubes in 4½ cups of hot water.

*Grain and Bean Dishes*

and stock. Bring to a boil over medium-high heat, then cover, reduce heat to very low, and cook 25 minutes. Remove from the heat and set the pilaf aside, without disturbing the lid, for at least 5 minutes before serving. Serve very hot.

---

Each serving provides:

| | | | |
|---|---|---|---|
| 265 | Calories | 52 g | Carbohydrate |
| 6 g | Protein | 218 mg | Sodium |
| 3 g | Fat | 6 mg | Cholesterol |
| 1 g | Dietary Fiber | | |

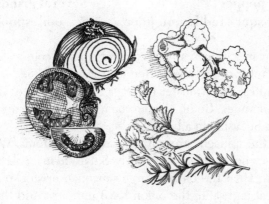

# Spinach and Rice Pilaf with Fresh Dill

*Here is another great standby rice dish. The dill, spinach, and lemon juice reveal its Greek inspiration. Try it with the Artichokes Braised with Parsley and Lemon (page 230) for an authentic combination. Vegans may simply omit the egg garnish.*

*Yield:* 6 side-dish servings

| | | |
|---|---|---|
| Eggs | 2 | large |
| Fresh spinach | 1 | pound |
| Olive oil | 1 | tablespoon |
| Onion | 1 | medium, diced |
| Uncooked long-grain white rice | 1½ | cups |
| Garlic | 2 | cloves, minced |
| Ground cumin | 1 | teaspoon |
| Fresh dill, minced | ⅓ | cup |
| Salt | ½ | teaspoon |
| Black pepper | Several grinds | |
| Fresh-squeezed lemon juice | 2 | tablespoons |

Put the eggs in a saucepan with several cups of cold water and bring to a boil over high heat. Reduce the heat to medium and boil 10 minutes, then transfer the eggs to a bowl of ice water to cool for 10 minutes. Remove from the ice water, peel, and chop them finely. Set aside in a bowl.

Wash the spinach carefully, discarding the stems. Without drying them, chop the leaves coarsely. Set aside in a colander to drain briefly. Heat the oil in a large saucepan or stockpot over medium heat and sauté the onion for 3 minutes. Add the rice, garlic, and cumin and stir and sauté 3 minutes. Add 2¼ cups water, ¼ cup of the dill, the salt, and pepper. Bring to a simmer over high heat, then mound the chopped spinach into the pan, reduce the heat to very low, cover, and cook 20 minutes. Remove from the heat and set the pilaf aside, without disturbing the lid, for at least 5 minutes. Transfer to a warmed serving bowl and toss with the lemon juice until the spinach is well distributed throughout the rice. Garnish with the chopped egg and the remaining minced dill.

---

Each serving provides:

| | | | |
|---|---|---|---|
| 245 | Calories | 43 g | Carbohydrate |
| 8 g | Protein | 255 mg | Sodium |
| 5 g | Fat | 70 mg | Cholesterol |
| 3 g | Dietary Fiber | | |

# Saffron Rice with Bell Peppers and Peas

*VEGAN*

*This dish was inspired by the classic preparation of Spanish rice. The vegetables are slow cooked for a while, then the rice is added and allowed to cook with some wine for a few minutes before the stock is added. It makes a delicious and versatile side dish.*

*Yield:* 6 side-dish servings

| | |
|---|---|
| Fresh pear tomatoes | ½ pound |
| Homemade Vegetable Stock* | 2 cups |
| Olive oil | 1 tablespoon |
| Red bell pepper | 1 medium, diced |
| Green bell pepper | 1 medium, diced |
| White onion, diced | ½ cup |
| Garlic | 2 cloves, minced |
| Uncooked long-grain white rice | 1 cup |
| Dry white wine | ¼ cup |
| Saffron threads | ½ teaspoon |
| Shelled peas, fresh or frozen | 1 cup |
| Fresh parsley leaves, minced | 2 tablespoons |

Cut out and discard the stem ends of the tomatoes, dice them, and set aside in a bowl. Heat the stock to the steaming stage and set aside until needed.

*If you do not have Homemade Vegetable Stock on hand, make some according to the directions on page 32 or dissolve 1 large low-sodium vegetable broth cube in 2 cups of hot water.

Heat the oil over medium heat in a large sauté pan or skillet that has a tight-fitting lid. Add the bell peppers, onion, and garlic and sauté for 5 minutes. Stir in the rice and tomatoes and cook for about 1 minute, then add the wine and cook 2 to 3 minutes, until the wine has been absorbed. Add the stock and saffron, increase the heat to high, and bring to a boil. Cover the pan, reduce the heat to low and cook 20 minutes. Remove the lid and stir in the peas and parsley, then replace the lid and remove the pan from the heat. Set aside in the covered pan for 5 to 10 minutes before serving.

---

Each serving provides:

| | | | |
|---|---|---|---|
| 187 | Calories | 35 g | Carbohydrate |
| 5 g | Protein | 62 mg | Sodium |
| 3 g | Fat | 0 mg | Cholesterol |
| 2 g | Dietary Fiber | | |

# Paella with Dried Tomato and Grilled Vegetables

*VEGAN*

*Paella is Spain's main contribution to the great rice dishes of the world. Traditional paella include seafood and sausage, but this meatless version is perfectly flavorful and satisfying. The preparation may seem like a bit of a production, but once you have tried it you will realize its simplicity. A tart salad, crusty bread, and fruity white wine would be perfect accompaniments.*

*Yield:* 6 main-course servings

| | | |
|---|---|---|
| Dried tomatoes | ⅓ | cup |
| Saffron threads | 1 | teaspoon |
| Homemade Vegetable Stock* | 4 | cups |
| Olive oil | 3 | tablespoons |
| Yellow onions | 2 | medium, diced |
| Garlic | 4 | cloves, minced |
| Paprika | 1 | teaspoon |
| Dried marjoram | 1 | teaspoon |
| Cayenne | ⅛ | teaspoon |
| Uncooked arborio rice | 2½ | cups |
| Dry white wine | ½ | cup |
| Salt | ¾ | teaspoon |
| Red bell peppers | 2 | medium |
| Fresh asparagus | 1½ | pounds |
| Fresh mushrooms | 1 | pound |
| Sherry vinegar | 1 | tablespoon |

*If you do not have Homemade Vegetable Stock on hand, make some according to the directions on page 32 or dissolve 2 large low-sodium vegetable broth cubes in 4 cups of hot water.

Preheat the oven to 375 degrees F. Place the dried tomatoes in a small bowl and pour 1 cup boiling water over them. Set aside for 10 minutes, then drain the tomatoes, reserving the soaking liquid. Thinly slice the tomatoes and set them aside. Combine the saffron with ¼ cup hot water and set aside.

Heat the stock until it is steaming and set it aside near the stove. Heat 2 tablespoons of the oil over medium heat in a paella pan or large, high-walled, ovenproof pan (such as a cast-iron Dutch oven). Add the onions and garlic and sauté, stirring frequently, 5 minutes. Stir in the saffron with its soaking liquid, along with the paprika, marjoram, and cayenne, then stir in the rice and wine. Cook 5 minutes, stirring almost constantly. Add the tomatoes and their soaking water, the hot stock, and ½ teaspoon of the salt and stir to combine. Bring to a simmer over medium-high heat, reduce the heat to medium, and simmer 5 minutes without stirring the contents of the pan.

Transfer the pan to the preheated oven and bake, uncovered, 20 to 25 minutes, until the rice is tender. Remove from the oven, cover with a clean tea towel, and set aside for 10 minutes before serving.

Meanwhile, preheat a coal or gas grill to medium-high. Cut the peppers in half lengthwise and discard their stems, seeds, and white membranes. Set aside. Rinse the asparagus spears and snap off the tough stem ends. Leave the spears whole. Remove the mushroom stems, reserving them for another use, such as soup stock. Wipe any visible dirt from the caps and gills of the mushrooms and leave them whole.

In a small bowl, combine the remaining 2 tablespoons oil with the sherry vinegar and the remaining ¼ teaspoon salt and brush or rub the vegetables liberally with this mixture. Place the vegetables on the preheated grill with the mushroom caps and the outside of the pepper halves down. Grill the vegetables 5 minutes, then turn the asparagus and mushrooms and grill 5 minutes longer. (Do not turn the peppers, you want their skin to completely char.) Grill a few minutes longer, if necessary, until the peppers are charred and the asparagus and mushrooms are fork-tender. Transfer the vegetables to a platter. Carefully peel off and discard the pepper skin and cut the peppers into thin strips. Cut the mushrooms into ½-inch slices.

Distribute the asparagus spears, pepper strips, and mushroom slices in a pretty pattern over the surface of the paella and sprinkle on the pine nuts. Transfer the pan directly to a trivet on the table and serve hot.

---

Each serving provides:

| | | | |
|---|---|---|---|
| 443 | Calories | 82 g | Carbohydrate |
| 103 g | Protein | 407 mg | Sodium |
| 8 g | Fat | 0 mg | Cholesterol |
| 4 g | Dietary Fiber | | |

# Falafel in Pita Bread
# with Cucumber Yogurt Sauce

*In the eastern Mediterranean, the falafel patty is frequently enjoyed
as an appetizer, but here it is combined with a delicious sauce in pita
bread and makes a very tasty main course at lunch or dinner.*

*Yield:* 6 main-course servings

### The falafel

| | | |
|---|---|---|
| French bread, cut into ¾-inch cubes | 1½ | cups |
| Cooked garbanzo beans, drained* | 1½ | cups |
| Fresh-squeezed lemon juice | 2 | tablespoons |
| Red onion, minced | ¼ | cup |
| Garlic | 2 | cloves, minced |
| Fresh cilantro leaves, minced | 2 | tablespoons |
| Ground cumin | ¼ | teaspoon |
| Ground coriander | ¼ | teaspoon |
| Salt | ¼ | teaspoon |
| Baking powder | ½ | teaspoon |
| Cayenne | A pinch | |
| Unbleached white flour | 2 | tablespoons |
| Olive oil | 3 | tablespoons |

*(continued)*

*Cook ¾ cup dried garbanzo beans according to the directions on page 29, or
use canned beans that do not contain additives.

## The yogurt sauce

| | | |
|---|---|---|
| Plain nonfat yogurt | 1 | cup |
| Garlic | 2 | cloves, minced |
| Fresh dill, minced | 1 | tablespoon |
| Cucumber | ½ | medium |
| | | |
| Whole wheat pita bread | 6 | rounds |
| Tomatoes | 2 | medium, diced |
| Red onion | 6 | thin slices |

Place the bread cubes in a bowl and add cold water to just cover them. Set aside for about 15 minutes. Preheat the oven to 375 degrees F. Place the garbanzo beans in a food processor and pulse until they are finely chopped. Add the lemon juice, onion, garlic, cilantro, cumin, coriander, salt, baking powder, and cayenne and process until smooth. Drain the bread and squeeze the water out then add to the food processor. Process until combined.

Form the mixture into 12 balls about 1 inch in diameter, flattening them slightly. Place the flour on a plate and dredge the patties in it to lightly coat. Use ¼ teaspoon of the oil to lightly coat a baking sheet. Place the patties on the sheet and bake for 6 minutes. Turn and continue to bake 6 minutes.

To make the sauce, whisk together the yogurt, garlic, and dill in a medium bowl. If the cucumber is waxed or its skin is bitter, peel it. Cut it in half lengthwise, then use a spoon to scrape out and discard the seeds. Finely dice the cucumber and stir it into the yogurt sauce. Set aside. Cut the pita breads in half, wrap in foil, and place in the oven to warm.

Heat 1 tablespoon of the remaining oil in a skillet over medium-high. When it is hot enough to sizzle a drop of water, add half of the patties to the pan. Cook them for 3 to 4 minutes until they are golden on the bottom. Add a bit more of the remaining oil, turn the patties, and continue to cook for 3 to 4 minutes. Remove them from the pan with a slotted spatula and place on a warmed platter. Cook the remaining patties, using the remaining oil as needed.

To serve, have each diner place 2 falafel patties in a warmed pita half, adding tomatoes and onion, and spooning some yogurt sauce into the sandwiches.

---

Each serving provides:

| | | | |
|---|---|---|---|
| 326 | Calories | 50 g | Carbohydrate |
| 14 g | Protein | 469 mg | Sodium |
| 8 g | Fat | 1 mg | Cholesterol |
| 6 g | Dietary Fiber | | |

# Risotto with Lemon,
# Peas, and Parmesan

*This versatile risotto may be enjoyed as a side dish or a simple main course, accompanied by a chunky vegetable side dish such as the Spicy Braised Broccoli (page 234). The tart lemon and pungent Parmesan infuse the rice with their delicious flavors.*

*Yield:* 4 side-dish servings

| | | |
|---|---|---|
| Homemade Vegetable Stock* | 3½ | cups |
| Olive oil | 1 | tablespoon |
| Shallots | 4 | medium |
| Uncooked arborio rice | 1 | cup |
| Dry white wine | ½ | cup |
| Lemon zest | 2 | teaspoons |
| Shelled peas, fresh or frozen | 1 | cup |
| Fresh-squeezed lemon juice | 3 | tablespoons |
| Parmesan cheese, finely grated | ⅓ | cup |
| Freshly grated nutmeg | ½ | teaspoon |

Heat the stock in a saucepan until just steaming and keep it handy near the stove. Peel and mince the shallots. Heat the oil in a heavy-bottomed saucepan over medium heat and sauté the shallots for about 2 minutes, stirring frequently. Add the rice, stir to coat it with oil and shallots, then pour in the wine and stir constantly until it is almost completely absorbed. Add the

*If you do not have Homemade Vegetable Stock on hand, make some according to the directions on page 32 or dissolve 1½ large low-sodium vegetable broth cube in 3½ cups of hot water.

*Grain and Bean Dishes*

stock, ½ cup at a time, stirring almost constantly and waiting until the liquid is almost completely absorbed before each addition.

When you stir in the last ½ cup of stock, add the lemon zest along with the peas and lemon juice. When this last addition has been absorbed and the rice is tender, stir in the Parmesan and nutmeg. Serve immediately.

---

Each serving provides:

| 307 | Calories | 52 g | Carbohydrate |
|---|---|---|---|
| 9 g | Protein | 271 mg | Sodium |
| 6 g | Fat | 5 mg | Cholesterol |
| 2 g | Dietary Fiber | | |

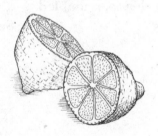

# Risotto with Tomatoes, Arugula, and Gorgonzola

*A wonderful blending of beloved Italian ingredients, this creamy rice preparation delivers a lot of flavor. Risotto is pure comfort food, and this is one of the best. It is intriguing and satisfying enough to serve as a main course with excellent crusty bread and a colorful hot vegetable dish on the side.*

*Yield:* 6 main-course servings

| | | |
|---|---|---|
| **Whole pear tomatoes**° | 1 | **28-ounce can** |
| **Unsalted butter** | 2 | **tablespoons** |
| **White onion** | 1 | **medium, diced** |
| **Salt** | ½ | **teaspoon** |
| **Garlic** | 2 | **cloves, minced** |
| **Fresh arugula leaves** | 4 | **cups, lightly packed** |
| **Homemade Vegetable Stock**°° | 5½ | **cups** |
| **Uncooked arborio rice** | 1½ | **cups** |
| **Dry white wine** | ½ | **cup** |
| **Gorgonzola cheese, crumbled** | 2 | **ounces (½ cup)** |
| **Black pepper** | | **Several grinds** |

°You may substitute 3 pounds fresh pear tomatoes—blanched, peeled, and seeded—for the canned variety. See the directions on page 28.

°°If you do not have Homemade Vegetable Stock on hand, make some according to the directions on page 32 or dissolve 2½ large low-sodium vegetable broth cubes in 5½ cups of hot water.

Drain the tomatoes, reserving the juice for another use. Coarsely chop the tomatoes and set them aside in a bowl.

Melt 1 tablespoon of the butter in a heavy-bottomed sauté pan or skillet over medium heat. Add the onion and cook, stirring frequently, until it is well browned, about 8 minutes. Stir in the tomatoes, salt, and 1 clove of the garlic and bring to a simmer over medium-high heat, then reduce the heat to medium-low and cook 5 minutes. Mound the arugula leaves on top of the tomato sauce and cover the pan. Cook for two minutes, then stir the arugula into the sauce. Cover the pan and remove from the heat.

Meanwhile, heat the stock in a saucepan until just steaming and keep it handy near the stove. Melt the remaining 1 tablespoon butter in a large, heavy-bottomed saucepan over medium-low heat and sauté the remaining 1 clove of garlic in it for about 30 seconds. Add the rice and stir for about a minute, then add the wine and stir constantly until it is almost completely absorbed. Add the hot stock ½ cup at a time, stirring almost constantly and waiting until the liquid is absorbed before each addition. When the last addition of stock has been absorbed and the rice is tender, stir in the cheese and tomato arugula sauce. Transfer to a warmed serving bowl and grind on plenty of black pepper.

---

Each serving provides:

| | | | |
|---|---|---|---|
| 302 | Calories | 50 g | Carbohydrate |
| 8 g | Protein | 676 mg | Sodium |
| 8 g | Fat | 18 mg | Cholesterol |
| 2 g | Dietary Fiber | | |

# Sweet and Sour Leeks with Rice

*Sweet and sour preparations date back to the ancient Romans, who dominated much of the Mediterranean region for centuries. This is sure to become a favorite dish on your family table.*

*Yield:* 8 side-dish servings

| | | |
|---|---|---|
| **Uncooked long-grain white rice** | 1 | **cup** |
| **Leeks** | 1¼ | **pounds** |
| **Olive oil** | 2 | **tablespoons** |
| **Whole cloves** | 4 | |
| **Whole bay leaves** | 2 | **large** |
| **Dry sherry** | 2 | **tablespoons** |
| **Red wine vinegar** | ¼ | **cup** |
| **Honey** | 1 | **tablespoon** |
| **Salt** | ½ | **teaspoon** |
| **Black pepper** | **Several grinds** | |

Bring 2 cups of water to a boil over high heat in a medium saucepan. Stir in the rice, reduce the heat to very low, cover, and simmer for 20 minutes. Remove from the heat and set aside in a warm spot, without disturbing the lid.

Meanwhile, trim off the root ends and all but about 2 inches of the green portion of the leeks. Slice them in half lengthwise and rinse under cold water to remove any dirt that may be lodged between the layers. Cut crosswise into ½-inch slices.

Heat the oil over medium heat in a sauté pan or skillet that has a tight-fitting lid. Add the cloves, bay leaves, and leeks. Stir to coat with the oil, then add the sherry and 2 tablespoons of water. Cover the pan and cook for 8 to 10 minutes. Remove the lid after 8 minutes to make sure there is still a little liquid in the pan; you want the leeks to brown slightly, but not scorch. If the liquid is gone but the leeks are not yet tender, add a tablespoon or two of water and replace the lid.

When the leeks are tender, increase the heat to high and add the vinegar, honey, salt, and pepper. Cook for about 2 minutes, stirring frequently, until the liquid has reduced to a syrupy consistency.

Fluff the rice with a fork and place it on a warmed serving platter. Top with the leeks and serve immediately.

---

Each serving provides:

| 150 | Calories | 27 g | Carbohydrate |
|---|---|---|---|
| 2 g | Protein | 141 mg | Sodium |
| 4 g | Fat | 0 mg | Cholesterol |
| 1 g | Dietary Fiber | | |

# Artichoke and Rice Casserole with Fresh Basil, Feta, and Tomatoes

*Keeping cooked rice in the refrigerator can make mealtime a snap. This delicious casserole is one example of a simple yet satisfying rice dish that will please friends and family without stressing out the cook.*

*Yield:* 4 main-dish servings

| | |
|---|---|
| **Canned artichoke bottoms** | 1  14-ounce can |
| **Whole pear tomatoes**° | 1  28-ounce can |
| **Garlic** | 2  cloves, minced |
| **Dried oregano** | 1  teaspoon |
| **Dried red chili flakes** | ¼  teaspoon |
| **Salt** | ⅛  teaspoon |
| **Olive oil** | ½  teaspoon |
| **Cooked brown rice** | 3  cups |
| **Feta cheese, crumbled** | 4  ounces (1 cup) |
| **Fresh basil leaves, chopped** | ½  cup |
| **Romano cheese, finely grated** | 2  tablespoons |

Drain the artichoke bottoms and coarsely chop them. Set aside. Drain the tomatoes, reserving the juice for another use. Coarsely chop them and place them in a skillet over medium heat, along with the garlic, oregano, chili flakes, and salt. Bring the tomatoes to a simmer and cook 5 minutes. Remove from the heat and set aside.

°You may substitute 3 pounds fresh pear tomatoes—blanched, peeled, and seeded—for the canned variety. See the directions on page 28.

Use the oil to rub down a 2-quart casserole dish. In a large bowl, toss together the rice, artichoke hearts, feta cheese, and basil until well combined. Transfer this mixture to the oiled dish and pat it down gently to create an even layer. Pour the tomato sauce over the top and shake the dish to settle the sauce a bit. Sprinkle evenly with the Romano cheese, cover, and bake for 20 minutes. Remove the lid and bake an additional 15 minutes. Serve very hot.

---

Each serving provides:

| | | | |
|---|---|---|---|
| 336 | Calories | 53 g | Carbohydrate |
| 13 g | Protein | 1045 mg | Sodium |
| 9 g | Fat | 28 mg | Cholesterol |
| 5 g | Dietary Fiber | | |

# Bulgur Pilaf with Garbanzo Beans, Caraway, and Fresh Mint

*VEGAN*

*This distinctive side dish goes well with any Mediterranean vegetable stir-fry or stew. Try it with Steamed Cauliflower with Garlic Paprika Sauce (page 242).*

*Yield:* 6 side-dish servings

| | |
|---|---|
| **Caraway seeds** | **1½ teaspoons** |
| **Whole coriander** | **1 teaspoon** |
| **Ground turmeric** | **1 teaspoon** |
| **Salt** | **½ teaspoon** |
| **Black pepper** | **Several grinds** |
| **Olive oil** | **1 tablespoon** |
| **White onion** | **½ medium, diced** |
| **Garlic** | **2 cloves, minced** |
| **Whole bay leaf** | **1 large** |
| **Uncooked bulgur wheat** | **1 cup** |
| **Cooked garbanzo beans, drained***  | **1½ cups** |
| **Fresh mint leaves, chopped** | **⅓ cup** |

*Cook ¾ cup dried garbanzo beans according to the directions on page 29, or use canned beans that do not contain additives.

Use a mortar and pestle to crush the caraway seeds and whole coriander together. Set aside in a small bowl with the turmeric, salt, and pepper. Heat the oil in a large saucepan over medium heat and sauté the onion for 3 minutes, stirring occasionally. Stir in the garlic and spices, then add 2 cups of water and the bay leaf. Bring to a boil over high heat. Add the bulgur and garbanzo beans and return to a simmer. Reduce the heat to very low, cover, and cook 20 minutes. Turn off the heat, remove the lid, and distribute the mint over the top of the pilaf. Replace the lid and set the pilaf aside, without disturbing the lid, for at least 5 minutes before serving. Remove the bay leaf and stir the mint into the pilaf until well combined. Transfer the mixture to a warmed serving bowl and serve hot.

---

Each serving provides:

| 184 | Calories | 32 g | Carbohydrate |
| 7 g | Protein | 186 mg | Sodium |
| 4 g | Fat | 0 mg | Cholesterol |
| 5 g | Dietary Fiber | | |

# Bulgur in Tomato Sauce with Thyme and Allspice

*ALMOST INSTANT, VEGAN*

*This side dish might appear on a family table in Lebanon or elsewhere in the eastern Mediterranean. It is simple, hearty, and delicious, with a moist rather than dry consistency. You may use the juice from the canned tomatoes where called for in this recipe, but for best results take a moment to strain out the seeds.*

*Yield:* 6 side-dish servings

| | | |
|---|---|---|
| Olive oil | 1 | tablespoon |
| Yellow onion | 1 | medium, diced |
| Garlic | 1 | clove, minced |
| Dried thyme | ½ | teaspoon |
| Ground allspice | ½ | teaspoon |
| Freshly ground black pepper | ½ | teaspoon |
| Dried bulgur wheat | 1½ | cups |
| Whole pear tomatoes, canned | 6, | chopped |
| Tomato juice | 1½ | cups |
| Salt | ¼ | teaspoon |

Heat the oil over medium heat in a heavy-bottomed saucepan with a tight-fitting lid. Sauté the onion, stirring frequently, for 5 minutes, then add the garlic, thyme, allspice, pepper, and bulgur. Stir and cook for 2 minutes, then add the chopped tomatoes, tomato juice, salt, and 1 cup of water. Bring the mixture to a simmer over medium-high heat, then cover, reduce the heat to very low, and cook 20 to 25 minutes, until all the liquid is absorbed and the bulgur at the bottom of the pan is browning just slightly. Transfer to a warmed serving bowl and serve very hot.

---

Each serving provides:

| 184 | Calories | 37 g | Carbohydrate |
| 6 g | Protein | 479 mg | Sodium |
| 3 g | Fat | 0 mg | Cholesterol |
| 6 g | Dietary Fiber | | |

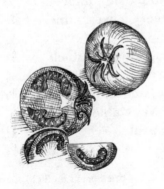

# Cannellini Beans with Peppers and Fennel Seed over Parmesan Polenta

*Here is another satisfying country supper. If you have precooked beans on hand, the dish comes together quickly. In Italy, a plate of grilled sausages might accompany the beans and polenta. Grilled baby vegetables and a tart, leafy salad would round out a meatless meal very nicely. We love our polenta enriched by Parmesan cheese; however, you may use a different variety of cheese, or none at all, if you prefer.*

*Yield:* 6 main-dish servings

| | | |
|---|---|---|
| Olive oil | 3 | tablespoons |
| Garlic | 4 | cloves, minced |
| Fennel seed | 1 | teaspoon |
| Dried red chili flakes | ½ | teaspoon |
| Red bell peppers | 2 | medium, diced |
| Cooked cannellini beans, drained* | 4 | cups |
| Fresh Italian parsley, minced | ⅓ | cup |
| Fresh rosemary leaves, minced | 1 | teaspoon |
| Salt | ½ | teaspoon |
| Bean cooking liquid or stock | ⅔ | cup |
| Dry white wine | ⅓ | cup |
| White onion, minced | ¾ | cup |
| Homemade Vegetable Stock** | 6 | cups |
| Yellow cornmeal | 1½ | cups |
| Parmesan cheese, finely grated | ¼ | cup |

*Cook 1½ cups of presoaked dried beans for 30 to 45 minutes (see page 29) until they are al dente. Alternatively, you may use canned beans that do not contain additives, rinsed and well drained.

**If you do not have any Homemade Vegetable Stock on hand, make some according to the directions on page 32 or dissolve 2 large low-sodium vegetable broth cubes in 6 cups of hot water.

Heat the oil in a large, heavy-bottomed sauté pan or skillet over medium heat. Add the garlic, fennel seed, and chili flakes and sauté for a moment, then add the bell peppers and reduce the heat to medium-low. Cook 5 minutes, stirring frequently. Add the beans, parsley, rosemary, and ¼ teaspoon of the salt and stir to combine, then stir in the bean cooking liquid and the wine (if you do not have bean cooking liquid on hand, replace with stock or water). Increase the heat to medium-high and cook 10 minutes, stirring gently from time to time. The liquid should cook down to a thick sauce consistency. Turn off the heat and stir in the onion. Set the beans aside in a warm spot until the polenta is ready.

Bring the stock to a boil with the remaining ¼ teaspoon salt in a large saucepan over high heat. Gradually pour in the cornmeal in a slow, steady stream, whisking constantly. Reduce the heat to medium-low and gently simmer about 20 minutes, stirring almost constantly with a wooden spoon. The polenta thickens as it cooks. When it is thick enough to pull away from the sides of the pan, it is done. Turn off the heat and stir in the Parmesan.

Reheat the bean mixture, if necessary. Distribute the polenta among 6 warmed individual serving bowls. Ladle equal portions of the beans over the top and serve hot or warm.

---

Each serving provides:

| 405 | Calories | 63 g | Carbohydrate |
| 17 g | Protein | 594 mg | Sodium |
| 9 g | Fat | 3 mg | Cholesterol |
| 8 g | Dietary Fiber | | |

# Cannellini Beans with Grilled Portobello Mushrooms

*Humble, yet elegant, this classic combination of Mediterranean flavors is fit for company. Serve it with Garlic Sautéed Arugula (page 229) and a good, crusty bread for a spectacular presentation. A leafy salad and a California pinot noir would round out the meal perfectly.*

*Yield:* 6 main-course servings

| | |
|---|---|
| **Uncooked cannellini beans** | 1½ **cups** |
| **Tomato paste** | 3 **tablespoons** |
| **Olive oil** | 2 **tablespoons** |
| **Garlic** | 4 **cloves, sliced** |
| **Dried thyme** | 1½ **teaspoons** |
| **Dried rosemary** | 1½ **teaspoons** |
| **Bay leaves** | 2 |
| **Salt** | ½ **teaspoon** |
| **Fresh portobello mushrooms** | 1 **pound** |
| **Parmesan cheese** | 1 **ounce, shaved** |
| **Black pepper** | **Several grinds** |

Sort the beans and place them in a large pan or bowl. Cover with boiling water, put on a lid, and soak for 2 hours, then drain in a colander. Bring 5 cups of fresh water to a boil in a large saucepan or stockpot and add the drained beans, the tomato paste, 1 table-spoon of the oil, the garlic, thyme, rosemary, and bay leaves. Bring the beans to a boil, reduce the heat to medium-high, and cook for 40 to 45 minutes, or until the beans are tender but not mushy. The liquid will cook down to form a thick sauce. Stir in the salt, cover the beans, and turn off the heat.

While the beans are cooking, preheat a coal or gas grill to medium high (see page 29). When the beans are almost ready, remove the stems from the mushrooms and reserve them for another use, such as soup stock. Gently brush or wipe the caps and gills of the mushrooms to remove any bits of dirt. Brush the mushroom caps with a bit of the remaining 1 tablespoon oil and place the mushrooms, cap side down, on the hot grill. Cook for about 7 minutes, brush the gill side of the mushrooms with a bit of oil, and turn. Grill 5 to 7 minutes longer. Remove them from the grill and cut them crosswise into thick slices.

Arrange equal portions of beans on warmed dinner plates and top each serving with slices of mushroom. Top with shaved Parmesan and a grinding of black pepper and serve immediately.

---

Each serving provides:

| | | | |
|---|---|---|---|
| 260 | Calories | 37 g | Carbohydrate |
| 16 g | Protein | 339 mg | Sodium |
| 7 g | Fat | 4 mg | Cholesterol |
| 4 g | Dietary Fiber | | |

# Lima Bean Puree
# with Garlic and Herbs

*VEGAN*

*This simple bean puree delivers tremendous flavor, reminiscent of the south of France. It goes well with any vegetable sauté or stew, or it can be served alongside a stuffed vegetable such as the Stuffed Zucchini with Walnuts, Olives, and Madeira (page 210).*

*Yield:* 4 side-dish servings

| | |
|---|---|
| Dried lima beans | 1 cup |
| Dry white wine | ⅓ cup |
| Garlic | 2 cloves, minced |
| Whole bay leaf | 1 large |
| Herbes de Provence (page 38) | 1 teaspoon |
| Extra virgin olive oil | 1 tablespoon |
| Salt | ¼ teaspoon |
| Black pepper | Several grinds |

Sort the beans, discarding any small pebbles or other foreign objects you may find. Place the beans in a colander and rinse them well under cold water. Place the beans in a stockpot or large saucepan with a tight-fitting lid and add 2¾ cups of water, the wine, garlic, and bay leaf. Bring to a simmer over medium-high heat, then reduce the heat to very low, cover, and cook 30 minutes. Stir in the herbes de Provence, increase the heat to medium, cover, and cook 20 to 25 minutes, until the beans are very tender and beginning to fall apart. Check the beans toward the end of the cooking time and add a few more tablespoons of water if the pan is too dry and the beans are not yet soft. When the beans are very tender and only a few tablespoons of liquid remain, discard the bay leaf and transfer the beans to a food processor. Add the oil, salt, and pepper. Puree until smooth and serve very hot. While pureeing you may add water to the mixture a tablespoon at a time if necessary to achieve a smooth texture.

---

Each serving provides:

| | | | |
|---|---|---|---|
| 195 | Calories | 29 g | Carbohydrate |
| 10 g | Protein | 143 mg | Sodium |
| 4 g | Fat | 0 mg | Cholesterol |
| 9 g | Dietary Fiber | | |

# Soft Polenta with Shallot and Porcini Mushroom Sauce

*Although you may associate polenta with the interior regions of northern Italy, it is also popular in the coastal areas that border the Adriatic Sea. This fragrant mushroom-laden dish is rich and delicious.*

*Yield:* 6 main-dish servings

| | | |
|---|---|---|
| **Dried porcini mushrooms** | 1 | ounce |
| **Button mushrooms** | 1 | pound |
| **Shallots** | 4 | medium |
| **Olive oil** | 2 | tablespoons |
| **Garlic** | 4 | cloves, minced |
| **Dry red wine** | ½ | cup |
| **Dried thyme** | 2 | teaspoons |
| **Homemade Vegetable Stock\*** | 6 | cups |
| **Salt** | ½ | teaspoon |
| **Yellow cornmeal** | 1½ | cups |
| **Parmesan cheese, finely grated** | ½ | cup |

Place the dried mushrooms in a bowl and pour 2 cups of boiling water over them. Set aside for 30 minutes. Meanwhile, brush or wipe any visible dirt from the button mushrooms and cut them into ¼-inch slices. Set aside.

Peel the shallots and mince them. Place the oil in a large sauté pan or skillet over medium heat and add the shallots. Sauté them, stirring frequently, until they are lightly browned, about 3 minutes. Add the button mushrooms, stir to combine with the shallots, and continue to cook until they begin to release their liquid, about 10 minutes.

\*If you do not have Homemade Vegetable Stock on hand, make some according to the directions on page 32 or dissolve 3 large low-sodium vegetable broth cubes in 6 cups of hot water.

*Grain and Bean Dishes*

Meanwhile, lift the porcini mushrooms out of their soaking liquid, reserving the liquid. Squeeze the mushrooms gently so that their juice drips back into the soaking liquid. Finely dice the mushrooms and set them aside. Strain the soaking liquid through a paper coffee filter and set it aside.

When the button mushrooms are beginning to release their liquid, add the porcini mushrooms and the garlic. Stir to combine, then add the wine and 1 teaspoon of the thyme. Sauté for about 2 minutes, stirring occasionally, then add the reserved mushroom-soaking liquid. Increase the heat to medium-high and bring to a rapid simmer. Cook for about 20 minutes, until the liquid has reduced by about half. Remove from the heat, cover the pan, and set aside in a warm spot.

Heat the stock to a simmer over medium-high heat in a heavy-bottomed saucepan. Crush the remaining 1 teaspoon thyme with a mortar and pestle until very fine, or thoroughly crumble with your fingers. Add to the stock, along with the salt. Gradually pour in the cornmeal in a slow, steady stream, whisking constantly. Reduce the heat to medium-low and gently simmer about 20 minutes, stirring almost constantly with a wooden spoon. As it cooks, the polenta will thicken. When it is thick enough to pull away from the sides of the pan, it is done. Turn off the heat and stir in the Parmesan.

Briefly reheat the mushrooms, if necessary. Transfer the polenta to a large warmed serving dish or platter. Use the back of a spoon to make a depression in the center and pour the mushrooms over the top. Serve immediately.

---

Each serving provides:

| | | | |
|---|---|---|---|
| 260 | Calories | 39 g | Carbohydrate |
| 9 g | Protein | 471 mg | Sodium |
| 8 g | Fat | 5 mg | Cholesterol |
| 4 g | Dietary Fiber | | |

# Soft Polenta with Gorgonzola and Sage Butter

*Polenta is always a treat, and this particular version is one of the best. Gorgonzola cheese combined with fresh sage leaves barely cooked in butter makes this a classic Italian side dish, perfect with any tomato-based sauce or stew.*

*Yield:* 4 side-dish servings

| | |
|---|---|
| **Garlic** | 2 cloves, minced |
| **Salt** | ¼ teaspoon |
| **Yellow cornmeal** | ⅔ cup |
| **Unsalted butter** | 2 tablespoons |
| **Fresh sage leaves, minced** | 3 tablespoons |
| **Gorgonzola cheese, crumbled** | 2 ounces (½ cup) |

Bring 2⅔ cups of water to a boil in a heavy saucepan over medium-high heat. Add the garlic and salt, then whisk in the cornmeal, adding it in a slow, steady stream. Reduce the heat to medium-low and gently simmer for about 20 minutes, stirring almost constantly with a wooden spoon. As it cooks, the polenta will thicken. When it is thick enough to pull away from the sides of the pan, it is done.

Melt the butter in a small skillet or saucepan and add the sage. Cook over medium-low heat for 1 minute, then turn off the heat and set the pan aside. When the polenta is done, transfer it to a warmed serving bowl and stir in the sage butter and gorgonzola. Serve very hot.

---

Each serving provides:

| | | | |
|---|---|---|---|
| 194 | Calories | 19 g | Carbohydrate |
| 5 g | Protein | 333 mg | Sodium |
| 11 g | Fat | 27 mg | Cholesterol |
| 1 g | Dietary Fiber | | |

# Acknowledgments

Thank you, readers, for embracing THE BEST 125 MEATLESS cookbook series. Creating this seventh book in the series was just as much fun as creating the first.

As usual, our colleagues at Prima Publishing were steadfastly supportive and essential to the process of birthing this book. Thanks especially to Andi Reese Brady, who kept the production schedule on track despite challenging circumstances.

Friends and family were on hand, as always, to let us know our efforts in the kitchen were appreciated. Our husbands ate heartily, critiqued honestly, and did dishes with enthusiasm. Thanks, guys.

Marvelous produce, grown in our California gardens or purchased at local farmers' markets, transported us to the sunny Mediterranean time and time again, a constant inspiration. For that, we have mostly Mother Nature to thank.

# Index

Mint, about, 11
 fresh, Bulgur pilaf with garbanzo
  beans, caraway, and, 286
 Bulgur salad with parsley, and tomatoes, 98
 French lentil salad with fresh basil
  and, 104
 fresh, Mushroom and lima bean stew
  with cabbage and, 142
 (ed) rice, dill, Green peppers stuffed
  with, 206
 Tomato and, salad with feta cheese, 106
 Zucchini and feta casserole with fresh
  mint, 184
Moussaka, Eggplant and artichoke, 197
Mushroom(s). See also Porcini mush-
  room(s), Portobello mushroom(s).
 about, 6
 and corn soufflé with tomato coulis,
  224
 and lima bean stew with cabbage and
  fresh mint, 142
 Tarragon creamed, au gratin, 254
 with cumin and sherry vinegar, 80
Mustard greens
 in Orecchiette with sauteed greens,
  158

Nicoise olive(s), about, 7
 in Salade Nicoise, 84
Nuts and Seeds. See also Almonds, Pine
  nuts, Sesame seeds, Walnuts.
 about, 6-7

Okra with olives, tomatoes, herbs, and
  lemon, 250
Olive(s), about, 7-8
 calamata, Spinach soup with oregano
  and, 118
 Couscous with feta, and walnuts, 176
 Fava beans with eggs and, 102
 Garbanzo bean and tomato stew with,
  and preserved lemons, 138
 green, Garlic marinated, 42
 green, in Caponata, 50
 Okra with, tomatoes, herbs, and
  lemon, 250
 Orzo with onions and, 156
 Saffron rice salad with, and grapes, 96
 Spanish, Potato salad with, 112
 Stuffed zucchini with walnuts, and
  Madeira, 210

tapenade, Black, 43
tapenade, Green, 44
Olive oil, about, 7
Onion(s), about, 4
 Caramelized, quiche, 220
 Pearl, pickled in sherry vinegar, 64
Ouzo, Rigatoni with, and roasted pepper
  sauce, 164
Orzo with onions and olives, 156

Paella with dried tomato and grilled veg-
  etables, 272
Parmesan cheese, about, 3
 Filo dough filled with zucchini and, 194
 polenta, Cannellini beans with pep-
  pers and fennel seed over, 290
 Risotto with lemon, peas, and, 278
Parsley, about, 12
 in Sour and sweet herb sauce, 56
Pasta and Couscous Dishes, 154-181
 See Contents for list of recipe titles.
Pasta
 about, 8
 al pesto frittata, 45
 Cold, with tomatoes, artichokes, and
  capers, 114
Pastry crust, 216
Pea(s)
 Creamed, and lettuce soup, 134
 Fresh, and shallots with Provençal
  herbs, 238
 Penne with, tarragon, walnuts, and
  goat cheese, 166
 Risotto with lemon, and Parmesan, 278
 Saffron rice with bell peppers and, 270
Pepper(s)
 Arugula and, salad with mustard fennel seed vinaigrette, 86
 bell, Saffron rice with, and peas, 270
 Cannellini beans with, and fennel
  seed over Parmesan polenta, 290
 Green, stuffed with dill minted rice,
  206
 red bell, tortilla of potatoes, artichokes, and, 76
 red, Linguine with, broccoli, basil,
  and Romano cheese, 172
 red, Stuffed with bread, walnuts, and
  fresh herbs, 208
 Roasted, in spicy marinade, 68
 roasted red, Garbanzo bean salad
  with, 100